2200 2100 2000 1900 1800

2134 Beginning of Egyptian Middle Kingdom

c. 2000 Hittite Empire founded

c. 1925 Abram leaves Ur

c. 1900 BC Asshur, capital of Assyria, founded

c. 1754 BC Code of Hammurabi

The Great Sphinx of Giza dates from c. 2570 BC.

Hittite cuneiform tablet.

ISRAELITES
KINGDOM OF JUDAH
KINGDOM OF ISRAEL
NEIGHBORING NATION
ASCENDANT NATION
CHRISTIANITY

Abram leaves Ur.

2200 2100 2000 1900 1800

200 300 400 500 600

MID-1ST CENTURY BC–END-4TH CENTURY AD Roman Rule

250 Emperor Decius persecutes Christians

284–305 Emperor Diocletian persecutes Christians

313 Christianity tolerated in Roman Empire

325–381 Arian controversy

325 Council of Nicaea

AD **390** Roman Empire divides between East and West

AD **410** Goths led by Alaric sack Rome

430 Patrick's mission to Ireland

450 Council of Chalcedon

Bethlehem star.

Caesar Augustus.

Emperor Constantine the Great c. 272–337 AD.

200 300 400 500 600

1700 1600 1500 1400 1300

2000–1600 BC Minoan palace civilization in Crete

c. 1900–1720 Isaac

c. 1280 Exodus from Egypt

c. 1800–1700 Jacob

c. 1750–1640 Joseph

c. 1700–1280 Israel in Egypt

c. 1640–1570 Hyksos rule in Egypt

c. 1450 Greek language written down for the first time

c. 1600 First urban civilization in China

1552 New Kingdom begins in Egypt

1332–1322 Pharaoh Tutankhamun

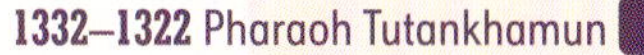

Code of Hammurabi.

Exodus.

Rameses II 1303–1213 BC.

1700 1600 1500 1400 1300

300 | 200 | 100 BC | 0 | AD 100

MID-6TH–MID-4TH CENTURIES Persia Ascendant

LATE-4TH–END-1ST CENTURIES Ptolemies Ascendant

LATE-4TH–MID-1ST CENTURIES Seleucids Ascendant

336–331 Darius III

336–323 Alexander the Great

283 Septuagint translation begins

217 Hannibal crosses the Alps

AD 33 Crucifixion of Jesus

214 Great Wall of China built

46–58 Paul's missionary journeys

175–163 Antiochus IV Epiphanes

60–100 Four Gospels written

167–140 Independent Hasmonean Kingdom

c. 167 Antiochus desecrates Temple

166–161 Judas Maccabeus

164 Temple rededicated

106–48 Pompey

c. 100 Dead Sea Scrolls

c. 100 Rise of the Essenes

63 Pompey captures Jerusalem

47–43 Antipater II

46–44 Julius Caesar

37 BC–AD 4 Herod the Great

27 BC–AD 14 Augustus

27 Establishment of the Roman Empire

4 BC–AD 39 Herod Antipas (Galilee)

4 BC–AD 34 Herod Philip (Iturea)

4 BC–AD 6 Archelaus (Judea)

c. 8/7 John the Baptist

c. 8/7 Birth of Jesus

AD 70 Romans destroy Jerusalem and Herod's Temple

Alexander the Great.

Dead Sea scroll.

300 | 200 | 100 BC | 0 | AD 100

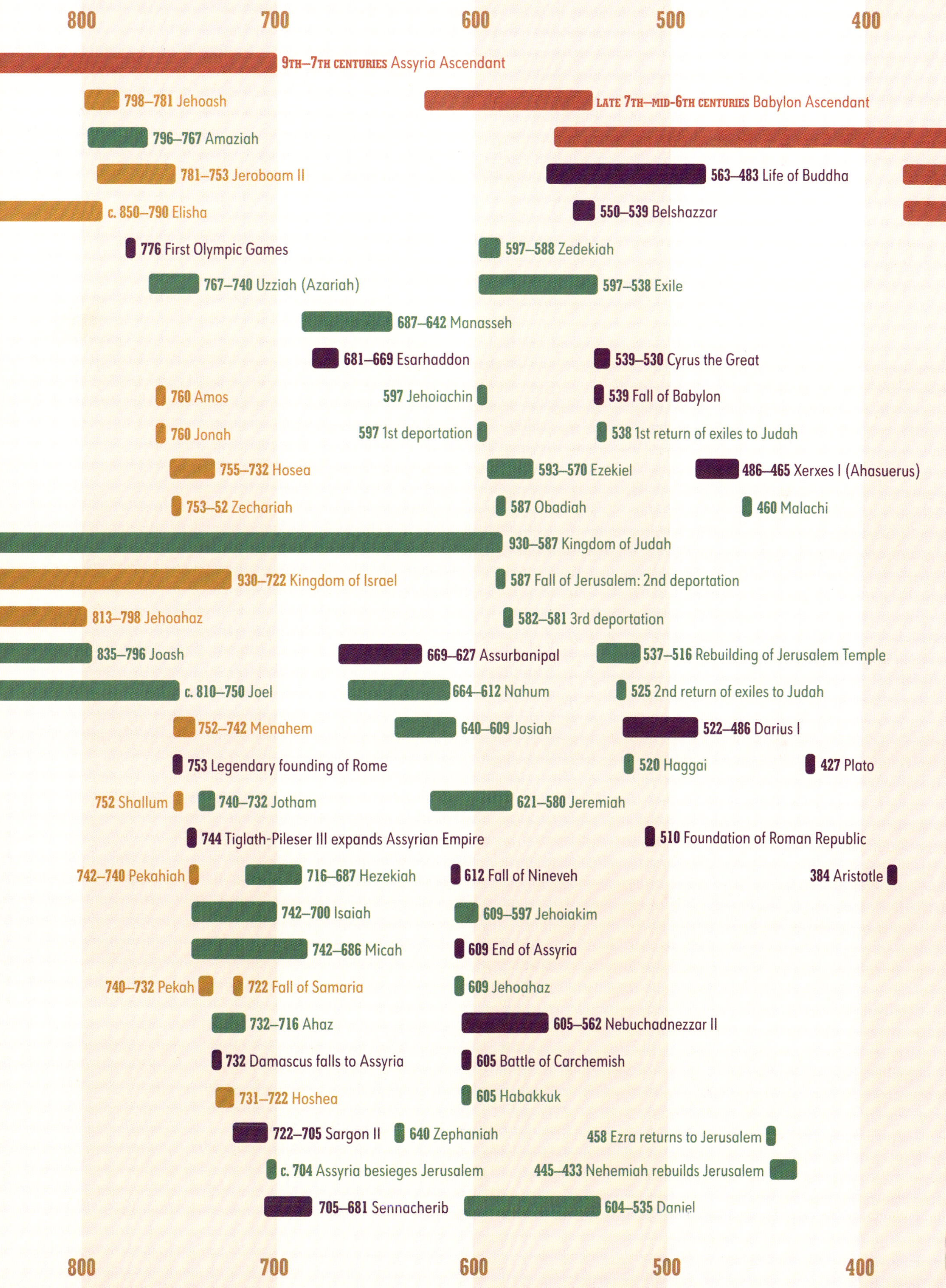
800
700
600
500
400
9th–7th centuries Assyria Ascendant
798–781 Jehoash
late 7th–mid-6th centuries Babylon Ascendant
796–767 Amaziah
781–753 Jeroboam II
563–483 Life of Buddha
c. 850–790 Elisha
550–539 Belshazzar
776 First Olympic Games
597–588 Zedekiah
767–740 Uzziah (Azariah)
597–538 Exile
687–642 Manasseh
681–669 Esarhaddon
539–530 Cyrus the Great
760 Amos
597 Jehoiachin
539 Fall of Babylon
760 Jonah
597 1st deportation
538 1st return of exiles to Judah
755–732 Hosea
593–570 Ezekiel
486–465 Xerxes I (Ahasuerus)
753–52 Zechariah
587 Obadiah
460 Malachi
930–587 Kingdom of Judah
930–722 Kingdom of Israel
587 Fall of Jerusalem: 2nd deportation
813–798 Jehoahaz
582–581 3rd deportation
835–796 Joash
669–627 Assurbanipal
537–516 Rebuilding of Jerusalem Temple
c. 810–750 Joel
664–612 Nahum
525 2nd return of exiles to Judah
752–742 Menahem
640–609 Josiah
522–486 Darius I
753 Legendary founding of Rome
520 Haggai
427 Plato
752 Shallum
740–732 Jotham
621–580 Jeremiah
744 Tiglath-Pileser III expands Assyrian Empire
510 Foundation of Roman Republic
742–740 Pekahiah
716–687 Hezekiah
612 Fall of Nineveh
384 Aristotle
742–700 Isaiah
609–597 Jehoiakim
742–686 Micah
609 End of Assyria
740–732 Pekah
722 Fall of Samaria
609 Jehoahaz
732–716 Ahaz
605–562 Nebuchadnezzar II
732 Damascus falls to Assyria
605 Battle of Carchemish
731–722 Hoshea
605 Habakkuk
722–705 Sargon II
640 Zephaniah
458 Ezra returns to Jerusalem
c. 704 Assyria besieges Jerusalem
445–433 Nehemiah rebuilds Jerusalem
705–681 Sennacherib
604–535 Daniel
800
700
600
500
400

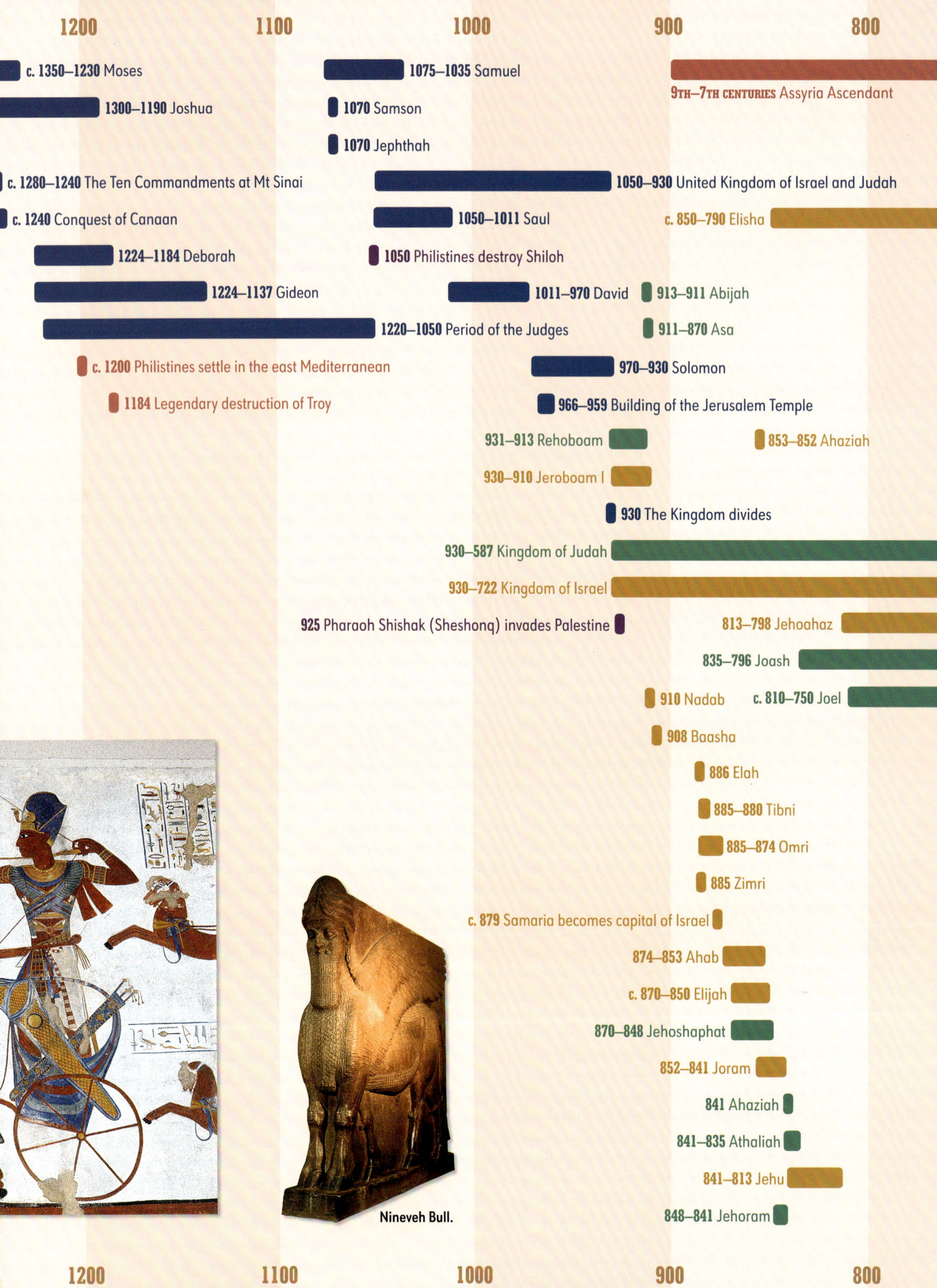

Nineveh Bull.

THE EVERYTHING BIBLE
THE ULTIMATE COLLECTION OF
BIBLE FACTS
TIMELINES, MAPS & CHARTS

THE EVERYTHING BIBLE

THE ULTIMATE COLLECTION OF

BIBLE FACTS

TIMELINES, MAPS & CHARTS

BroadStreet Publishing Group, LLC.
Savage, Minnesota, USA
Broadstreetpublishing.com

The Everything Bible: The Ultimate Collection of Bible Facts, Timelines, Maps and Charts

9781424569380
9781424569397 (eBook)

Typesetting and design by bounford.com

Editorial services by Tim Dowley Associates Ltd, London

Printed in China.

24 25 26 27 28 29 30 7 6 5 4 3 2 1

Contents

Contents

New Testament

Contents

Contents

Old Testament

What is the Bible?

The Protestant Bible is made up of a "library" of 66 books, 39 in the Old Testament, 27 in the New. The Roman Catholic New Testament contains exactly the same books as the Protestant New Testament, but the Catholic Old Testament consists of 46 books.

The Old Testament

The writings of the Old Testament first appeared as separate scrolls in Hebrew. We do not know exactly how or when they were first gathered into a single volume. But there is clear evidence that books, as we know them, first appeared during the first and second centuries AD (see the section titled How the Bible came down to us on page 177). We also need to remember that, before the Old Testament Hebrew Scriptures were written down, there were likely many centuries when traditions were passed on by word of mouth, or "orally." The patriarch, Abraham, for example, probably lived during the period 2000–1800 BC. From his time on, it is believed traditions about the divine Covenant were preserved orally until the time of Moses (c. mid-2nd millennium BC), who is accepted as the editor and recorder of the first Hebrew Scriptures.

The books of the Old Testament vary in authorship and style, and can be divided into four main groupings:

1. **Law**
   Sometimes called the "Books of Moses" or the Pentateuch—"five scrolls." The Jews call these five books the "Torah," Hebrew for instruction. They contain all the details of the Law Covenant that governed all aspects of daily life for God's people.
2. **History**
   Books that trace the story of God's people from their entry into the Promised Land to the Exile.
3. **Poetry and wisdom**
   Books full of proverbs, riddles, parables, warnings, and wise sayings.
4. **Prophecy**
   God's prophets explain what happened in the past, speak out against evil in the present, and foretell what God will do in the future.

The Apocrypha

The Apocrypha is a collection of books, and additions to Old Testament books, written between 300 BC and AD 100. They are sometimes also known as "deuterocanonical" books—belonging to a second "canon" of Scripture. These writings were not accepted by the Jews as part of their Scripture, and most Protestant churches do not accept them either. Some are included in the Roman Catholic Bible.

These books are interesting and valuable historical documents, and range from historical narratives to pious fiction.

The New Testament

The 27 books of the New Testament were written in Greek. Like the Old Testament, they can be divided into different types of writing:

1. **History**
   The book of Acts and the four Gospels. The Gospels are not simply historical records; they form portraits of Jesus as the Messiah and were written to persuade readers to believe in Jesus.
2. **Letters**
   In older Bibles they are often called "epistles." They include the Apostle Paul's letters to groups of Christians or churches in various cities, Paul's letters to individual Christians, and letters written by other apostles.
3. **Revelation**
   This book opens with letters to seven different churches in Asia Minor, urging them to remain constant in their faith in the midst of severe persecution. The book continues with disturbing visions about the Last Days. However, importantly, the visions begin and end with the clear message that the Kingdom of God will endure forever.

Ten major discoveries in biblical archaeology

1. The Nag Hammadi Library
In 1945 two peasants discovered a thirteen-volume library of Coptic texts hidden under a boulder near the town of Nag Hammadi, upper Egypt. This reintroduced the largely forgotten, heretical Gnostic beliefs in early Christianity.

2. 'Ain Dara Temple
A temple in northern Syria that is the most similar known structure to Solomon's Temple. Its plan, size, date, and architectural details are typical of sacred architecture of the area between the tenth and the eighth centuries BC.

3. Tel Dan "David" Stela
A ninth-century BC inscription that provides the first evidence for King David outside of the Bible.

4. Mona Lisa of Galilee
More than sixteen centuries after an earthquake destroyed the Roman city of Sepphoris, west of the Sea of Galilee, this richly colored mosaic portrait of an unnamed woman was discovered among the ruins.

5. Peter's House
This simple first-century AD home in Capernaum may have been occupied by Jesus during his Galilean ministry. It seems to have become a place for gatherings linked with Jesus and his disciple Peter.

6. Siloam Pool
In 2004, archaeologists excavated part of this monumental pool south of Jerusalem's Temple Mount, on the ridge known as the City of David. This is where Jesus restored the sight of a blind man, in John's Gospel.

7. Ashkelon's Arched Gate
The oldest known monumental arch, built during the Middle Bronze Age, circa 1850 BC, and discovered in southern Israel in 1992.

8. The Dead Sea Scrolls
This hugely important library of more than 800 manuscripts, most likely belonging to the Jewish sect of the Essenes, dates from between c. 250 BC and AD 68. They were discovered in 1947 by a Bedouin shepherd in caves near the Dead Sea, and give unique insights into contemporary Judaism, religious culture, and the Bible.

9. Two synagogues at Magdala
Mary Magdalene is usually thought to mean "Mary of Magdala". At the site of Magdala a synagogue dating to AD 50–100 BC was discovered in 2009, and a second synagogue dating to the same period in 2021. This was the first time two synagogues of this period have been found at one site.

10. Siloam Inscription, Hezekiah's Tunnel, Jerusalem
Discovered by two boys playing in the tunnel in 1880, this inscription describes the moment when quarrymen from each end met in the middle, throwing light on 2 Kings 20:20.

Siloam inscription.

The Books of the Old Testament

Genesis
The beginnings, describes creation, the rebellion and sin of man, and the early history of God's people, through whom he introduces his plan of redemption via his covenant with Adam at creation, Noah, Abraham, Isaac, and Jacob.

Exodus
The story of Israel's escape from Egypt and the leadership of Moses; God's covenant with Israel; the giving of the Law; and the construction of the Tabernacle.

Leviticus
The laws through which God's people can worshipfully approach, and sustain fellowship with God.

Numbers
A census of the people and their wanderings in the wilderness, as God prepares them to enter the Promised Land.

Deuteronomy
Before his death, Moses emphasizes the covenant and the Law to the people.

Joshua
Israel enters Canaan and divides the land among the tribes.

Judges
The story of the Israelites in Canaan as they learn that turning from God leads to oppression by enemies, followed by repentance and deliverance through a judge.

Ruth
A story of tragedy and love in the lives of ancestors of David—a story of redemption that points to Jesus.

1 Samuel
The history of Israel from the rule of Samuel, the last judge, to the reign of King Saul.

2 Samuel
The record of David's reign.

1 and 2 Kings
The last days of David's reign through the reign of his son, Solomon, and the division of the kingdom, after which both kingdoms are presented in chronological order until the release of Jehoiachin from prison in Babylon, about 561 BC.

1 and 2 Chronicles
The official histories of the kingdoms of Judah and Israel, including the genealogies and history, from the reigns of David and Solomon through the captivity.

Ezra
The return of the Jews from Babylonian captivity and rebuilding of the Jerusalem temple.

Nehemiah
A further account of the return from exile; the rebuilding of the walls of Jerusalem and the renewal of the covenant.

Esther
The story of a Jewess who becomes Queen of Persia and saves her people from destruction, foiling the plot of Haman the Agagite, a Persian courtier who hated the Jewish people.

Job
The sufferings and faith of a man who learns to accept the—sometimes baffling—will of God.

Psalms
Poems, prayers, and praises written by David and others.

Proverbs
The wise and practical sayings of Solomon and other wise men.

Ecclesiastes
How the search for happiness and satisfaction in earthly things apart from God always ends in futility.

Camp at Mount Sinai.

The Books of the Old Testament continued

Song of Songs
A love song recounting the courtship and marriage of a man and a woman, illustrating the relationship between God and his people, and Christ and his church.

Isaiah
Prophecies concerning Judah and Jerusalem, vivid messages of redemption for God's people, and hope for a Messiah.

Jeremiah
Prophecies predicting the fall of Judah, the people's sufferings, and exile at the hands of the Babylonian armies; and, finally, the overthrow of their enemies.

Lamentations
Grief for the fall of Jerusalem and destruction of the Temple by the Babylonians.

Ezekiel
God's judgment on the Jews and messages of comfort, along with promises of renewal in the midst of their Babylonian captivity.

Daniel
Some of the events of the captivity, and prophecies of Christ and the end-times.

Hosea
Hosea's grief over his unfaithful wife illustrates God's relationship with Israel.

Joel
God's judgment of Judah—and the blessings that will follow repentance.

Amos
Judgment against Israel because of idolatry and the oppression of the poor, and against surrounding nations—with glimpses of the Messiah's kingdom.

Obadiah
Prophecies of the destruction of Edom, and the deliverance that will be found in Zion.

Jonah
The story of the prophet Jonah, and God's mercy toward nations that are willing to repent—such as the Assyrian city of Nineveh.

Micah
Judgment on Israel and Judah; the prediction of restoration and the Messiah's reign.

Nahum
Prediction of the downfall of Assyria.

Habakkuk
Prediction of the Babylonian invasion, the destruction of Babylon, and restoration of God's people.

Zephaniah
Prediction of the overthrow of Judah because of idolatry, pride, and materialism; a foreshadowing of the ultimate deliverance and restoration of God's people.

Haggai
Prophecies and exhortations about the rebuilding of the Temple.

Zechariah
Prophecies about rebuilding the Temple, the coming of the Messiah, and the triumph of the kingdom of God.

Malachi
Judgment for Israel's sins, and predictions of blessings for the repentant; and the coming of Christ.

The ten oldest men in the Bible

Methuselah
969 years
GENESIS 5:21-27

Jared
962 years
GENESIS 5:18-20

Noah
950 years
GENESIS 9:29

Adam
930 years
GENESIS 5:5

Seth
912 years
GENESIS 5:8

Cainan/Kenan
910 years
GENESIS 5:9-14

Enos
905 years
GENESIS 5:6-11

Mahalalel/ Mahalaleel
895 years
GENESIS 5:12-17

Lamech
777 years
GENESIS 5:31

Enoch
365 years—after which "he was not"
GENESIS 5:18-24

Zechariah.

Some Bible Firsts

First man
Adam

First woman
Eve

First child
Cain

First death
Abel

First person not to die
Enoch

First clothes
aprons of fig leaves

First boat
the ark

First twins
Esau and Jacob

First king
Melchizedek of Salem

First king of Israel
Abimelech

First disciples of Jesus
Peter and Andrew

First of Jesus' miracles
turning water to wine at Cana

First Christian martyr
Stephen

Adam and Eve.

Genesis

Author
Moses.

Date
Between 1520 and 1400 BC.

Outline
The story of humankind 1:1–11.30
The story of Abraham 11:31–25:18
The story of Isaac 25:19–27:40
The story of Jacob 27:41–37:1
The story of Joseph 37:2–50:26

Purpose
Genesis gives the origin of all things, both the cosmic order of the universe and the covenant relationship of God's people, via the persons of Adam, Noah, Abraham, Isaac, and Jacob. We find the beginning of the heavens and the earth, but also the origin of nations, with God's choice of the Hebrews as the people through whom the redeemer will come to the world. Genesis is the foundation upon which all revelation rests.

Author
The book of Genesis is part of the larger collection of books known as the Pentateuch. Moses is traditionally recognized as the author of the first five books of the Bible, called the Torah, the law of Moses, or Book of Moses.

God's promise to Abram (GENESIS 15:5).

Major themes in Genesis

Origin of Creation
The God of Abraham, Isaac, and Jacob created the heavens and the earth and everything in it. The origin of the God-man relationship; Eden, a bliss-filled paradise, the home of Adam and Eve; and the origins of sin and ensuing fallout. Because Adam and Eve ate what was forbidden, sin, pain, and death entered the world. Yet, from the beginning, God had a plan to rescue humanity.

Blessed to be a blessing
"Blessing" holds Genesis together and connects it to the rest of the Hebrew Scriptures. For instance, God blessed Joseph, and in turn blessed his life, the lives of his family, and the lives of the nations.

Origin of God's people, expressed in the revelation of the Divine Covenant
Genesis 12 is a sort of second creation account, in which God's holy people are "created" through an act of grace. Abram, who became Abraham, is invited into a loving covenant relationship in order to birth a nation.

Faith in God's promises
Perhaps the greatest hero of faith is Abraham.

History of God's redemption
Father God did what any good father would do when a child fails: he assured them of his love. This love was expressed via the unveiling of his plan of redemption.

The days of Creation

Day 1
Light was created and separated from darkness to make day and night.
GENESIS 1:3-5

Day 2
God made the sky to separate the water on earth from the water above.
GENESIS 1:6-8

Day 3
Water on earth was gathered to form seas separate from land. Vegetation was created, and able to reproduce from seeds.
GENESIS 1:9-13

Day 4
Heavenly bodies—sun, moon, and stars—were created to provide light and to mark the seasons.
GENESIS 1:14-19

Day 5
Birds and fish.
GENESIS 1:20-23

Day 6
God created land creatures, and finally humankind—male and female.
GENESIS 1:24–2:1

Day 7
God rested.
GENESIS 2:2-3

Creation.

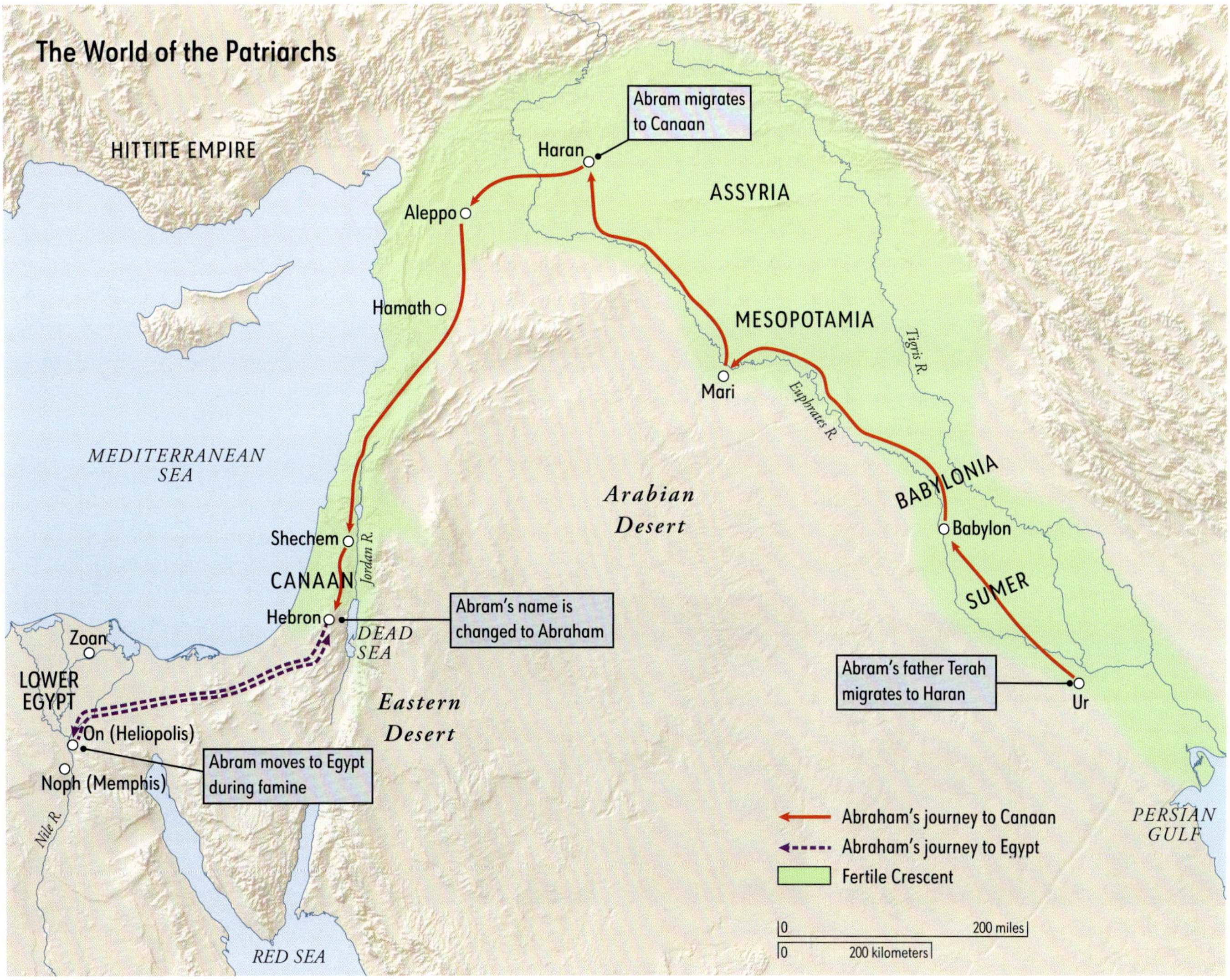

The World of the Patriarchs

HITTITE EMPIRE
Abram migrates to Canaan
Haran
ASSYRIA
Aleppo
Hamath
MESOPOTAMIA
Tigris R.
Mari
Euphrates R.
MEDITERRANEAN SEA
Arabian Desert
BABYLONIA
Babylon
Shechem
Jordan R.
CANAAN
SUMER
Hebron
Abram's name is changed to Abraham
DEAD SEA
Zoan
LOWER EGYPT
Abram's father Terah migrates to Haran
Ur
Eastern Desert
On (Heliopolis)
Abram moves to Egypt during famine
Noph (Memphis)
Nile R.
PERSIAN GULF
Abraham's journey to Canaan
Abraham's journey to Egypt
Fertile Crescent
0 200 miles
0 200 kilometers
RED SEA

The first generations

Adam
The first person created by God. When he ate the forbidden fruit, he brought sin into the world, and, with Eve, had to leave the Garden of Eden.
GENESIS 2–3; LUKE 3:38; ROMANS 5:14-19; 1 CORINTHIANS 15:22, 45

Eve
The first woman, and mother of all human beings. Tempted by the serpent, she disobeyed God and gave Adam forbidden fruit to eat.
GENESIS 2:18–3:20

Cain
Adam and Eve's eldest son. God rejected his offering of produce, but accepted his brother's sacrifice. This so enraged Cain that he murdered Abel.
GENESIS 4:1-25; HEBREWS 11:4

Abel
Adam and Eve's second son, murdered by his jealous brother, Cain.
GENESIS 4:1-25; HEBREWS 11:4

Noah
The only blameless man in a corrupt world. On God's instructions, he built an ark in which he and his family were kept safe during the great flood.
GENESIS 5–9; LUKE 3:36; 1 PETER 3:20; 2 PETER 2:5

Entering Noah's ark.

Ham
Probably Noah's second son.
GENESIS 5:32; 9:18–10:6

Shem
Noah's eldest son, an ancestor of Jesus.
GENESIS 5:32; 9:18-23; 10:21-29; 11:10-26; LUKE 3:36

Japheth
Probably Noah's youngest son.
GENESIS 5:32; 9:18-23; 10:2-5

Methuselah
969 when he died; renowned for being the oldest man to have lived.
GENESIS 5:21-27; LUKE 3:37

Enoch
One of only two people—the other is Elijah—translated to heaven without dying.
GENESIS 5:18-24

Job
A godly man who endured terrible, undeserved sufferings. He lost his family, wealth, status, and health. Three friends—Eliphaz, Bildad, and Zophar—tried unsuccessfully to advise him, as did a younger man, Elihu. Nothing helped, until he humbled himself before God.
JOB 1–42

Jacob and Isaac.

Abraham (Abram)
Abraham was originally known as Abram (Genesis 11–14), but then God changed his name to Abraham (meaning "Father of many nations"), after promising to confirm his divine covenant with the patriarch (Genesis 17:5). Abraham was the founder of the Jewish nation. Answering God's call, he set off from Ur and traveled to Canaan. He believed God's promise that a great nation would descend from him.
GENESIS 11:10–25:11; MATTHEW 1:1-2; ACTS 7:2-3; HEBREWS 11:8-19

Sarah
Abraham's wife, mother of Isaac in old age.
GENESIS 17:1–18:15; 20:1–21:7; HEBREWS 11:11; 1 PETER 3:6

Terah
Born in Ur, he traveled with his son Abram, to Haran, where he died.
GENESIS 11:24-32; LUKE 3:34

Lot
Abraham's nephew, who chose to live in the evil, immoral town of Sodom, escaping just before it was destroyed.
GENESIS 11:31–14:16; 19

Isaac
The long-awaited son whom God had promised to Abraham and Sarah. As a boy, he went with Abraham to Mount Moriah to be sacrificed, but was spared at the last moment. Isaac and his wife, Rebekah, had twin sons, Esau and Jacob. In his old age, Isaac was tricked by Jacob—his younger son—into giving him the blessing he had reserved for Esau, his first-born son.
GENESIS 21:1–27:40; MATTHEW 1:2

Jacob
The son of Isaac and Rebekah, and younger twin brother of Esau, whom he supplanted to inherit God's blessing. Jacob escaped to Mesopotamia, where he married his uncle Laban's two daughters, Leah and Rachel. As he returned to Canaan, he wrestled with an angel and was renamed Israel. His sons were the founders of the twelve tribes of Israel.

GENESIS 25:21–35:29; 37:1; 42:1–50:14

Rachel
Jacob worked for Laban for fourteen years to gain his daughter Rachel in marriage. Joseph and Benjamin were their sons.

GENESIS 29–30; 35:16-20

Leah
Laban's eldest daughter, passed off to Isaac as a wife by her father. Mother of Reuben, Simeon, Levi, Judah, Issachar, and Zebulun.

GENESIS 29–31; 33–35; 46; 49

Bilhah
Jacob also kept Bilhah—Rachel's maid-servant—as a concubine, who bore two sons to him: Dan and Naphtali.

GENESIS 35:25

Zilpah
Jacob also kept Zilpah—Leah's maid-servant—as a concubine, who bore two sons to him: Gad and Asher.

GENESIS 35:26

Rebekah
The wife of Isaac. Rebekah suggested Jacob should trick Isaac into giving him his blessing.

GENESIS 24–28

Esau
The son of Isaac and Rebekah, elder twin of Jacob, and a skillful hunter. He was the founder of the nation of Edom.

GENESIS 25:1–28:9; 32–33; 36; HEBREWS 12:16-17

Hagar
Sarah's servant, and Abraham's secondary wife. When Ishmael was born to Hagar and Abraham, the childless Sarah was jealous of Hagar. After Isaac was born, Hagar and Ishmael were sent away.

GENESIS 16; 21:8-21; GALATIANS 4:21-31

Ishmael
The son of Hagar. Sarah made Abraham expel Ishmael and Hagar into the desert, where an angel led them to water. Ishmael had twelve sons.

GENESIS 16–17; 25:12-18; 1 CHRONICLES 1:28-31

Melchizedek
The king of Salem (Jerusalem), priest of the most high God, he blessed Abraham. Melchizedek was a prophetic symbol of Jesus Christ, who was both king and priest. One of the Bible's most mysterious figures.

GENESIS 14:18-20; PSALM 110:4; HEBREWS 5:6; 7

Jacob's dream.

Abraham's Timeline

Event	Age	Reference in Genesis
Abram departs from Haran, enters Canaan	75	12:4-5
Abram fathers Ishmael with Hagar	85-86	16:3-4
Abraham fathers Isaac with Sarah	100	21:5
Abraham's wife Sarah dies	137	23:1-2
Abraham's son Isaac marries Rebekah	140	25:20

The Abrahamic Covenant

God made his covenant with Abram when he was living in Ur of the Chaldees, promising a land, descendants, and blessing.
GENESIS 12:1–3

Abram went with his family to Haran and lived there for a time, before leaving, aged seventy-five.
GENESIS 12:4–5

After Lot separated from Abram, God again promised the land to him and his descendants.
GENESIS 13:14–17

This covenant was ratified when God passed between the sacrificial animals Abram laid before God.
GENESIS 15:1–21

When Abram was ninety-nine, God renewed his covenant, and changed Abram's name to Abraham ("father of a multitude/many nations"). The sign of the covenant: circumcision.
GENESIS 17:1–27

Confirmation of the covenant because of Abraham's obedience.
GENESIS 22:15–18

Exodus

Author
Moses.

Date
c. 1400/1200 BC.

Outline
Israel in Egypt 1:1–22
Moses the deliverer 2:1–4:31
Freedom from bondage 5:1–18:27
The law and the covenant 19:1– 24:18
The construction of the Tabernacle 25:1-31:18; 35:1–40:38
Failure—and renewal 32:1– 34:35

Major themes in Exodus

Freedom
Exodus opens with the Israelites under the yoke of slavery in Egypt. Their deliverance was not easily achieved, but when it happened it was complete.

The Lamb of God
The Passover lamb is a picture of the Lamb of God—an anticipation of the death of Jesus Christ, God's Son, on the cross—a reminder that we have been released from the bondage of sin.

Law of the Covenant
The freed Hebrew slaves were reminded that God expects obedience to his covenant law. The ten commandments constitute a moral code for all people in all times.

Worship
After Israel had been set free they were told how to worship God. The Tabernacle was a visual reminder of God's presence with his people.

The Tabernacle.

Who are the Pharaohs mentioned in Scripture?

King	Identity	Scripture
Unnamed	Befriended Abraham and took Sarah into his household.	Genesis 12:14-20
Unnamed	Put Joseph in charge of food supply in Egypt.	Genesis 41:37-57
Sety I (Sethos) 1291-79 BC	Possibly the "New King" who was Pharaoh during the Hebrews' slavery in Egypt.	Exodus 1–14
Rameses II 1279-12 BC	Followed Sety I and may be the Pharaoh at the time of the Exodus.	Exodus 1–14
Unnamed	Father of King Solomon's Egyptian wife.	1 Kings 3:1; 7:8
Shishak 945-924 BC	Raided the Jerusalem Temple in the reign of Rehoboam of Judah; let Jeroboam of Israel hide in his palace.	1 Kings 14:25-26; 2 Chronicles 12:2-9
727-720 BC	Maybe Pharaoh Osorkon IV, sent a message by King Hoshea of Israel before the Israelites rebelled against the King of Assyria.	2 Kings 17:1-4
Tirhakah 690-664 BC	"King of Ethiopia" who battled with Assyria during the reign of King Hezekiah of Judah.	2 Kings 19:9; Isaiah 37:9
Neco 610-595 BC	Killed King Josiah of Judah at Megiddo, replaced Jehoahaz with Jehoiakim as Judah's ruler, and was defeated by King Nebuchadnezzar of Babylon.	2 Kings 23:29-34; 2 Chronicles 35:20–36:4
Hophra 589-570 BC	Prophet Jeremiah said Hophra would be captured by his enemy Nebuchadnezzar of Babylonia.	Jeremiah 43:6-13; 44:30
Other unnamed kings, about whom little is known.		1 Kings 11:14-22; 1 Chronicles 4:17-18

An Egyptian pharaoh.

Chephren Pyramid, Egypt.

What were the ten plagues of Egypt?

Moses warned Pharaoh of ten plagues that would come upon Egypt if he did not release the Hebrews from their captivity. The plagues amounted to attacks on the Egyptian deities, demonstrating God's power over them.

1. **Water to blood**
   The Nile River was turned into blood. This represented a direct attack on the Egyptian river god, Hopi, and demonstrated God's power over it. (EXODUS 7:14–24)
2. **Frogs**
   Frogs, a symbol of fertility, overran the land, and when they died polluted Egypt. (EXODUS 7:25–8:15)
3. **Gnats**
   A small stinging insect, such as the sand flea, is probably meant by "gnat." Egypt's magicians could not repeat this miracle and told Pharaoh it was the work of God. (EXODUS 8:16–19)
4. **Flies**
   Swarms, possibly of biting swamp flies, infested Egypt. (EXODUS 8:20–32)
5. **Death of cattle**
   Some believe the plague that struck the cattle of Egypt was anthrax. The Israelite cattle were immune, showing that God distinguished between his people and their oppressors. (EXODUS 9:1–7)
6. **Boils**
   Probably skin anthrax, carried by the bites of the flies that fed on the rotting frogs. (EXODUS 9:8–12)
7. **Hail**
   A hailstorm ruined the Egyptians' barley and flax, but the land of Goshen, occupied by the Israelites, was spared. (EXODUS 9:13–35)
8. **Locusts**
   Locusts stripped the land of any remaining crops. (EXODUS 10:1–20)
9. **Darkness**
   The sun was darkened for three days—a terrifying darkness. (EXODUS 10:21–29)
10. **Death of the firstborn**
    The final plague killed the firstborn in every Egyptian household, but left the Israelites unharmed. Pharaoh's stubborn resistance was finally broken, and he urged Moses to take Israel out of his land. (EXODUS 11:1—12:33)

Frogs plague.

Locust plague.

Numbers in the Bible

One

Represents monotheism, uniqueness, and unity.

"The LORD is our God, the LORD alone." DEUTERONOMY 6:4 NLT

"There is one Lord, one faith, one baptism." EPHESIANS 4:5 NLT

Three

Represents completeness or totality. Many ancient religions considered three a divine number.

Three men visited Abraham at Mamre. GENESIS 18:1-15

Three annual pilgrimage festivals: Unleavened Bread, Harvest, and Shelters. EXODUS 23:14-19

Number of days and nights Jonah was inside the big fish. JONAH 1:17

Number of days between Jesus' death and resurrection. MARK 8:31; 1 CORINTHIANS 15:4

Four

Most cultures speak of four winds or directions, and divide the year into four seasons.

Number of rivers flowing out of the garden of Eden. GENESIS 2:10

Four living creatures of Ezekiel's vision. EZEKIEL 1:4-5; see also REVELATION 4:1-8

Four horses and riders of John's vision. REVELATION 6:1-8

Seven

Represents completeness and perfection. Like three, considered a sacred number in many cultures in the ancient world.

Number of days in the week in the Creation story. GENESIS 1:1–2:3

The seventh day is a holy day of rest, or Sabbath. EXODUS 20:8-11

The Israelites were to let the land rest every seventh, or sabbatical, year. EXODUS 23:10, 11

Every fiftieth year (7 x 7 + 1) the Israelites were to celebrate a Year of Celebration, or Jubilee, to mark a time of freedom and forgiveness. LEVITICUS 25:8-55

Number of times blood was sprinkled during sacrifices. LEVITICUS 4:6, 17; 14:7; NUMBERS 19:4

Number of some items in Revelation, such as lampstands, stars, churches, seals, trumpets, and bowls. REVELATION 6–11; 15; 16

Number of times Jesus said to forgive—seventy-seven or seven times seventy. MATTHEW 18:21-22

Ten

Ten is the sum of three and seven, and sometimes represents complete perfection.

The number of times "God said" is repeated in the Hebrew text of the Creation story. GENESIS 1:1-31

The Ten Commandments. EXODUS 20:1-17; DEUTERONOMY 5:1-22

Twelve

Another number of completeness and perfection.

Number of Jacob's sons, and of the tribes of Israel. GENESIS 35:23-26; 49:1-28

Number of gates to Jerusalem in Ezekiel's vision. EZEKIEL 48:30-34; see also REVELATION 21:11-21

Number of Jesus' apostles. MATTHEW 10:1-4; MARK 3:13-19; LUKE 6:12-16; see also ACTS 1:12-26

Forty

A long, but limited, period of time.

Number of days it rained during the Great Flood. GENESIS 7:4, 17-18

Number of days Moses stayed on Mount Sinai. EXODUS 24:17-18

Number of years the Israelites wandered in the wilderness. NUMBERS 14:33-34; DEUTERONOMY 2:7; 29:4-6

Number of days Jesus went without eating in the desert. MATTHEW 4:2; MARK 1:12-13; LUKE 4:2

Ezekiel's vision of four creatures.

It rained forty days during the Great Flood.

The Tribes of Israel

Named after the sons of Jacob

Why thirteen tribes when we speak of the "twelve tribes of Israel"? Unlike the other tribes, Levi did not receive territory. Also, Joseph's sons were considered heads of tribes—both of which received an inheritance of land. In some Old Testament lists, Joseph is counted as one of the twelve. In others, Levi isn't counted and Ephraim and Manasseh are named as separate tribes.

1. Reuben (mother, Leah)
2. Simeon (Leah)
3. Levi (Leah) the priestly tribe, allotted no territory
4. Judah (Leah)
5. Dan (mother, Bilhah)
6. Naphtali (Bilhah)
7. Gad (mother, Zilpah)
8. Asher (Zilpah)
9. Issachar (Leah)
10. Zebulun (Leah)
11. Ephraim (son of Joseph)
12. Manasseh (son of Joseph)
13. Benjamin (mother, Rachel)

The Ten Commandments

Then God gave the people all these instructions:

I am the LORD your God, who rescued you from the land of Egypt, the place of your slavery.

You must not have any other god but me.

You must not make for yourself an idol of any kind or an image of anything in the heavens or on the earth or in the sea. You must not bow down to them or worship them, for I, the LORD your God, am a jealous God who will not tolerate your affection for any other gods. I lay the sins of the parents upon their children; the entire family is affected—even children in the third and fourth generations of those who reject me. But I lavish unfailing love for a thousand generations on those who love me and obey my commands.

You must not misuse the name of the LORD your God. The LORD will not let you go unpunished if you misuse his name.

Remember to observe the Sabbath day by keeping it holy. You have six days each week for your ordinary work, but the seventh day is a Sabbath day of rest dedicated to the LORD your God. On that day no one in your household may do any work. This includes you, your sons and daughters, your male and female servants, your livestock, and any foreigners living among you. For in six days the LORD made the heavens, the earth, the sea, and everything in them; but on the seventh day he rested. That is why the LORD blessed the Sabbath day and set it apart as holy.

Honor your father and mother. Then you will live a long, full life in the land the LORD your God is giving you.

You must not murder.

You must not commit adultery.

You must not steal.

You must not testify falsely against your neighbor.

You must not covet your neighbor's house. You must not covet your neighbor's wife, male or female servant, ox or donkey, or anything else that belongs to your neighbor.

EXODUS 20:1–17, NLT

What happened to the Israelites during the Exodus?

1. The Israelites were told to leave Egypt by Pharaoh. The years of slavery were over. EXODUS 12:29–37
2. The Israelites traveled to the region of the Bitter Lakes. EXODUS 12:37–39; 13:17—14:4
3. Pharaoh changed his mind and pursued his escaped slaves, trapping the Israelites at the sea. EXODUS 14:5–12
4. God told Moses to hold out his staff over the sea. The waters were driven back and the people crossed on dry land. The Egyptians were drowned when the water flowed back. EXODUS 14:13–31
5. After three days, the Israelites arrived at Marah—but the water there was too bitter to drink. EXODUS 15:22–26
6. God provided manna and quails for the Israelites to eat. EXODUS 16
7. God provided the Israelites with water from a rock. The Amalekites attacked and were defeated. EXODUS 17
8. Israel received the Law from God at Mount Sinai. EXODUS 19—32
9. Miriam became leprous because of her rebellion against her brother Moses. NUMBERS 12:1–16
10. Eleven days after leaving Mount Sinai, Moses sent twelve spies into Canaan. NUMBERS 13:1–24
11. The spies returned. Ten brought bad reports, leading the people to rebel. They wanted a new leader, to take them back to Egypt. NUMBERS 13:25—14:10
12. As punishment, God sent the Israelites to wander in the desert for forty years, before entering Canaan. NUMBERS 14:11–38

Joseph, Moses, and the Israelites

Joseph
Rachel and Jacob's first son was given a "coat of many colors" by his father. His brothers sold him as a slave. Wrongfully thrown into prison in Egypt, Joseph was freed after he interpreted Pharaoh's dreams. This supernatural ability was a gift from God. Pharaoh made him prime minister of Egypt, responsible for storing food, before the seven years of famine that he predicted.
GENESIS 30:22–24; 37–50

Pharaoh
The pharaoh in the time of Moses was Rameses II, who forced the Hebrews to be slaves.
GENESIS 40–41; EXODUS 1–15

Benjamin
Jacob's youngest son. When Benjamin went to Egypt, Joseph detained him, accusing him of stealing a silver cup.
GENESIS 35:18, 24; 42:4, 36; 43–45

Ephraim
Joseph's second son, and brother of Manasseh. Though he was the younger of Joseph's sons, Jacob gave him the blessing of the firstborn. Ancestor of one of the twelve tribes of Israel.
GENESIS 41:52; 46:20; 48; 50:23

Zipporah
One of seven daughters of Jethro, a priest in Midian. Zipporah became Moses' wife: they had two sons, Gershom and Eliezer.
EXODUS 2:16–22; 4:24–26; 18:2–4

Miriam
Moses' sister. As a child, she helped hide her baby brother and kept watch until he was rescued. She became a prophetess. When she opposed Moses' leadership, she was punished with leprosy temporarily.
EXODUS 2:4, 7–8; 15:20–21; NUMBERS 12; 20:1

Aaron
Moses' elder brother, and spokesman to Pharaoh. In the desert, Aaron helped the Israelites make a golden calf. He became Israel's first high priest, in charge of the tabernacle.
EXODUS 4:14, 30; 5–12; 28–29; 32

Joshua
Spiritual and military leader of the Israelites. He spied out the land of Canaan and—with Caleb—encouraged the people to attack. He eventually led the people to victory in Canaan, taking over leadership on Moses' death. At the end of his life, Joshua challenged the Israelites to follow God faithfully.
EXODUS 17:9–13; 24:13; NUMBERS 13–14; JOSHUA 24

Judah
Fourth son of Jacob and Leah, gained the birthright that Reuben forfeited. When his brothers plotted to kill Joseph, Judah persuaded them to sell him to traders instead.
GENESIS 29:35; 37:26–28; 38; 43:3–10

Levi
Third son of Jacob and Leah, and ancestor of the Levites, the Israelite tribe who served in the Tabernacle, and later in the Temple.
GENESIS 29:34; 34:25–31; 49:5–7

Manasseh
Joseph's elder son, Manasseh, was adopted—along with his brother Ephraim—by his grandfather Jacob, and so an ancestor of one of the tribes of Israel. Jacob, however, gave the blessing for the firstborn to Ephraim, and not Manasseh.
GENESIS 41:51; 48

Potiphar
High-ranking Egyptian official who put Joseph in charge of all his household and later threw him in prison, after his wife falsely accused Joseph of attempted rape.
GENESIS 37:36; 39

Reuben
First of Jacob and Leah's six sons, Reuben tried to rescue Joseph when his brothers planned to kill him.
GENESIS 29:32; 35:22–23; 37:21–29; 42:37–38

Simeon
Jacob and Leah's second son. With his brother Levi, he avenged his sister Dinah's rape by slaughtering the people of Shechem.
GENESIS 29:33; 34:25–30; 49:5–7

Joseph, Moses, and the Israelites continued

Caleb

One of the twelve who Moses sent to spy out the Promised Land. He and Joshua said that, with God's help, they could conquer the land. Of all those who left Egypt, only Joshua and Caleb entered Canaan.

NUMBERS 13–14; 26:65

Achan

Achan stole treasures from the conquered city of Jericho and hid them in his tent, which led to Israel's defeat at Ai. When his crime was discovered, he was stoned to death and Ai successfully captured.

JOSHUA 7:1–8:29

Moses

As a baby, Moses was saved from death by Pharaoh's daughter, who found him in a basket in the Nile River. She brought him up as her son, a prince of Egypt. After killing an Egyptian taskmaster, Moses fled to Midian, where he became a shepherd and married Zipporah. He saw a burning bush in the desert, and God called him to return to Egypt to rescue his people. Moses confronted Pharaoh, but only after Egypt had been devastated by plagues and all firstborn Egyptian sons had died did Pharaoh allow them to leave.

After leading the people to safety on dry land through the Red Sea, Moses brought them to Mount Sinai, where God gave him the Ten Commandments, together with rules for daily living and instructions for building the Tabernacle. Moses led his often rebellious people through the desert for forty years. Moses was the first and greatest of the prophets. He gave the Law, and revealed God as "Yahweh"–"I am."

EXODUS 2–DEUTERONOMY; LUKE 9:28-36; HEBREWS 11:23-29

Moses at the burning bush.

Leviticus

Author

Moses.

Date

c. 1400/1200 BC.

Outline

Sacrifices 1:1–6:23

Offerings 6:24–7:38

Appointment of the priests 8:1–10:20

Purity and impurity 11:1–15:33

The Day of Atonement 16:1-34

Rules for holy living 17:1–22:33

The religious calendar 23:1–25:55

Obedience–and disobedience 26:1–27:34

Major themes in Leviticus

Holiness

God is holy: the basis for all of the Law.

Justice

God's holiness and justice go hand in hand. God deals justly with his people: they must deal justly with each other.

Covenant

God had made his covenant with Israel; they must live in the pattern he had set. Keeping his laws was not optional.

Thankfulness

Everything the Israelites had was given by God—including the laws and sacrifices that made it possible to renew their relationship with him when they sinned.

Numbers

Author
Moses.

Date
c. 1400/1200 BC.

Outline

Organizing Israel 1:1–10:36

Adventures in the wilderness 11:1–25:18

Looking to the Promised Land 26:1–33:49

Preparing to enter Canaan 33:50–36:13

The Hebrew title for the book of Numbers is "In the Desert." The book begins with the people of Israel camped in the wilderness. The Lord commands Moses to count the people, and gives the Israelites rules for their time of traveling and instructions for worship.

The people begin their journey to the promised land of Canaan, pass through the land of Kadesh, and try to enter Canaan from the south, but are forced to detour around the country of Edom.

Numbers also describes the people's disobedience and how they grumbled against the Lord during their years in the desert. After the Lord chooses Joshua to be the leader of the people after Moses' death, the Israelites defeat the Midianites, and finally come to the mountains overlooking the promised land.

Major themes in Numbers

Divine provision
How God provides for his people.

Divine guidance
Despite persistent backsliding, God led his people all through their wanderings with the cloud and fire.

Noah releases the dove.

Five Covenant stages in the Old Testament—and the New Covenant

There is one over-arching covenant that spans both Old and New Testaments. It is the divine Covenant of Redemption, which is made up of five stages in the Old Testament, plus the promise of a New Covenant, followed by its fulfilment in Jesus Christ in the New Testament—six stages in all.

1. The Covenant of creation
   Made with creation itself, including Adam and Eve, whereby God instructed how humankind was to live as steward of the world God had brought into being (cf. GENESIS 1—3; HOSEA 6:7; JEREMIAH 33:19–22).
2. The Noahic Covenant
   Made between God and the whole creation. It was unconditional, with no human obligations. After Noah's flood, God promised never again to use a flood to destroy the earth (cf. GENESIS 9).
3. The Abrahamic Covenant
   God made promises to Abraham and his family, who were called upon to remain in relationship with, and obedient to, God (cf. GENESIS 12, 15, 17).
4. The Mosaic, or Sinaitic, Covenant
   The major covenant with Israel. Moses acted as go-between when it was set up between God and Israel at Sinai (cf. EXODUS 19–24; LEVITICUS; DEUTERONOMY).
5. The Davidic Covenant
   God made special promises to David concerning his descendants (cf. 2 SAMUEL 7).
6. The promise of a New Covenant
   Jeremiah (33) and Ezekiel (36:24–32) reveal God's promise of a new covenant relationship, in which God's law will be written on people's hearts and they will know and follow God. This New Covenant is fulfilled in the person of Jesus Christ.

Deuteronomy

Author
Moses.

Date
c. 1400/1200 BC.

Outline
Moses' first speech 1:1–4:43
Commitment to God 4:44–11:32
God's laws 12:1–26:19
Blessing and cursing 27:1–28:68
Looking backward—and forward 29:1–30:20
Moses' final days 31:1–34:12

Major themes in Deuteronomy

The Covenant
The heart of the Book of Deuteronomy is God's covenant with his people, and all the ramifications it holds for the people of God. All the themes listed below can be regarded as sub-themes of this dominant motif.

God's power
God is not only the Lord of the covenant and sovereign over Israel, but the God of history, sovereign over the world, controlling nations and nature. He has the power to carry out his promises.

God's faithfulness
Israel knew that God is totally dependable.

Love
The covenant was based on love. God's love started the covenant and made possible its continuation. The first demand on us is that we love God. Without love, a relationship with God cannot exist.

Commitment
God wants total commitment, undivided allegiance, and whole-hearted devotion from his people. This involves following God's will in every sphere of life.

The Cities of Refuge

In Old Testament times six cities of refuge were located in Israel to provide a place of safety for people who had accidentally killed someone (cf. JOSHUA 20:7–8). Such protection was necessary because a relative might feel a duty to kill the perpetrator. Three cities were situated on each side of the Jordan River.

Bezer
A walled city in the territory of Reuben, in the wilderness plateau of Moab.

Golan
East of the Sea of Galilee, in the area known as Bashan.

Hebron
Twenty miles south of Jerusalem, Hebron was the southernmost of the cities of refuge.

Kedesh, or Kedesh Naphtali
In Galilee, in the mountains of Naphtali.

Ramoth, or Ramoth Gilead
Important walled city east of the Jordan river, in the tribal lands of Gad.

Shechem
In the mountains of Ephraim, this is where the Lord appeared to Abraham and promised to give him this land.

Tomb of the Patriarchs, Hebron.

Joshua

Author
Probably Joshua.

Date
c. 1350/1150 BC.

Outline
Entering the land 1:1–5:12
Conquering the land 5:13–12:24
Dividing the land 13:1–22:34
Farewell and burial in the land 23:1–24:33

About
Joshua became leader of God's people after the death of Moses. This book is the hinge of Israel's history: the wilderness wandering was over and the promised land before them.

As the sixth book of the Bible, Joshua begins the section on Israel's history. Joshua through Esther make up the history of the Jewish people.

Purpose
Joshua—a book of conquest—describes the transition of God's chosen people from wilderness wanderers to courageous conquerors.

The Israelites march around Jericho.

Major themes in Joshua

The land of promise

God promised this land from the day he called out the man—Abraham—who would birth the nation.

Covenant and the obedience of God's people

The land given to the children of Israel is at the heart of the covenant God made with them generations before. Throughout Joshua, the Ark of the Covenant went before the people as a reminder of this relationship, symbolizing God's mercy, power, and holiness. Obedience was at the core of this relationship, realized and renewed in Joshua. The people who still lived in the land with their pagan gods challenged the obedience of God's people.

The typology of Jesus

Joshua is a type of Jesus. For the follower of Christ, the Promised Land becomes a picture of the untold blessings that are ours in Christ.

Priests carry the Ark of the Covenant across Jordan.

Deities of Bible times

Name	Country	Description	Scripture
Artemis (Diana)	Asia	many-breasted fertility goddess	Acts 19:28
Asherah	Canaan	goddess of the sea wife of Baal symbol—a pole	Judges 3:7 1 Kings 18:19 2 Kings 21:3
Ashtoreth (Astarte Queen of Heaven)	Canaan Sidon	mother goddess fertility goddess	Judges 2:13; 10:6 1 Samuel 12:10 1 Kings 11:5, 33 Jeremiah 7:18; 44:17-25
Baal	Canaan	young storm god chief god of Canaan until the Exile	Judges 2:13; 1 Kings 16:31-32;18:18-29
Baal-Zebub	Philistia	god of Ekron	2 Kings 1:2
Castor and Pollux	Greece	twin sons of Zeus	Acts 28:11
Chemosh	Moab	national god of war	Numbers 21:29 Judges 11:24 1 Kings 11:7, 33 Jeremiah 48:7
Dagon	Philistia	national god of rain/agriculture	Judges 16:23 1 Samuel 5:2-7
Hermes (Mercury)	Greece	messenger god, god of cunning, theft	Acts 14:12
Marduk (Bel)	Babylon	young storm/war god chief god	Isaiah 46:1 Jeremiah 50:2; 51:44
Molech (Malcam) (Milcom) (Moloch)	Ammon Israel	national god worshiped with child sacrifice	Zephaniah 1:5 Jeremiah 49:1, 3 1 Kings 11:5, 7, 33 Acts 7:43
Nebo (Nabu)	Babylon	son of Marduk god of wisdom, literature, arts	Isaiah 46:1
Nergal	Babylon	god of hunting, the underworld	2 Kings 17:30
Rimmon (Hadad)	Damascus	god of thunder, lightning, rain	2 Kings 5:18
Tammuz	Babylon	fertility god	Ezekiel 8:14
Zeus	Greece	chief of Greek gods	Acts 14:12

( ) = alternative name

Judges

Author
Samuel the prophet.

Date
1200–970 BC.

Outline
Disobedience: Israel turns from God 1:1–2:5
Victory and defeat 1:1-36
Divine mercy 2:1-5
Discipline: The Lord punishes Israel 2:6–16:31
Israel's disobedience and defeat 2:6–3:6
Othniel, Ehud, and Shamgar 3:7-31
Deborah and Barak 4:1–5:31
Gideon 6:1–8:32
Abimelech 8:33–9:57
Tola and Jair 10:1–5
Jephthah 10:6–12:7
Ibzan, Elon, and Abdon 12:8–15:20
Samson 13:1–16:31
Disgrace: Israel falls into anarchy 17:1–21:25
Idolatry 17:1–18:31
Immorality 19:1-30
Civil war 20:1–21:25

About
Judges describes the men and women who distinguished themselves in the period between the book of Joshua and the establishment of a kingdom, in 1 Samuel. For 400 years, Israel had no king or prophet to guide them. Instead, twelve consecutive judges led them. The judges were not law-court justices: God chose them to deliver Israel from enemy oppression, lead the people of God in revival, and restore their national identity.

Purpose
The book of Judges explores one of the most crucial periods in the history of Israel: the transition from slaves of Egypt to citizens of a kingdom. It shows how Israel failed to live up to the covenant that God lovingly entered into with them, and the resulting disastrous downfall.

Major themes in Judges

Idolatry and apostasy on trial

Judges recounts Israel's lapses into idolatry and apostasy: worshiping false gods and living as they pleased. They forgot the wonders in the wilderness, the manna, the split rock that gave them water. Not only did Israel settle among the Canaanites, Hittites, Amorites, Perizzites, Hivites, and Jebusites, but they also intermarried and served false gods.

Disobedience and deliverance

A cyclical pattern in Judges is repeated seven times: Israel does what is evil in God's sight; the people are delivered to their enemies; Israel cries out to God; he answers their prayer; God raises up a leader and delivers Israel; the people return to the Lord, and peace is regained for a time.

Spirit-empowered leadership

Under Joshua, the people did what was right. However, once he died, the next generation forgot God and all he had done for Israel (2:10). But the Lord did not abandon his people; he raised up deliverers to rescue them.

Samuel hears God's call.

Significant persons in the time of the Judges

Judges were rulers of Israelite tribes at the time that the Israelites were settling in the Promised Land. A judge was a military leader who rescued his tribe, or group of neighboring tribes, from the enemy, and became a peacetime governor.

Samson
Famed for his strength, Samson ruled Israel for twenty years and tried to free the Israelites from forty years of domination by the Philistines. Dedicated to God as a Nazirite, he never cut his hair—but foolishly revealed to Delilah, his Philistine wife, that his strength lay in his long hair, as a result of her nagging him for his secret. While asleep, she had his hair cut, and then betrayed him to her people, after which the Philistines blinded him and took him prisoner. When his hair grew back and strength returned, he destroyed a Philistine temple, killing himself and many Philistines.
JUDGES 13–16; HEBREWS 11:32

Jael
Jael murdered Sisera, commander of the Canaanite army, driving a tent peg through his head.
JUDGES 4:17–21; 5:24–27

Barak
Commander of the Israelite army, Barak defeated Jabin, king of Canaan, and freed the Israelites.
JUDGES 4–5

Deborah
The only female judge. Deborah's general, Barak, defeated the Philistines, commencing forty years free of foreign domination.
JUDGES 4–5

Jephthah
Israel's eighth judge, who rashly vowed that, if he beat the Ammonites, he would sacrifice the first person to come out of his house to meet him. His daughter met him, and he fulfilled his vow. It is possible that this vow entailed not her physical death, but a vow dedicating her to perpetual celibacy, and therefore, childlessness.
JUDGES 11–12

Abimelech
Gideon's son, who ruled Israel as judge for three years. He was crushed to death by a millstone.
JUDGES 8–9

Hannah
Wife of Elkanah. She prayed for a son, whom she vowed to dedicate to God's service. God gave her a son, Samuel, who she presented to Eli to serve in the sanctuary at Shiloh.
1 SAMUEL 1–2

Eli
Priest and judge of Israel. As priest at Shiloh, he trained Samuel. He failed to discipline his sons, Hophni and Phinehas, which brought God's judgment on Israel.
1 SAMUEL 1–4

Gideon
Gideon had little self-confidence. At God's command, he reduced his army to 300, and overcame vast numbers of Midianites. After this victory, Gideon became judge over his tribe.
JUDGES 6–8

Samuel
Son of Elkanah and Hannah, the last great warrior-judge of Israel, and one of the first prophets. Samuel's rule marked the transition between the period of judges and kings. In old age, he yielded to the Israelites' wish to be like other nations and have a king, anointing Saul as Israel's first king. When Saul betrayed his early promise, Samuel anointed David as his successor.
1 SAMUEL 1–4; 7–16

The following three people were highly significant persons who held a place in the genealogy of Jesus Christ (cf. MATTHEW 1; LUKE 3). They all lived during the time of the Judges.

Naomi
Ruth's mother-in-law. With her husband, Elimelech, she moved from Bethlehem to Moab, where he and their two sons died. Naomi's daughter-in-law Ruth returned with her to Bethlehem.
RUTH

Ruth
Wife of Naomi's son, Mahlon. When he died, she left Moab to go to Naomi's home in Bethlehem, where she married Naomi's relative, Boaz. Ruth's son, Obed, was father of Jesse, one of whose sons was King David.
RUTH; MATTHEW 1:5

Boaz
A wealthy landowner who married Ruth and became great-grandfather of King David.
RUTH; MATTHEW 1:5; LUKE 3:32

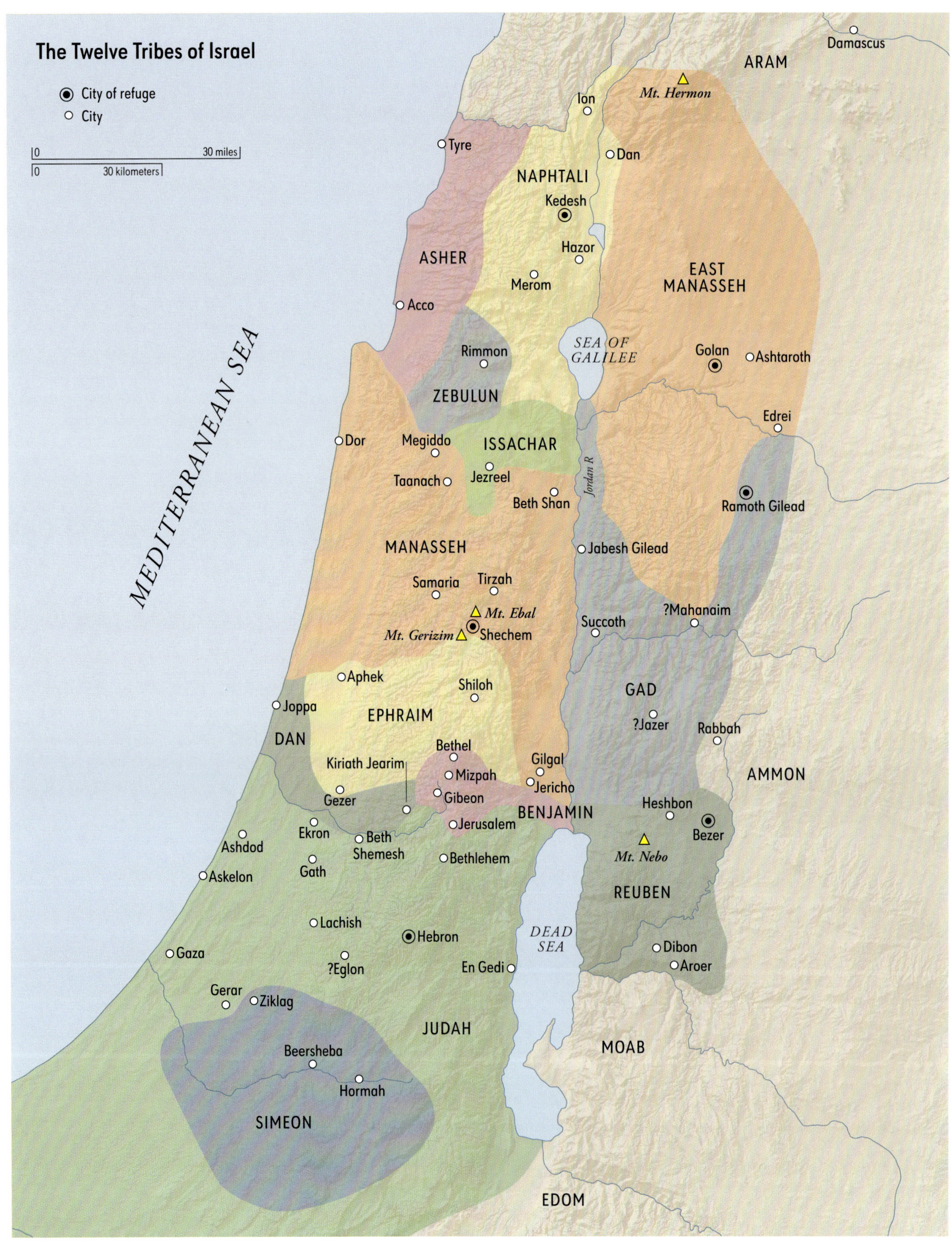
The Twelve Tribes of Israel
City of refuge
City
0 30 miles
0 30 kilometers
MEDITERRANEAN SEA
Damascus
ARAM
Mt. Hermon
Ion
Tyre
Dan
NAPHTALI
Kedesh
ASHER
Hazor
EAST MANASSEH
Merom
Acco
SEA OF GALILEE
Rimmon
Golan
Ashtaroth
ZEBULUN
Edrei
Dor
Megiddo
ISSACHAR
Taanach
Jezreel
Jordan R.
Beth Shan
Ramoth Gilead
MANASSEH
Jabesh Gilead
Samaria
Tirzah
Mt. Ebal
?Mahanaim
Mt. Gerizim
Shechem
Succoth
Aphek
Shiloh
GAD
Joppa
EPHRAIM
?Jazer
Rabbah
DAN
Bethel
Kiriath Jearim
Gilgal
Mizpah
AMMON
Jericho
Gezer
Gibeon
Heshbon
BENJAMIN
Jerusalem
Bezer
Ekron
Beth Shemesh
Ashdod
Mt. Nebo
Gath
Bethlehem
Askelon
REUBEN
Lachish
Hebron
DEAD SEA
Gaza
Dibon
?Eglon
En Gedi
Aroer
Gerar
Ziklag
JUDAH
MOAB
Beersheba
Hormah
SIMEON
EDOM

The Israelite Conquest of Canaan

When the Israelites came to the Promised Land, God told them they must defeat the Canaanite tribal nations and take over the land: First, because he had promised this land to Abraham and his descendants; second, to punish the Canaanite nations that tried to harm God's people and prevent them from entering the Promised Land.

Moabites
One of Lot's sons, Moab, became father of the Moabites (GENESIS 19:36-37), who settled southeast of the Jordan River. They tried to stop the Israelites entering the Promised Land by hiring Balaam to curse them (NUMBERS 22–24).

Ammonites
Lot's other son, Ben-Ammi, became father of the Ammonites (GENESIS 19:38), who settled east of the Jordan River.

Edomites
Esau, Jacob's twin, became the father of the Edomites (GENESIS 36:9), who lived south of the Moabites, and refused to let the Israelites pass through their land on the way to the Promised Land.

Amalekites
The Amalekites lived in the Negev, the southern part of what became Israel (NUMBERS 13:29).

Jebusites
The Jebusites lived in the hill country (NUMBERS 13:29) in and around Jerusalem.

Hittites
Originally from Anatolia (Turkey), the Hittites spread out, some coming to live in the hill country of Canaan (NUMBERS 13:29, JOSHUA 12:7-8).

Amorites
The Amorites lived in the hill country (NUMBERS 13:29).

Canaanites
The Canaanites were descended from Ham (Noah's son) and his son Canaan, and lived near the sea and along the Jordan River (NUMBERS 13:29).

Philistines
Descendants of Ham and his son Egypt (GENESIS 10:6-14), the Philistines were also called Caphtorim (DEUTERONOMY 2:23, JEREMIAH 47:4). Part of a group called the Sea People, they settled along the Mediterranean coast and remained enemies of Israel until King David defeated them.

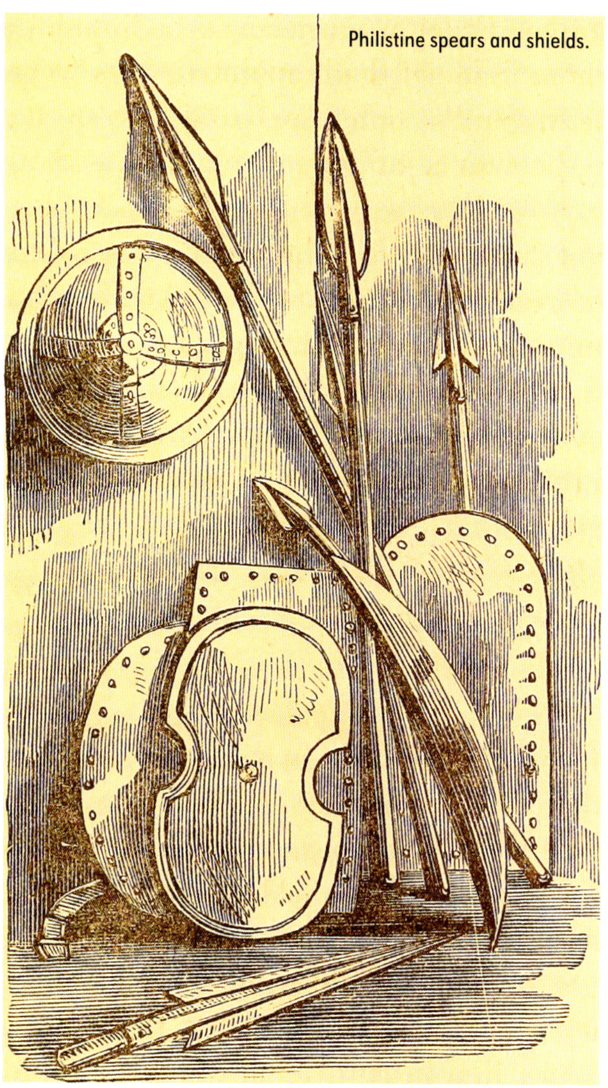
Philistine spears and shields.

Amorite clay tablet.

The judges of Israel and their adversaries

Judge Oppressor	Actions	Years the judge led Israel Years of oppression	Reference in book of Judges
Cushan, King of Aram		8	3:8
Othniel	Freed Israel from Mesopotamian oppressors	40	3:7-11
Eglon, King of Moab		18	3:14
Ehud	Freed Israel from Moabite oppressors	80	3:12-30
Shamgar	Freed Israel from Philistine oppressors	10	3:31
Jabin, King of Canaan		20	4:2
Deborah	With Barak, freed Israel from Canaanite oppressors	40	4:4–5:31
Midianites		7	6:1
Gideon	Freed Israel from Midianite oppressors	40	6:11–8:35
Abimelech	Terrorized the people as self-proclaimed King of Israel	3	9
Tola		23	10:1-2
Jair		22	10:3-5
Ammonites		18	10:7-9
Jephthah	Freed Israel from Ammonite oppressors	6	10:6–12:7
Ibzan		7	12:8-10
Elon		10	12:11-12
Abdon		8	12:13-15
Philistines		40	13:1
Samson		20	13–16
Eli	High priest and judge	40	1 Samuel 1:1–4:18
Samuel	High priest and judge	21	1 Samuel 1:11–25:1
Joel/Abijah			1 Samuel 8:1-2

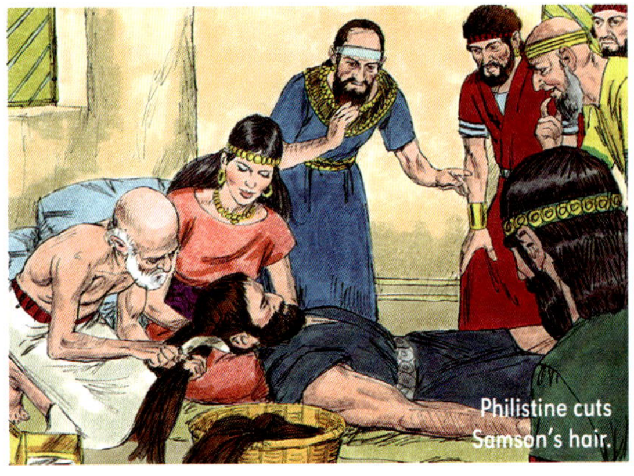
Philistine cuts Samson's hair.

Samuel confronts King Saul.

The Holy Land
Damascus
Mt. Hermon
Litani R.
Dan
MEDITERRANEAN SEA
Galilean Hills
LAKE GALILEE
Mt. Carmel
Jezreel Valley
Mt. Tabor
Yarmuk R.
Jordan R.
Plain of Sharon
Gilead
Jordan Valley
Mt. Gerizim
Hill-country of Ephraim
Coastal Plain
Shephelah
Jerusalem
Mt. Nebo
Central Highlands
Wilderness of Judea
DEAD SEA
Arnon R.
Eastern Desert
Beersheba
Negeb
Arabah
Wilderness of Zin
0
50 miles
0
50 kilometers

Ruth

Author

Traditionally, Samuel the prophet.

Date

Likely during the early monarchy (1030–970 BC), about 80 to 100 years before David.

Outline

Love's resolve: Ruth's noble choice 1:1-22

Love's response: Ruth's lowly service 2:1-23

Love's request: Ruth's tender appeal 3:1-18

Love's reward: Ruth's joy 4:1-22

Purpose

Ruth showcases the faithfulness of God, partly by the establishment of the genealogy of David and Jesus. The book of Ruth contains one of the most beautiful love stories in the Old Testament.

Major themes in Ruth

Outsiders become insiders

Ruth, a Moabite from a gentile nation, is an example of faithfulness to the law, contrasting with Israel's idolatry and faithless living. This non-Jewish outsider played a vital role in God's promise of salvation, standing in the long line of women leading to the birth of Jesus.

Our circumstances, God's faithfulness

Ruth reveals the sovereignty of God, focusing on two women, and how he overrules circumstances for his good purposes. The most painful time of Ruth's life became her most vital, propelling her to a destiny she never could have imagined.

God's kinsman-redeeming love

There is a Hebrew word at the center of this story that means "kinsman-redeemer." If a widow was childless, under the law a close male relative could redeem her through marriage and buy back her property. Naomi had relatives in Bethlehem who could be her kinsman-redeemer, one of whom was Boaz. Boaz is a picture of our Lord Jesus Christ, our Kinsman-Redeemer.

Gleaning grain.

1 Samuel

Author

Traditionally, Samuel.

Date

Probably 10th century BC.

Outline

Eli and Samuel 1:1–7:17

Samuel and Saul 8:1–15:35

Saul and David 16:1–31:13

Major themes in 1 Samuel

Prayer and praise

God's man seeks guidance when it comes to making important decisions.

Rules for service

There are basic conditions for spiritual progress which cannot be ignored if we are to know God's blessing.

Spiritual gifts

God specially gifts those who would serve him. When God's Spirit came on them, they were able to do what they could not naturally do before. Yet this change may not be permanent, nor may they live holy lives afterward. There is no substitute for a continuous relationship with God.

Some Bible giants

Og, king of Bashan

He possessed an iron—or possibly stone—bedstead, nine cubits long and four cubits wide—roughly 13 x 6 feet, or 4 x 2 meters. (JOSHUA 12:4)

Goliath, the giant Philistine killed by David.

He was six cubits and a span tall—about 10 feet, or almost 3 meters. (1 SAMUEL 17:4)

An Egyptian giant five cubits tall, who owned a spear like a weaver's beam. (1 CHRONICLES 11:23)

Three Philistine giants, one of whom had six fingers on each hand, six toes on each foot. (1 CHRONICLES 20)

Travels of the Ark of the Covenant

The Lord calls Samuel, sleeping in the tent of meeting, "where the ark of God was." 1 SAMUEL 3:3

Philistines capture the Ark for seven months. 1 SAMUEL 4

Philistines bring the Ark to Ashdod, placing it next to the idol, Dagon, which God destroys the following morning. 1 SAMUEL 5:1–7

Philistines bring the Ark to Gath. 1 SAMUEL 5:8–9

Philistines send the Ark to Ekron. 1 SAMUEL 5:10–12

Philistines return the Ark to Beth-shemesh. 1 SAMUEL 6:10–15

God strikes 70 men dead for looking into the Ark. 1 SAMUEL 6:19–21

Men of Kiriath-jearim take the Ark to the house of Abinadab, where it remains for 20 years. 1 SAMUEL 7:1–2

Saul commands Ahijah to bring the Ark to the camp. 1 SAMUEL 14:18

David starts moving the Ark to Jerusalem on an ox-drawn cart, contrary to God's instructions, which required that it be carried on the shoulders of Levites and those of the house of Kohath. 2 SAMUEL 6:2–5

The Lord strikes Uzzah dead for touching the Ark, even though he was trying to prevent it falling off the cart. 2 SAMUEL 6:6–7

David takes the Ark to the house of Obed-edom, where it stays three months. 2 SAMUEL 6:10–11

David brings the Ark to Jerusalem, and places it inside a tent. 2 SAMUEL 6:12–17

Zadok brings the Ark to David, who tells him to carry it back to Jerusalem. 2 SAMUEL 15:24–25

Zadok and Abiathar take the Ark to Jerusalem. 2 SAMUEL 15:29

2 Samuel

Author

Probably an unnamed prophet, using writings of Nathan and Gad.

Date

Probably 10th century BC.

Outline

The death of Saul 1:1-27

David, King of Judah 2:1–4:12

David, King of all Israel 5:1–9:13

Victory—and defeat 10:1–12:31

Civil war 13:1–20:26

Gibeonites and Philistines 21:1-22

David's testimony 22:1–24:25

Major themes in 2 Samuel

Son of David

God's agreement with David—"the Davidic covenant" (2 SAMUEL 7)—was that all future and true kings of Israel would come from his family. For this reason the Jews in Jesus' day were looking for a Messiah—that is, an "anointed one"—who would fulfil all the ideals of kingship as David's descendant.

David's Lord

David owed everything he had to God, whose character shines through this book.

Treachery

There is a great deal of deceitfulness and wickedness in this book. David's men, family, and subjects all failed him. Perhaps it was because David did not know who he could trust that he put such trust in God.

The First Kings of Israel—along with family, friends, and foes

Saul (first king)
A Benjamite, the son of Kish, Saul was anointed by Samuel as Israel's first king. A courageous military leader, he was also a man of God, but grew proud and disobedient, so God rejected him. In his times of madness, David calmed him by playing the harp, but Saul became jealous of David's popularity and drove him from the country. Saul was wounded in battle against the Philistines at Mount Gilboa and killed himself.
1 SAMUEL 8–31; 2 SAMUEL 1

Jesse (family)
A grandson of Ruth and Boaz, and father of King David.
RUTH 4:16–22; 1 SAMUEL 16–17

Jonathan (family)
King Saul's eldest son. He knew that David—not he—would be the next king, but remained David's closest friend. Jonathan was killed in battle against the Philistines.
1 SAMUEL 13–14, 18–20, 23, 31; 2 SAMUEL 1

Goliath (foe)
A Philistine champion, more than 3 meters (10 feet) tall. A stone from David's sling felled him.
1 SAMUEL 17; 22:10

Ish-Bosheth (king of the Northern tribes of Israel)
Saul's son, crowned king of the northern tribes of Israel after Saul's death. When Ish-Bosheth died, David became king of Judah and Israel.
2 SAMUEL 2–4

David (second king—first as ruler of Judah (7½ years), and then of all Israel)
Despite spectacular failures, including adultery with Bathsheba and the murder of her husband, Uriah, David was Israel's greatest king. The youngest son of Jesse, he played the harp, wrote some of the psalms, killed the giant Goliath, defeated Israel's enemies, established Jerusalem as capital, and ushered in a golden age for Israel—"a man after God's own heart."
1 and 2 SAMUEL; in particular, 2 SAMUEL 2; 5ff; 1 CHRONICLES 11–29

Absalom (family)
Much loved, but ill-disciplined, son of David, whose throne he tried to usurp. Civil war ensued. As Absalom fled for his life, his long hair was caught in a tree. Against David's orders, Joab killed him.
2 SAMUEL 3:3; 13–19

Michal (family)
Saul's younger daughter and David's first wife. She saved David's life when Saul attempted to kill him.
1 SAMUEL 18–19; 25:44; 2 SAMUEL 3:13; 6

Bathsheba (family)
David committed adultery with Bathsheba, had her husband Uriah killed, and married her. The prophet Nathan rebuked David for this sin. Bathsheba and David's first son died, but their next son, Solomon, succeeded David as king.
2 SAMUEL 11–12; 1 KINGS 1–2.

Joab (friend)
King David's nephew and commander-in-chief. Joab killed David's son Absalom when he rebelled against David. Solomon had Joab killed for slaying Abner and Amasa, two other army commanders.
2 SAMUEL 2–3; 14; 18–20; 1 KINGS 2:28–35

Solomon (third king)
The son of Bathsheba and King David, whom he succeeded as king of Israel. Solomon built the temple in Jerusalem. Solomon excelled in diplomacy, strengthening his kingdom with trading partnerships and marriage alliances. Renowned for his wisdom, however his many foreign wives led him to lose his love of God. High taxes to finance his building projects left his country impoverished, and people angry.
2 SAMUEL 12:24; 1 KINGS 1–11; 1 CHRONICLES 22; 28; 29; 2 CHRONICLES 1–9

Uriah the Hittite (friend)
A loyal officer in David's army. David, who committed adultery with Uriah's wife, Bathsheba, arranged for Uriah to fight in the most dangerous position in the front line of battle, where he was killed.
2 SAMUEL 11–12

Abigail (friend)
Abigail protected her husband, Nabal, from David's anger with gifts of food. David married Abigail after her husband died.
1 SAMUEL 25; 27:3; 30:5; 2 SAMUEL 2:2

Adonijah (family)
David's fourth son, who tried unsuccessfully to take the throne of Israel from his elderly father.
2 SAMUEL 3:4; 1 KINGS 1:1–2:25

The First Kings of Israel—along with family, friends, and foes continued

Hiram (friend)
King of Tyre and ally of David and Solomon. Hiram supplied pine logs and cedars from Lebanon for building the Temple.
2 SAMUEL 5:11; 1 KINGS 5; 9:11-14

Amnon (family)
King David's first son, who raped his half-sister Tamar. Absalom, Tamar's brother, killed him two years later.
2 SAMUEL 3:2; 13:1-39

Abner (both foe and friend)
The commander of Saul's army who crowned Ish-Bosheth king on Saul's death.
1 SAMUEL 14:50; 17:55-58; 26:7-16; 2 SAMUEL 2:12–3:39

Ahithophel (foe)
When David's son, Absalom, revolted, Ahithophel deserted David and joined Absalom. After Absalom rejected Ahithophel's advice, the latter committed suicide.
2 SAMUEL 15–17

Abiathar (friend of David)
Saul had Abiathar's father and many other priests killed for assisting David. Abiathar, the only survivor, became joint high priest with Zadok under King David. Later, Abiathar helped David's son Adonijah attempt to usurp the throne, and for this was banished by Solomon.
1 SAMUEL 22–23; 2 SAMUEL 8:17; 1 KINGS 1:7, 19; 2:26-27;
1 CHRONICLES 15:11-15; 18:16

Zadok (friend)
Joint high priest with Abiathar during David's reign. Though Abiathar supported Adonijah's claim to the throne, Zadok remained faithful to David and crowned Solomon as next king of Israel. Solomon retained Zadok as high priest.
2 SAMUEL 8:17; 15:24-36; 17:15; 19:11; 1 KINGS 1:8; 2:35

1 Kings

Author
Unknown, but Jewish tradition claims Jeremiah.

Date
Possibly 6th century BC.

Outline
Death of David 1:1–2:11
Solomon's years of glory 2:12–10:29
Solomon's decline and death 11:1–12:24
The nation divides 12:25–15:24
Israel alone 15:25–16:34
Elijah: God's man 17:1–19:21
Ahab: weakness and greed 20:1–22:53

Major themes in 1 Kings

The sovereignty of God
God is involved in human history.

Righteousness
God expects his people to be obedient and loyal. 1 Kings describes the reigns of eight kings of Israel and four kings of Judah after the land was divided.

Weakness
1 Kings presents an unvarnished picture of God's servants. We see their faults as well as their good points; God accepted and used them as they were.

Solomon dedicates the Temple.

Tiphsah
Euphrates R.
Orontes R.
HAMATH
Hamath
Arvad
Kadesh
Tadmor
MEDITERRANEAN
SEA
Byblos
PHOENICIA
Sidon
Damascus
Tyre
Dan
ARAM
Kedesh
Hazor
Acco
Ashtaroth
Megiddo
Ramoth Gilead
Taanach
Beth Shan
Shechem
Jordan R.
AMMON
Joppa
PHILISTIA
Gezer
Rabbah
Gibeah
Ashdod
Medeba
Jerusalem
Ashkelon
Gath
DEAD
SEA
Ziklag
Hebron
Beersheba
MOAB
Kadesh Barnea
EDOM
Sinai
The Kingdoms of Saul, David, and Solomon
Saul's Kingdom
Kingdom of David and Solomon
Territory controlled by Solomon
0
100 miles
0
100 kilometers

Miracles of Elijah and Elisha

Elijah

Fed by ravens	1 KINGS 17:1–7
Meal and oil for the widow of Zarephath	1 KINGS 17:16
Fire on the altar	1 KINGS 18:38
Taken in a whirlwind	2 KINGS 2

Elisha

Jordan River purified	2 KINGS 2:19–22
Mockers killed by bears	2 KINGS 2:24
Widow's oil multiplied	2 KINGS 4:1–7
Widow's son raised from dead	2 KINGS 4:32–36
Naaman's leprosy cured	2 KINGS 5:10–14
Axe-head restored	2 KINGS 6:1–7
Arameans struck with blindness	2 KINGS 6:8–23
Syrian army put to flight	2 KINGS 7:6–7

Elijah's sacrifice.

2 Kings

Author
Unknown, but Jewish tradition claims Jeremiah.

Date
6th century BC.

Outline
Elijah hands over his prophetic mantle to Elisha 1:1–3:27
Elisha the prophet 4:1–8:29
Kings Jehu and Joash 9:1–12:21
War—and peace 13:1–17:41
Judah stands alone 18:1–21:26
The end of Judah 22:1–25:30

Major themes in 2 Kings

Response

God is sovereign but this doesn't mean our actions or prayers do not matter. God responds to us, and his dealings with us depend on our response to him.

Righteousness

God rewards righteousness and punishes evil. 17:7–18 is a summary of this message, and acts as a sort of obituary for the nation of Israel.

Retribution

The people of Israel, along with their rulers, were guilty of violating God's covenant, committing many sins. For these acts of disobedience, there was inevitable retribution from God—resulting ultimately in the destruction of the Northern Kingdom of Israel at the hands of the Assyrian armies.

The Divided Kingdom
Northern Kingdom: Israel
Southern Kingdom: Judah
0
50 miles
0
50 kilometers
MEDITERRANEAN SEA
PHOENICIA
ARAM
Tyre
Dan
Jeroboam builds a sanctuary
Hazor
SEA OF GALILEE
Megiddo
Bethshan
Ramoth-gilead
ISRAEL
Jordan R.
Samaria
Shechem
Shiloh
AMMON
Jeroboam builds a sanctuary
Bethel
Rabbah
Jericho
Ashdod
Jerusalem
Bethlehem
Gath
Ashkelon
Hebron
Gaza
DEAD SEA
JUDAH
PHILISTIA
Beer-sheba
MOAB
Kir-hareseth
EDOM
Kadesh-barnea

Kings of Assyria

The Hebrews suffered severely at the hands of Assyrian kings, whose cruelty was proverbial.

Assur-nasirpal II 883–859 BC
His formidable fighting machine extended Assyrian might to the Mediterranean.

Shalmaneser III 858–824 BC
The first Assyrian king to clash with Israel. Ahab fought against him at Qarqar and Jehu paid him tribute.

Shamshi-Adad V 823–811 BC

Adad-nirari III 810–783 BC
He and other weak emperors until 747 BC allowed Uzziah of Judah and Jeroboam II of Israel to rule long and prosperously.

Shalmaneser IV 782–773 BC

Assur-dan III 772–755 BC

Assur-nirari V 754–745 BC

Tiglath-Pileser III 745–727 BC
Carried northern Israel into exile in 734 BC.

Shalmaneser V 727–722 BC
Besieged Samaria.

Sargon II 722–705 BC
Took Samaria in 722 BC.

Sennacherib 705–681 BC
A great conqueror, though he failed to take Jerusalem.

Esarhaddon 681–699 BC
Rebuilt Babylon and conquered Egypt.

Ashurbanipal 668–627 BC
The last great emperor.

626–607 BC
Disintegration and fall of this cruel empire.

Assyrian warriors.

Kings of Babylon

Nabopolassar 626–605 BC

Nebuchadnezzar II 605–562 BC

Evil-Merodach 562–560 BC

Neriglissar 560–556 BC

Labasi-Marduk 556 BC

Nabonidus 556–539 BC

1 Chronicles

Author
Traditionally Ezra.

Date
5th century BC.

Outline
The family histories of Israel 1:1–9:44
The story of David's reign 10:1–29:30
David's last words 28:1–29:30

Major themes in 1 Chronicles

Failure
David's sin in taking a census shows that we need always to be alert to temptation. David was in the wrong. How he suffered the consequences; what he learned; how he reacted; and how good came of it in the end.

Election
God chose David and his family to reign over Israel in Jerusalem (16:13; 28:4–6,10; 29:1).

2 Chronicles

Author
Traditionally, Ezra.

Date
5th century BC.

Outline
Solomon's reign 1:1–9:31
The reigns of Solomon's successors 10:1–36:23

Major themes in 2 Chronicles

Wisdom and the building of the Temple

Solomon's request
Why God was pleased—and what resulted from it (1:7–17). Both Solomon and Huram (Hiram) of Tyre are gifted with wisdom (i.e. skills) by the Spirit of God in the building of the Temple—the dominant feature of Solomon's reign in the narrative of the Chronicler in this second part (chapters 1—9).

Idealizing the reign of Solomon
Unlike the accounts of Solomon's failures in 1 Kings 11, the Chronicler makes no mention of Solomon's fall from grace, nor any of his failures, nor the political struggles he encountered. The royal figure of King Solomon in 2 Chronicles (like David in 1 Chronicles) should be seen as typifying the future Messianic King, not solely as the Solomon of history.

Suffering and judgment
The suffering and judgment from the hand of God by both people and kings, following the reign of Solomon (chapters 11—36) is not absolute. Rather, it is to be seen as divine chastisement for the nation's violation of their covenant commitment to God. But in the end God fulfils his promise to return his people to their homeland, after their exile to Babylon (36:20–23).

Inconsistent godliness
2 Chronicles contains examples of kings who change from better to worse—and vice-versa. The reigns of many kings were a mixture of godliness and ungodliness. Two prime examples of this were Manasseh (33:1–20) and Josiah (34–35).

Rebuilding Jerusalem.

Ezra

Author
Ezra.

Date
5th century BC.

Outline
The Jews return under Cyrus 1:1–6:22
The Jews return under Artaxerxes 7:1–10:44

Major themes in Ezra

Experience
Ezra was aware that God was at work in his life and guiding his movements.

Ambition
Ezra's passion in life was the word of God (7:10). He studied it, obeyed it, and taught it. Study and obedience must go together.

Giving
The returning Jews gave spontaneously to God (2:68–69).

Failure
Ezra (9:1—10:44) teaches that failure needs to be faced: confessing, mourning, and putting right. Only then can true forgiveness be known.

Faith
Ezra was very brave to return to Jerusalem without an armed escort (8:21–23).

Nehemiah

Author
Nehemiah.

Date
5th century BC.

Outline
Nehemiah returns and rebuilds the walls 1:1–7:73
A new community 8:1–10:39
Nehemiah continues his task 11:1–13:31

Major themes in Nehemiah

Nehemiah: man of God
Nehemiah is the ideal worker for God: a man of patriotism and courage, fearless, enthusiastic, and enterprising. He was a man of prayer and hard work, and one who feared God, and sought his blessing. His life was marked by a balance between prayer and hard work.

Patriotism
Patriotism in itself is not wrong. Nehemiah had a deep concern for his own people (1:3–11). True patriotism is concerned for the state of the nation.

Prayer
Nehemiah turned to prayer at all times and under all circumstances.

Dedication
Nehemiah took the work God gave him seriously—he was thorough. He knew the sacredness of his work and inspired others to work too.

Perseverance
Nehemiah was unmoved by opposition, whether from within or without. He met ridicule and scorn by reliance on God (2:19–20). He refused to be distracted from the task in hand (6:2–3).

Spiritual failure
Despite the many godly reforms overseen by Nehemiah during his leadership of the people of Judah after the exile, there were a number of spiritual failures on the part of this community—failures which greatly distressed Nehemiah (13:1–30).

Esther

Author
Esther.

Date
5th century BC.

Outline
A disobedient queen 1:1–22
Mordecai, Esther, and Haman 2:1–3:6
The Jews in danger 3:7–4:17
Esther acts 5:1–7:10
The Jews delivered 8:1–9:19
Festival of Purim 9:20–10:3

Major themes in Esther

Esther
Meek and attractive (2:1–18); dependent on God (4:15–17); brave (4:16); diplomatic (5:1–8; 7:1–6).

Mordecai
Mordecai was essentially a godly man, motivated by love for God's people (see 2:7, 19–23; 4:1–17; 10:3). He was acutely aware of the need to protect Queen Esther and the Jewish community from the attacks of those conspiring to destroy the Jewish community in Persia. He was of Jewish heritage, a descendant of the tribe of Benjamin.

Haman
His downfall was caused by greedy ambition (5:10–12), aided by his wife (5:14), and by her change of mind (6:13). He had a long way to fall (3:1–2). Haman was also an Agagite, a descendant of the Amalekite ruler, Agag, who had attacked the Israelites after their escape from Egypt (cf. EXODUS 17:8–16). This drew down the curse of God against this nation, who charged Israel with the task of "blotting out the memory of Amalek from under heaven" (cf. DEUTERONOMY 25:17–19).

Job

Author
Unknown.

Date
Possibly as early as 10th century BC.

Outline
Job is tested 1:1–3:26
The first debate 4:1–14:22
The second debate 15:1–21:34
The third debate 22:1–31:40
Elihu speaks 32:1–37:24
God speaks to Job 38:1–42:6
The story ends 42:7-17

Major themes in Job

God's character and works

God is sovereign. Even the devil cannot act without his permission. Job and his friends were aware of this, and that God made the world and keeps it going. This book is filled with God's greatness, wisdom, and grace. This latter divine attribute characterizes God's dealings with Job throughout the book.

Human weakness

Job's situation illustrates our weakness, ignorance, sinfulness, and the shortness of our lives. His plea for justice really demanded a life beyond this, where God could punish the wicked and right the wrongs of this world.

Wisdom

God's wisdom, that is, God's mind, intelligence and purpose, are described as beyond our reach (28:1–28). If we are let into some of his secrets, it will not be due to our cleverness. Only as we submit to him will we begin to understand something of his ways.

Comforting others

Job's friends provide an example of how not to do it. Many of the things they said were true—but beside the point and hurtful.

Mountains in the Bible

Throughout Scripture, God met with his people on mountains.

Mount Ararat
In modern Turkey. Where Noah's ark came to rest.
GENESIS 8:4

Mount Carmel
Where Elijah defeated the prophets of Baal.
1 KINGS 18:9-42

Mount Ebal
Where Moses ordered an altar to be built after the Hebrews entered the Promised Land.
DEUTERONOMY 11:26-29

Mount Gerizim
Where Jesus spoke to a Samaritan woman at the well.
JOHN 4:20

Mount Gilboa
Where King Saul and his sons were killed in battle.
1 CHRONICLES 10:1, 8

Mount Hermon
Mountain range at the northern border of Canaan.
JOSHUA 11:3, 17

Mount Lebanon
Source of cedar wood for Solomon's Temple.
1 KINGS 5:14, 18

Mount of Olives
Where Jesus taught about his second coming.
MATTHEW 24:3

Mount Pisgah, or Nebo
From which Moses viewed the Promised Land and where he was buried.
DEUTERONOMY 34:1-6

Mount Sinai, or Horeb (near Egypt)
Where God gave the Law to Moses.
EXODUS 19:2-25

Job.

The Hebrew Calendar

Month	Name (before Exile)	Modern equivalent	Weather	Harvests/agriculture	Festivals/Holy days
1	Nisan (Abib)	March/April	Rain ("latter rain")	Flax harvest	14th Passover 15th–21st Unleavened Bread 16th Firstfruits
2	Iyyar (Ziv)	April/May	Dry	Barley harvest	14th Second Passover
3	Sivan	May/June	Warm and dry	Wheat harvest	6th Pentecost (Harvest, Firstfruits, Shavuot, Weeks)
4	Tammuz	June/July	Hot and dry		
5	Abu (Ab)	July/August	Very hot and dry		
6	Elul	August/September	Very hot and dry	Date harvest Grape harvest Summer fig harvest	
7	Tishri (Ethanim)	September/October	Rain begins	Olive harvest Grape harvest	1st Trumpets (Rosh Hashanah) 10th Day of Atonement (Yom Kippur) 15th–21st Tabernacles (Ingathering, Succoth, Booths) 22nd Simchat Torah (Solemn Assembly)
8	Heshvan (Bul)	October/November	Rainy ("former rain")	Olive harvest (Marcheshvan) Ploughing	
9	Chislev	November/December	Cool and rainy	Winter fig harvest Sowing	25th–2nd Tebeth Dedication (Hanukkah, Lights)
10	Tebeth	December/January	Cold, hail and snow	Sowing	
11	Shebat	January/February	Warmer and rainy	Almond blossoms Sowing	
12	Adar	February/March	Thunder and hail	Citrus fruit harvest Sowing	14th–15th Purim (= Lots)

The Jewish year is strictly lunar, with lunar months averaging 29.5 days, giving 354 days in a year. A thirteenth month, Veadar, was added roughly every three years to align the calendar with the solar year.

The Kings and Prophets of Judah and Israel

Judah			Israel		Assyria
King	Prophet	Date BC	King	Prophet	
Rehoboam	Shemaiah	931	Jeroboam I	Ahijah	
Egypt invades Jerusalem					
Abijah	Iddo	913	*War with Judah*		
Asa	Azariah	911			
	Hanani	910	Nadab		
		909	Baasha	Jehu	
Allies with Syria against Baasha		886	Elah		
		885	Zimri		
		885	Tibni		
		885	Omri		883-859 Ashurnasirpal II
			Samaria becomes capital		
		874	Ahab	Elijah, Micaiah	
Jehoshaphat	Jehu	870	*Allies with Judah against Syria*		
	Jahaziel	853	Ahaziah	Elisha	858-824 Shalmaneser III
	Eliezer	852	Jehoram Joram		
Jehoram (Joram)		848			
Ahaziah		841	Jehu		
Athaliah		841			
Jehoash (Joash)	Joel	835			
	Zechariah	814	Jehoahaz		
		798	Jehoash Joash		
Amaziah		796	*Fights Amaziah*		
		782	Jeroboam II	Jonah	782-773 Shalmaneser IV
Uzziah (Azariah)		767		Amos	
	Isaiah	753	Zechariah	Hosea	
Jotham regent		752	Shallum		
		752	Menahem		744-727 Tiglath-Pileser III
		742	Pekahiah		
			Pays tribute to Assyria		

The Kings and Prophets of Judah and Israel continued

Judah			**Israel**		**Assyria**
King	Prophet	Date BC	King	Prophet	
Jotham		740	Pekah	Oded	
			Fights Assyria		
			Many deported		
Ahaz	Micah	732	Hoshea		
Tribute to Assyria			*Tribute to Assyria*		726-722 Shalmaneser V
		722	*Fall of Samaria*		721-705 Sargon II
Hezekiah		715			704-681 Sennacherib
Sennacherib invades		701			
Manasseh		687			680-669 Esarhaddon
Amon		642			
Josiah	Nahum	640			
Religious reform	Zephaniah				
	Habakkuk	612			*Nineveh falls*
Jehoahaz	Jeremiah	609			
Jehoiakim	Uriah	609			
		605			*Egypt loses battle of Carchemish*
Tribute to Egypt					
Jehoiachin		598			
Many deported to Babylon					
Zedekiah		597			
Fall of Jerusalem		587/86			

Kings of Judah

After Solomon's death, the united kingdom of Israel split in two, with ten tribes forming the northern kingdom of Israel and two tribes forming the southern kingdom of Judah.

Rehoboam
King Solomon's son and successor, who inherited a kingdom seething with discontent. When he refused to reduce the taxes, the Israelites rebelled. Only the tribes of Benjamin and Judah remained loyal to Rehoboam and the house of David.
1 KINGS 12; 14:21-31; 2 CHRONICLES 10–12

Abijah
Judah's second king, son of King Rehoboam. Though not a godly king, when an emergency situation arose he cried to God for help and won a great victory.
1 KINGS 14:31–15:8; 2 CHRONICLES 12

Asa
Asa, Judah's third king, tried to erase pagan worship from Judah and restored silver and gold items to the Temple.
1 KINGS 15:9-24; 2 CHRONICLES 14–16

Jehoshaphat
Asa's son, and Judah's fourth king. He allied himself with wicked King Ahab, but was a godly king, destroying idols and upholding God's laws.
1 KINGS 22; 2 KINGS 3; 2 CHRONICLES 17:1–21:3

Jehoram
Son and successor of Jehoshaphat, he married Athaliah, daughter of Jezebel and Ahab, who lured him away from his father's godly ways. Edomites, who had been subject to Judah, rebelled during his reign and established their own king.
2 KINGS 8:16–24; 2 CHRONICLES 21:4-20

Ahaziah
Sixth king of Judah, the son of Jehoram. Influenced by his mother, Athaliah, he "did evil in God's sight." He was killed by Jehu while visiting his uncle, Joram, King of Israel.
2 KINGS 8:25-29; 9:14-29; 2 CHRONICLES 22:1-9

Athaliah
Judah's only queen. When her son King Ahaziah died, she murdered her grandchildren to gain the throne. Only Joash survived, hidden until the age of seven, when he was proclaimed king and Athaliah was murdered.
2 KINGS 11; 2 CHRONICLES 22:10–23:21

Joash
Son of King Ahaziah, Joash became king of Judah when he was seven. Influenced by the priest Jehoiada, he restored the Temple and erased Baal worship. When Jehoiada died, Joash let idol worship return. He ruled for forty years before officials murdered him.
2 KINGS 11–12; 2 CHRONICLES 23–24

Amaziah
Son of Joash, he gradually turned from God's ways and reintroduced idols. Assassinated at Lachish, after twenty-nine years' rule.
2 KINGS 14:1-22; 2 CHRONICLES 25

Azariah
Also called Uzziah, Azariah was Amaziah's son, becoming king aged sixteen. He failed to remove idolatrous high places. For usurping the role of priest, he was infected with leprosy and had to live in isolation.
2 KINGS 15:1-6; 2 CHRONICLES 26

Jotham
A king who followed in the godly rule of his father, Uzziah. He was crowned in Uzziah's lifetime, after Uzziah was forced to live in isolation.
2 KINGS 15:32–38; 2 CHRONICLES 27

Ahaz
Son of Jotham who encouraged Baal worship and even sacrificed his own sons. When the armies of Aram and Israel marched against him, he ignored Isaiah's advice and asked Tiglath-Pileser III of Assyria for help, ending up as his subject.
2 KINGS 16; 2 CHRONICLES 28; ISAIAH 7

Hezekiah
Unlike his father, Ahaz, Hezekiah remained faithful to God and introduced religious reform. He rebelled against Assyria. When the Assyrians called on him to surrender, he turned to God, who routed them.
2 KINGS 18–20; 2 CHRONICLES 29–32; ISAIAH 36–39

Manasseh
Manasseh, son of Hezekiah, burned his own son as a sacrifice, took advice from fortune-tellers, and practiced magic. Captured by the Assyrians and exiled to Babylon, he returned to Judah a reformed man, trusting God.
2 KINGS 21:1-18; 2 CHRONICLES 33:1-20

Amon
Son of Manasseh who succeeded his father as king and followed the same sinful path. He was murdered by palace officials.
2 KINGS 21:18-23; 2 CHRONICLES 33:20-25

Kings of Judah continued

Josiah
Boy-king of Judah, crowned when he was eight, after his father, Amon, was killed. During his reign, idolatry was purged and the Temple repaired. A copy of the lost scroll of the Law was found, which Josiah followed. He reintroduced observance of Passover.
2 KINGS 21:26–23:30; 2 CHRONICLES 33:25–25:27

Jehoahaz
During his three-month reign, he reverted to previous evil practices. He was captured and carried off to Egypt, where he died.
2 KINGS 23:31-35

Jehoiakim
Babylon was becoming a serious threat. At first Jehoiakim paid tribute, but he eventually rebelled. Jehoiakim reversed reforms introduced by his father, Josiah, and restored Baal worship. He opposed the prophet Habakkuk and burnt the prophet Jeremiah's scrolls.
2 KINGS 23:36–24:7; 2 CHRONICLES 36; JEREMIAH 36

Jehoiachin
Appointed king by the Babylonians in place of his father, Jehoiakim. Just fourteen weeks later, he was exiled to Babylon by Nebuchadnezzar, along with 10,000 officers, soldiers, craftsmen, and artists in the first exile.
2 KINGS 24:8-16; 2 CHRONICLES 36:9-10; JEREMIAH 52:31-34

Zedekiah
The last king of Judah, who took over from his nephew Jehoiachin. Despite being Nebuchadnezzar's puppet king, Zedekiah rebelled, bringing about Jerusalem's destruction.
2 KINGS 24:17-25; 2 CHRONICLES 36:10-23; JEREMIAH 21; 32; 34; 37–39

Prophets of Judah

Isaiah
Isaiah prophesied in Jerusalem during the reigns of Uzziah, Jotham, Ahaz, and Hezekiah—about forty years. His call came in a vision of the holiness of God (Isaiah 6). Isaiah is the first to portray the Messiah as a suffering servant, killed for the sins of his people. He was an adviser of kings, warning against foreign political alliances and preaching the need to trust God.
ISAIAH, especially 1:1; 6; 7:3; 8:1; 53; 61

Habakkuk
Prophet who wrote during the reigns of Jehoiakim and Josiah. He warned that Babylon would capture Judah, as God's punishment for their violence, idolatry, and corruption. He stressed the importance of personal faith. He also prayed that God would remember mercy in the midst of his wrath, and was confident that God would ultimately bring salvation to his people.
HABAKKUK

Nahum
Prophet who encouraged the people of Judah when they faced defeat by the Babylonians. He predicted the overthrow of Nineveh, capital of the Assyrians, who had long oppressed the Israelites.
NAHUM

Jeremiah
Prophet who lived in the dark time of the last five kings of Judah: Josiah, Jehoahaz, Jehoiakim, Jehoiachin, and Zedekiah. His prophecies are in Jeremiah and Lamentations. People called him a traitor when he urged them not to resist the Babylonian armies, because the impending destruction of Jerusalem was God's judgment against idolatry. He portrays the horror he felt as he saw the destruction of his homeland. After Jerusalem fell to Nebuchadnezzar in 587 BC, Jeremiah was probably taken to Egypt.
JEREMIAH, LAMENTATIONS

Micah
Prophesied against the southern kingdom of Judah during the reigns of Jotham, Ahaz, and Hezekiah; and against the northern kingdom of Israel during the reigns of Pekah and Hoshea. He denounced evil practices and announced God's impending judgment, but was also a prophet of hope, predicting a great ruler of Israel would come from Bethlehem.
MICAH

Zephaniah
Great-great-great-grandson of King Hezekiah whose judgment on Judah was given during Josiah's reign. He predicted a small number—a remnant—would return to Jerusalem.
ZEPHANIAH

Obadiah
Prophesied against the people of Edom, Judah's persistent enemy.
OBADIAH

Huldah
A prophetess consulted by Hilkiah the priest on behalf of Josiah, after the book of the Law was discovered in the Temple.
2 KINGS 22:14-20; 2 CHRONICLES 34:22-28

Kings of Israel

In the 210 years between Jeroboam I and Hoshea, the northern kingdom of Israel had nine dynasties and nineteen kings. Kings' sons did not succeed their fathers, as in the southern kingdom—which had a single dynasty. The kings of Israel were often ambitious and bloodthirsty officials or military leaders.

Jeroboam I

Jeroboam was a talented young officer in Solomon's court, in charge of the country's labor force. The prophet Ahijah prophesied he would become king of the ten northern tribes. Solomon tried to kill him, so he fled to Egypt until Solomon died. Jeroboam became Israel's first king after Israel split into two kingdoms. To stop his people traveling to Jerusalem to worship, he set up rival religious sanctuaries in Bethel and Dan. Warned by God through signs–including a withered arm–he refused to repent.

1 KINGS 11:26–14:20

Nadab

Nadab was the son of Jeroboam, who followed his father's example. He was killed by Baasha, who succeeded him.

1 KINGS 15:25-32

Baasha

Baasha also followed the path of Jeroboam. The prophet Jehu predicted the downfall of his family.

1 KINGS 15:33–16:7

Elah

Elah was the son of Baasha, murdered by Zimri, one of his chariot officers.

1 KINGS 16:8-14

Zimri

Zimri had murdered his predecessor, Elah, and succeeded him as king. Some Israelites supported the rival claimant, Omri. When Zimri saw he was losing, he committed suicide, burning the palace down with himself inside.

1 KINGS 16:15-20

Omri

Omri was the commander-in-chief of Elah's army, he became king after defeating Zimri. Omri established the strategic hill town of Samaria as Israel's new capital.

1 KINGS 16:15-28

Tibni

Tibni was crowned as a rival to Omri, but did not succeed.

1 KINGS 16:15-28

Ahab

Ahab was the son and successor of Omri, Ahab was one of Israel's most successful–but evil–kings. He married Jezebel, daughter of Ethbaal, king of the Sidonians, and began to worship Baal. He set up an altar for Baal in a temple he built. Ahab's death, during war against Syria, was seen as God's punishment on one of Israel's wickedest kings.

1 KINGS 16:29–18; 20:1–22:40; 2 KINGS 9:30-37

Ahaziah

Ahaziah was the king who followed his father, Ahab, and consulted Baal-Zebub, the god of Ekron, rather than the Lord.

1 KINGS 22:51-53; 2 KINGS 1

Jehoram (Joram)

Jehoram was allied with Judah's king, Jehoshaphat, to defeat the Moabites. During his reign, Samaria was besieged by the Arameans. Like his brother Ahaziah, Jehoram did evil, though he attempted to end Baal worship. He was murdered by Jehu.

2 KINGS 3; 6:24–7:20; 9:14-29

Jehu

Jehu was the army commander anointed by a prophet to be the next king of Israel. He killed Jehoram, Jezebel, the royal family, and all priests of Baal. Though he promised he would worship God, he retained the false worship introduced by Jehoram.

2 KINGS 9–10

Jehoahaz

Jehoahaz was Israel's eleventh king, leading the Israelites away from God, and was defeated by Hazael and Ben-Hadad, kings of Syria.

2 KINGS 13:1-9

Jehoash

Jehoash was sometimes known as Joash. He consulted the dying prophet Elisha, who told him he would defeat Syria three times. Despite this, he worshiped idols.

2 KINGS 13:10–14:16

Jeroboam II

Jeroboam II recovered Damascus and Hamath for Israel, fulfilling a prophecy of Jonah, but continued Baal worship.

2 KINGS 14:23-29

Zechariah

Zechariah was the son of Jeroboam II; reigned six months before he was assassinated. Not to be confused with Zechariah the prophet.

2 KINGS 15:8-12

Kings of Israel continued

Shallum
Shallum was crowned king, but was assassinated a month later.
2 KINGS 15:13-15

Menahem
Menahem was a violent, evil man. He taxed the wealthy to pay an indemnity to save his country from destruction by Assyria.
2 KINGS 15:16-22

Pekahiah
King Pekahiah was assassinated by Pekah, one of his chief officers.
2 KINGS 15:23-26

Pekah
The Assyrians closed in on Israel during Pekah's long reign. He was assassinated by Hoshea.
2 KINGS 15:27-31

Hoshea
Hoshea was the last king of Israel. During his reign, final disaster struck the northern kingdom. After a three-year siege, Shalmaneser captured Samaria, the capital of Israel, and deported the Israelites to Assyria. In this way the prophetic warnings were fulfilled, and Israel was punished for worshiping other gods and disobeying God's law.
2 KINGS 15:30; 17–18

Prophets of Israel

Elijah
Elijah was the most prominent prophet of his time in Israel. He opposed Ahab and Jezebel in their attempts to make Baal worship the religion of Israel. God sent a severe drought, during which he was fed by ravens. Elijah also multiplied food for a widow and brought her son back to life. He challenged Ahab and 450 prophets of Baal to a contest on Mount Carmel. Baal's prophets failed, but fire came on Elijah's sacrifice, in answer to his prayer. Elijah fled to the wilderness, where God spoke to him in a still, small voice. Elijah was one of only two recorded biblical figures who did not pass through physical death (cf. 2 KINGS 2:1-12). The other one was Enoch (cf. GENESIS 5:24). Elijah was caught up in a chariot of fire and taken straight to heaven. He then appeared with Moses at Jesus' transfiguration (cf. LUKE 9:28-36).
1 KINGS 17–19; 21; 2 KINGS 1:1–2:18; LUKE 9:28-36

Elisha
Elisha was Elijah's disciple, assistant, and successor as God's faithful prophet in Israel. He was a prophet for fifty-five years, during the reigns of Joram, Jehu, Jehoahaz, and Joash. Fourteen miracles were performed through Elisha, notably the healing of Naaman's leprosy, which was then passed on to Gehazi—Elisha's dishonest servant, who secretly accepted gifts from Naaman, which Elijah had declined.
1 KINGS 19:16, 19–21; 2 KINGS 2–9; 13:14-20

Amos
Amos was a shepherd and cultivator of sycamore-fig trees in Judah, whom God sent to Israel to prophesy against corruption, dishonesty, mistreatment of the poor, and luxurious living.
AMOS

Joel
Joel warned the southern kingdom of Judah that God's judgment would fall on Judah like a plague of locusts if they failed to follow God.
JOEL

Hosea
Hosea was a prophet who denounced Israel for idolatry, likening them to his adulterous wife, Gomer, in their unfaithfulness to God. Hosea showed that, just as he loved his wife and brought her back, so God loves his wayward people and brings them back to himself.
HOSEA

Jonah
Jonah was the first Hebrew prophet who was sent to a pagan country. God told Jonah to warn the people of Nineveh to turn from their sins. Running away from this hard task, he was swallowed by a great fish. When eventually he did preach in Nineveh, and the people turned to God, Jonah was furious. Jonah had to learn that God cares for people of all nations.
JONAH

Exile and Return

Sennacherib

Sennacherib was the king of Assyria who defeated the Babylonians and besieged King Hezekiah of Judah. After 185,000 Assyrian soldiers mysteriously died in the night, Sennacherib returned to Nineveh, where two of his sons killed him.

2 KINGS 18:17–19:37; 2 CHRONICLES 32; ISAIAH 36–37

Nebuchadnezzar

Nebuchadnezzar was the king of Babylon who defeated the Israelites of Judah, captured Jerusalem, and exiled most of its people to Babylon. Nebuchadnezzar built impressive palaces and temples in Babylon. He was insane for seven years—God's punishment for his pride.

2 KINGS 24–25; 2 CHRONICLES 36:6–20; DANIEL 1–4

Ezekiel

Ezekiel was a prophet with a priestly heritage. He lived in Jerusalem until 597 BC, when he was deported to Babylon, with the king and most of the ruling families. After the destruction of Jerusalem, Ezekiel preached a message of hope, prophesying a future return to Jerusalem. He demonstrated that faith in God could continue in a foreign land and without the Temple. He often acted out his prophecies in dramatic—sometimes strange—ways.

EZEKIEL

Abednego

Abednego (or Azariah) was one of Daniel's three close friends among Jewish exiles in Babylon. With Shadrach (Hananiah) and Meshach (Mishael), he refused to worship the statue of Nebuchadnezzar. For this, he was thrown into a furnace, but miraculously survived unscathed.

DANIEL 1–3

Belshazzar

Belshazzar was a co-regent, and successor to Nebuchadnezzar. Belshazzar was Babylon's last king. During a banquet, Belshazzar called Daniel to examine writing that appeared on a wall. Daniel interpreted it that Belshazzar had been weighed in God's balances and found wanting—and was about to lose his throne to the Medes and Persians. He died the same night, bringing to an end the power of Babylon.

DANIEL 5

Cyrus II

Cyrus II was the royal founder of the Persian Empire who captured Babylon in 539 BC. Cyrus was noted for his humane rule and permitted the exiled Jews to return to Jerusalem and rebuild the Temple.

EZRA 1–6

Daniel

Daniel was a young Jewish man, exiled to Babylon in his teens. He rose to high rank in the Babylonian, and then Persian, kingdoms. He was noted for his courage and wisdom, including a God-given ability to interpret dreams. Daniel refused to deny his faith and was thrown into a lions' pit, but was miraculously preserved.

DANIEL

Darius

Darius the Mede succeeded Belshazzar as king of Babylon, and was tricked into having Daniel thrown to the lions.

DANIEL 6

Nehemiah

Nehemiah grew up in Babylon during the Jewish Exile, and rose to become cupbearer to King Artaxerxes of Persia. When Jews were allowed back to Jerusalem, he was troubled after he heard that the returned exiles had not rebuilt the walls. Nehemiah asked to return to Jerusalem to rebuild. His building program was opposed by Sanballat, Tobiah, the Arabs, the Ammonites, and men of Ashdod, but with hard work and prayerful vigilance the wall was rebuilt.

NEHEMIAH

Ezra

Ezra was a priest and scribe who led the third group of Israelites back to Jerusalem from Babylonian exile. He gained permission to enforce God's law as the law of the land. The temple had been rebuilt, but he discovered the people were neglecting God's laws.

EZRA

Zerubbabel

Zerubbabel was leader, and later governor, of the first group of Israelites to return to Jerusalem from exile in Babylon. With the encouragement of the prophets Haggai and Zechariah, and against violent opposition, he rebuilt and dedicated the Temple.

EZRA 1–5; HAGGAI

Esther

Esther was a young Jewess who grew up in Susa, capital of Persia. King Xerxes chose her as his consort after Queen Vashti fell from favor. At first, Esther did not reveal she was Jewish, but when Haman the Agagite planned to massacre the Jews in his empire, she devised a bold plan to save her nation.

ESTHER

Xerxes (Ahasuerus)

Xerxes was king of Persia who married Esther, after dismissing his first wife, Vashti.
ESTHER

Haggai

Haggai was a prophet who rebuked the returned exiles for living in expensive houses while the Temple lay in ruins. Zerubbabel, Judah's governor, and Jehozadak, the high priest, followed Haggai's instructions and rebuilt the Temple.
HAGGAI

Haman (the Agagite)

Haman was the prime minister to Xerxes, king of Persia. He hated Mordecai and masterminded the massacre of the Jewish people in Persia. There is evidence that suggests his hatred was based on his heritage: he was most likely a descendant of Agag, the Amalekite king, who opposed and attacked the Hebrews in the desert after their escape from Egyptian captivity (cf. EXODUS 17:8-16; 1 SAMUEL 15:20) His plan would have succeeded, but for Esther. Haman was hanged on gallows he had built for the execution of Mordecai.
ESTHER 3–9

Malachi

After the exile, Malachi was a prophet who rebuked the Jews for replacing enthusiasm for God with ritualism in the new Temple.
MALACHI

Sanballat

Sanballat, governor of Samaria, with Tobiah and Geshem, opposed Nehemiah's governorship, and strove—unsuccessfully—to prevent the rebuilding of Jerusalem's walls.
NEHEMIAH 2:19-20; 6:1-14; 13:28-29

Tobiah

Tobiah the Ammonite, with Sanballat, and Geshem the Arab, fought against Nehemiah's rebuilding of Jerusalem.
NEHEMIAH 2:19-20; 4:3-9; 6; 13:1-9

Zechariah

Zechariah was a priest and prophet who roused the Jews who returned to Jerusalem from apathy and evil behavior. Born in exile in Babylonia, he returned with the first group of Jews and prophesied alongside Haggai.
ZECHARIAH

The Three Jewish Returns from Exile

	First return	Second return	Third return
Scripture	Ezra 1	Ezra 2–6	Ezra 7–10, Nehemiah 1–2
Date	538 BC	525 BC	458 BC, 445 BC
King of Persia	Cyrus the Great 559-530 BC	Cambyses II 530-522, Darius 522-486	Artaxerxes I 465-425
Leader of return	Zerubbabel	Ezra	Nehemiah
Leader's role	Governor	Priest	Governor
Number of returnees	49,897	1,774	Armed escort
Other Jewish leaders	Joshua the priest	Nehemiah, Malachi, Haggai, Zechariah	Ezra, Malachi
Result	Temple foundations laid	Work finished in 516	Law taught. Jerusalem's people separated from non-Jews. Jerusalem's walls rebuilt. Work stops

Psalms

Author

There were several authors, including David, Solomon, Asaph, the prophetic singers of Korah's clan, and Moses.

Date

From the monarchy through the postexilic era.

Outline

Psalms of man and creation PSALMS 1–41

Psalms of suffering and redemption PSALMS 42–72

Psalms of worship and God's house PSALMS 73–89

Psalms of our pilgrimage on earth PSALMS 90–106

Psalms of praise and the Word PSALMS 107–150

Author and audience

Most are by David, King of Israel. He wrote them during particular periods in his life: when he was on the run from Saul, grateful for God's protection and provision; scared for his future; mournful over his sin; and praising God. Other authors include David's son Solomon, Moses, Asaph, and the prophetic singers of Korah's clan.

Major themes in Psalms

Praise

As long as we have breath we should praise the Lord. The Psalms release a flood of God-inspired insights that lift heaviness from the human heart.

Prayer

Each Psalm is a prayer. The early church regularly recited and sang the Psalms.

Wisdom

The Psalms unlock mysteries and parables.

Poetry of prophecy

Prophetic insights rest upon the Psalms.

Poetry of Jesus Christ

We should read the Psalms in two ways:

1. As the original audience heard them in the ancient Hebrew world
2. As the fulfillment of messianic prophesies: these poems point to Jesus Christ.

We could say every Psalm is messianic as each finds its fulfillment in Christ. They all point to our Lord, whom God has chosen as King over all.

The Shepherd Psalm

Psalm 23 is probably the best known and most loved of the psalms. This psalm has been set to music many times as a hymn and an anthem, and is frequently spoken or sung at funerals.

1 The Lord is my shepherd; I have everything I need.
2 He lets me rest in green meadows; he leads me beside peaceful streams.
3 He renews my strength. He guides me along right paths, bringing honor to his name.
4 Even when I walk through the dark valley of death, I will not be afraid, for you are close beside me. Your rod and your staff protect and comfort me.
5 You prepare a feast for me in the presence of my enemies. You welcome me as a guest, anointing my head with oil. My cup overflows with blessings.
6 Surely your goodness and unfailing love will pursue me all the days of my life, and I will live in the house of the Lord forever.

PSALM 23, NLT

Eastern shepherd.

The Seven Penitential Psalms

Psalms of confession and penitence.

Psalm 6 "O Lord, hear me as I pray."
Psalm 32 "Oh, what joy for those whose rebellion is forgiven."
Psalm 38 "O Lord, don't rebuke me in your anger!"
Psalm 51 "Have mercy on me, O God, because of your unfailing love."
Psalm 102 "Lord, hear my prayer! Listen to my plea!"
Psalm 130 "From the depths of despair, O Lord, I call for your help."
Psalm 143 "Hear my prayer, O Lord; listen to my plea!"
ALL FROM NLT

King David.

Messianic Psalms

Many of the Psalms anticipate the life and ministry of Jesus Christ, the Son of David, who came centuries later as the promised Messiah. The messianic prophecies in the Psalms take different forms and refer to Christ in a variety of ways.

Psalm	Portrayal	Fulfilled
2:7	The Son of God	Matthew 3:17
8:2	Praised by children	Matthew 21:15-16
8:6	Ruler of all	Hebrews 2:8
16:10	Rises from death	Matthew 28:7
22:1	Forsaken by God	Matthew 27:46
22:7-8	Derided by enemies	Luke 23:35
22:16	Hands and feet pierced	John 20:27
22:18	Lots cast for clothes	Matthew 27:35-36
34:20	Bones unbroken	John 19:32-33, 36
35:11	Accused by false witnesses	Mark 14:57
35:19	Hated without cause	John 15:25
40:7-8	Delights in God's will	Hebrews 10:7
41:9	Betrayed by a friend	Luke 22:47
45:6	The eternal King	Hebrews 1:8
68:18	Ascends to heaven	Acts 1:9-11
69:9	Zealous for God's house	John 2:17
69:21	Given vinegar and gall	Matthew 27:34
109:4	Prays for enemies	Luke 23:34
109:8	His betrayer replaced	Acts 1:20
110:1	Rules over his enemies	Matthew 22:44
110:4	A priest forever	Hebrews 5:6
118:22	The chief stone of God's building	Matthew 21:42
118:26	Comes in the name of the Lord	Matthew 21:9

Proverbs

Author
Mostly Solomon, king of Israel, but others too.

Date
10th century BC and later.

Outline
Collection I: Wisdom 1:1–9:18

Collection II: Sayings of Solomon, Part 1 10:1–22:16

Collection III: Sayings of the wise 22:17–24:22

Collection IV: More sayings of the wise 24:23-34

Collection V: Sayings of Solomon, Part 2 25:1–29:27

Collection VI: Sayings of Agur and Lemuel 30:1–31:31

About Proverbs
Proverbs is a book of wisdom from above, clothed in metaphors, symbols, and poetic imagery.

Major themes in Proverbs

The art of successful living
Insights that touch on universal problems and affect us all.

Lady wisdom, revelation-knowledge, living-understanding
Throughout Proverbs, wisdom is personified by Lady Wisdom, who dispenses knowledge and understanding, and is a figure of speech for God. Wisdom is personified as a guide (6:22), a beloved sister or bride (7:4), and a hostess. In Proverbs, wisdom is inseparable from knowledge and understanding.

The fear of the Lord
We gain the essence of wisdom and cross the threshold of true knowledge only when we fear the Lord.

God is transcendent and immanent
Proverbs teaches that God is both the author of (transcendent), and actor in (immanent), our human story. God is above, and outside, the world as Creator; and he is part of, and involved with, the world.

Wise and fool, righteous and wicked
There are two kinds of people in the world: the wise righteous, and wicked fools. The wise person has God's knowledge and understanding—and is just, peaceful, upright, blameless, good, trustworthy, and kind. The wicked fool is greedy, violent, deceitful, cruel, and speaks perversely.

Wealth and poverty
Solomon teaches seven things about having wealth and being poor, and how wisdom and foolishness affect both. The righteous are blessed with wealth by God himself; foolishness leads to poverty; fools who have wealth will soon lose it; poverty results from injustice and oppression; the wealthy are to be generous with their wealth; gaining wisdom is far better than gaining wealth; and the value of wealth is limited.

Jesus and the church
Read Proverbs in the light of Jesus and his ministry. Throughout the gospels, Jesus associates himself with wisdom.

The wisdom of Solomon.

Ecclesiastes

Author
Probably Solomon in his old age.

Date
10th century BC and later.

Outline
Life is pointless 1:1–2:26
How God made things 3:1-22
Poverty, riches and God 4:1–6:6
Making the best of it 6:7–7:29
Answering to man and God 8:1-17
How to live 9:1–12:14

Major themes in Ecclesiastes

Man
Through all the questioning, we come to an important insight into how God made us. The fact that we worry about such things, that we need a purpose in life, witnesses to a dignity in humans as God created us (3:10–11). It also tells of our woeful, natural ignorance of spiritual things (7:23–24; 8:16–17; 11:5–6), and that we are not as God intended (7:20, 27–29).

Fearing God
Our proper response to God is to fear him, that is, acknowledge him to be God, and live our lives in that attitude. We should worship him and seek to please him in all we do. He sees all we do and one day we will answer to him.

Wisdom
Wisdom belongs to God alone, but he gives it to men and women (2:26). The preacher's final warning is that life is not a matter of knowing, but doing (12:12–14).

Song of Songs

Author
Solomon, King of Israel.

Date
The reign of Solomon, 970–931 BC.

Outline
The dream of the bride for her beloved 1:1–3:5
The bridegroom arrives 3:6-11
In praise of the bride 4:1–5:1
The bride's night thoughts 5:2–6:3
The bride's beauty 6:4–7:9
The beauty of love 7:10–8:14

About Song of Songs
The Song of Songs is full of symbols, subtle art forms, poetry, and nuance.

Major themes in Song of Songs

Interpreting Song of Songs
This divine song is one of the most difficult books to interpret. Over the centuries there have been six main ways that people have understood it: typical, dramatic, mythological-cultic, dream, literal, and allegorical.

Christ's divine love for his bride
This song speaks of God's saving love, keeping love, forgiving love, and embracing love. The allegory of the bride and bridegroom-king speaks of the passionate pursuit of our loving God.

Divine romance
The symbol of the bride (Christians) pursuing and being given to the Bridegroom-King (Jesus) also represents the *community* of brides, the church. The king's vineyard is a picture of the church, those called to follow Jesus.

Passionate devotion
Throughout this love song, different symbols are used to speak of our passionate, emotional devotion to our bridegroom-king-lover. *Lilies* symbolize our pure devotion to Christ in our inner being; *foxes* are the compromises hidden in our hearts that keep the fruit of devotion to Christ from growing within us; *hair* is a symbol of our devotion to Christ; *pomegranates* represent human passion.

Isaiah

Author
Isaiah.

Date
740–700 BC.

Outline
God's vision for Judah and Jerusalem 1:1–5:30
Isaiah's vision and prophetic call 6:1-13
God's signs, judgment, and deliverance 7:1–12:6
God's judgments against the nations 13:1–23:18
God's victory over the nations 24:1–27:13
The false hope of trusting the nations 28:1–33:24
Enemies judged, the redeemed return 34:1–35:10
Vision about Hezekiah 36:1–39:8
Vision about God's promises 40:1–48:22
Vision about redemption and restoration 49:1–55:13
God, our judge and redeemer 56:1–66:24

About Isaiah
Isaiah, the first of the major prophets, was not just a teacher or preacher, but also a seer and intercessor for God's people. The book of Isaiah is a vast collection of prophecies that span the plan of the ages.

Isaiah contains God's glorious message of overcoming, hope, comfort, and the restoration of all things. Because of Christ's appearing with love for all the world, Isaiah's words are now seen as prophetic insights into the death, resurrection, and glory of our King.

Purpose
This book includes every nation on earth in its scope. Isaiah's vision includes impending judgment for sins; coming comfort for future destruction; and the hope of eventual redemption. Particularly important is his insight into the person and work of Jesus—the Faithful Servant, Chosen Servant, Teacher-Servant, and Suffering Servant.

Isaiah teaches about the virgin birth of Christ. We see Jesus as the Man of Sorrows and Conquering King.

Isaiah's prophecies are unrivaled in Scripture and present cataclysmic judgments, the survival of a holy remnant, and the canopy of glory that is coming to earth.

Major themes in Isaiah

The Bible in one book
The first 39 chapters of Isaiah include woes, judgment, and promises; there is a focus on the Hebrew people and their history and the destined future of God's people is unveiled. The last 27 chapters of Isaiah—beginning with Isaiah 40—herald the coming of the Messiah, who brings the message of life and hope.

Judgment for the rebellious
An outpouring of wrath, not only on nations who have turned their backs on the Lord, but on God's people who have rejected the Holy One of Israel. Israel and Judah had become estranged and alienated from God, offering defiled sacrifices and tainted worship.

Unveiling the Messiah
More than any other place, revelation concerning God's Anointed One is given here for the benefit of God's people. Isaiah 42 introduces to us the Lord Jesus, the Messiah, the Chosen Servant of the Lord, sustained by God, sent on a divine mission to bring light and freedom to the hearts of his covenant people.

Starting with chapter 42, Isaiah gives us four Servant Songs:

1. The Faithful Servant, who brings light to the nations. 42
2. The Chosen Servant, bringing salvation to the nations and restoring Israel. 49:1–13
3. The song of the Obedient Servant, who reveals the Father. 50:4–9
4. The Suffering Servant. 52:13—53:12

Isaiah.

Jeremiah

Author
Jeremiah.

Date
c. 627–580 BC.

Outline
Introduction 1:1–19
Prologue to judgment 2:1–6:30
Speech for the prosecution 7:1–10:25
Anticipated sentence 11:1–13:27
Shadow of doom 14:1–20:18
Life and death 21:1–24:10
Conclusion 25:1–38

Babylonian warriors.

Major themes in Jeremiah

Sin
The people had the wrong idea about sin: it had come to mean the neglect of religious duties—as if God was concerned only with what happened on one day of the week, but it was none of his business what went on the other six days.

Preaching through pictures
Jeremiah uses many illustrations to ensure people remember what he has said. He speaks about marriage, divorce, and prostitution; tents and vines; battles, chariots and childbirth; birds in cages, camels in the deserts.

Set in history
The book of Jeremiah cannot properly be understood apart from history. Jeremiah was active for forty years, through the reigns of five kings, and through probably the most violent period of Israel's history.

Prophecy is also theology
In the "Second Book of Judgment" (chapters 46—51), where judgment is pronounced against ten groups of people, the spotlight is on Babylon (50:1–46; 51:1–64). Babylon has a special significance in the Bible, starting with the rebellion against God at Babel (another name for Babylon) in Genesis 11, and concluding with the announcement of the fall of Babylon in Revelation 18.

Lamentations

Author
Possibly Jeremiah.

Date
Soon after 586 BC.

Outline
Cry of the mourner 1:1–22
God against his people 2:1–22
Personal lament and prayer 3:1–66
Jerusalem past and present 4:1–22
Prayer for help 5:1–22

Major themes in Lamentations

Honesty and hope in trouble
Openly and honestly, the writer describes his sorrow, loneliness, and sense of bereavement.

The writer identifies with his people
This is apparent throughout the book.

The Message of the Prophets

Eighth century BC

Amos and Hosea, the only writing prophets of the northern kingdom, worked at this time, as did Isaiah and Micah in the southern kingdom.

Amos

Great prosperity and great corruption in the northern kingdom.

God's judgment on injustice must be taken seriously.

Hosea

Great prosperity and great corruption in the northern kingdom.

God loves the people deeply and is hurt by their idolatry and corruption. Because he takes them seriously, they will be judged.

Isaiah 1–39

The country was prosperous, profiting from problems in surrounding countries and enemies being occupied elsewhere. A big gap had opened up between rich and poor; the judicial system benefited the rich at the expense of the poor.

God is great and will judge injustice and oppression.

Isaiah 40–55

The Exile is assumed to have happened, judgment has fallen, and Israel can now look ahead to a new future.

God is great and will save. Looks forward to the coming of the Servant of God, the Messiah.

Isaiah 56–66

Isaiah looks further ahead, to the situation after the return from Exile, when the nation was re-established.

There is disappointment that hopes for the future had not worked out as the people expected. God is great, even when life does not appear to be so great.

Micah

There is great prosperity and great corruption in the southern kingdom.

God will judge the people for their injustice and immorality; but for those who repent there is a great future and hope.

Up to the Exile

Four prophets—Nahum, Zephaniah, Habakkuk, and Jeremiah—began work during the seventh century BC.

Nahum

There is cruelty and sin in Nineveh, Assyria's capital.

Judgment upon Nineveh.

Zephaniah

There is sin and irreligion in Judah.

Repent while there is still time.

Habakkuk

There is corruption in Judah alongside the wickedness of her enemies.

Amid confusion and doubt, the reality of God remains.

Jeremiah

Babylon was attacking and Judah about to be conquered.

This is a deserved judgment from God, who will not intervene to save his people.

Transform your lifestyle, accept punishment, and wait in hope for God to bring salvation.

Obadiah

Obadiah prophesies the destruction of Edom for her gloating over the devastation of Israel by foreign powers.

Watch out, Edom! Israel's God is sovereign.

Jonah

There is cruelty and sin in Nineveh, Assyria's capital.

Repent—or face destruction. God cares about the nations.

Repentance is followed by mercy.

Joel

Faithlessness and covenant disobedience continues amongst the nation of God's people.

God will act. Calamity will follow disobedience in the form of a locust plague—a precursor of the great and dreadful "Day of the LORD"; and then blessing will follow righteousness.

The Exile—and beyond

Ezekiel

Ezekiel lived and prophesied in Babylon during the exile.

His message may be summarized by: Accept your punishment, love God, and hope for the future.

Daniel

Daniel was both a Jewish statesman in the court of Babylon during the exile and a prophet, gifted with the God-given ability to interpret dreams. The book named after him contains stories of respect and resistance, dreams and visions of the Messianic future of God's people, and the victory of the divine Kingdom at the end of time.

Haggai

Haggai returned from Exile with the remnant of Judah; but the Temple had not been rebuilt.

His message may be summarized by: Put God first if you are to prosper.

Zechariah

Zechariah was a contemporary of Haggai, and also returned from the Exile. But the glory had departed. However, along with Haggai, Zechariah witnessed the re-building of the Temple.

His message was a mixture of exhortation (call to repentance), prophetic visions, and oracles of judgment and salvation that predicted the future of the people of God, culminating in the coming of the promised Messiah and the victory of the Kingdom of God.

Malachi

Malachi witnessed the on-going struggle in the Judean community after the exile to maintain devotion and obedience to their covenant obligations. The people still believed in God their redeeemer, but were uncommitted.

His message: Take action. If you do, you will be overwhelmed by blessings; if you don't, you will be overwhelmed by judgment.

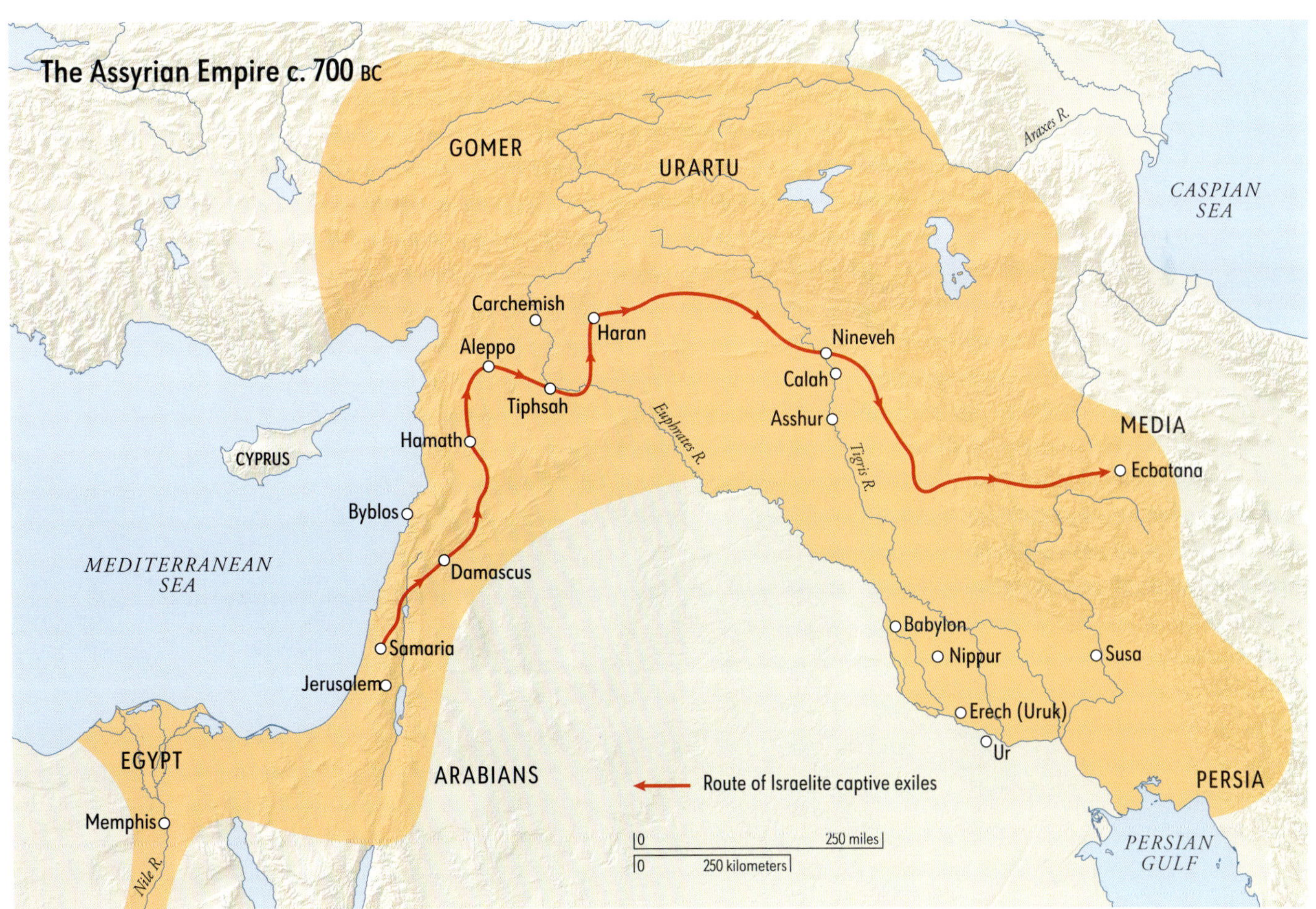

Parables in Ezekiel

Wood of the vine
How Judah had become useless to the Lord and now served no purpose except to be consumed in judgment.
EZEKIEL 15:1-8

The foundling
Judah's betrayal of God's love and compassion.
EZEKIEL 16

The eagles and the cedar
The folly of Zedekiah; his rebellion would bring Nebuchadnezzar's troops to destroy Jerusalem.
EZEKIEL 17

The fiery furnace
God was going to purify his people through the siege of Jerusalem.
EZEKIEL 22:17-22

The two harlots
The spiritual adultery of Israel and Judah.
EZEKIEL 23

The cooking pot
How God was going to cleanse Jerusalem of its impurities.
EZEKIEL 24:1-14

The shipwreck
The judgment that was going to fall on Tyre.
EZEKIEL 27

The irresponsible shepherds
The worthless leaders of Jerusalem and how God would deal with them.
EZEKIEL 34

Dry bones
The spiritual renewal of the nation of Israel.
EZEKIEL 37

Ezekiel

Author
Ezekiel.

Date
593-570 BC.

Outline
The prophet's call 1:1–3:27
Judgment on Jerusalem 4:1–12:28
The sins of Jerusalem and Israel 13:1–24:27
Prophecies against the nations 25:1–32:32
Prophecies for the future 33:1–39:29
The new Jerusalem 40:1–48:35

Major themes in Ezekiel

God's honor
The Israelites thought the honor of Israel was the same as the honor of God, so God would never let Israel be destroyed. This was mistaken; Israel had brought dishonor to God's name. For the sake of his glory, God acted, first to punish, then to save.

God's care
God continued to care for Israel, even when he had to punish her.

Responsibility
Everyone is responsible before God for what they do. Family and circumstances cannot be blamed for the way we turn out. We make a choice—to serve God and keep serving him, or not.

The watchman
Ezekiel took very seriously his call to be a watchman, warning his peers that God's judgement was coming, and to turn and accept the way of escape God provided.

The Vision of a New Jerusalem
The final nine chapters of Ezekiel's prophecy (40—48) are devoted to an extended vision of the construction of a new and eternally everlasting new Temple. The rebuilding includes physical details of reconstruction, as well as the clear indication that, when the Messiah comes, the glory of the Lord will return—and will never again leave (cf. ch. 43). This suggests that this new Temple will move into the eternal realm of the new heavens and the new earth, at the end of time.

Valley of dry bones.

Daniel

Author
Probably Daniel.

Date
Probably 6th century BC.

Outline
The story of Daniel in Babylon 1:1–6:28
Daniel's visions 7:1–12:13

Major themes in Daniel

The first six chapters of Daniel tell the story of Daniel and his three friends, young Hebrew men living in exile in Babylonia. Daniel and his friends—who are faithful to the Lord and under his protection—are training to become court officials of King Nebuchadnezzar. Daniel, already renowned for his wisdom, becomes famous as an interpreter of dreams and mysterious writings. God saves Daniel's friends from Nebuchadnezzar's flaming furnace. Others at court become jealous of Daniel's success and try to undermine him, even attempting to use Daniel's faith to destroy him. The enemies succeed in having Daniel thrown into a pit of lions, but God sends an angel to protect him. At chapter seven, the narrative changes to a series of accounts of Daniel's visions and dreams, which are explained to him by an angel. Together, the first and second parts of Daniel honor God as the one who controls the universe and all human events, offering hope and consolation to God's people living under foreign rule.

The end times

The book of Daniel is prophetic, containing unusual pictures and symbolism. It is primarily concerned with the end times.

Jesus taught that we are not intended to know exactly when the end will come (Mark 13:32–4). The information in Daniel does not allow us to work out the precise time of the end—but we are not left without any clues.

The 70 sevens

Many solutions to the mystery of the "sevens" have been proposed, and there is no scholarly consensus on their definitive meaning. The first period of "7 sevens" may refer to the period of exile, from 587/6 BC when Jerusalem fell, to 538/7 BC, when Cyrus ordered the rebuilding of Jerusalem. The two latter groups of "sevens"—comprising "62 sevens," and one final group of "7 sevens"—may possibly refer, respectively, to the period spanning the return of the Jews to their homeland from captivity until the coming of the Messiah. In which case the final group could embrace the ministry of Jesus Christ, his death, resurrection and ascension, and his inauguration of the New Covenant era, culminating in the new heavens and the new earth.

The Anointed One

Most people agree that the Anointed One (the meaning of the Hebrew word, Messiah) refers to Christ. And it is often suggested that between the 69 weeks and the final week—that is, between the first and second comings of Christ—there is a long "pause" during which the good news is to be preached.

Daniel in the lions' den.

Hosea

Author
Hosea.

Date
755–710 BC.

Outline
God's family and Hosea's 1:1–3:5
The corruption of Israel 4:1–5:15
God's love rejected 6:1–8:6
Judgment is inevitable 8:7–10:15
Repentance is still possible 11:1–14:9

Prophet Hosea.

Major themes in Hosea

Relationship
The basis of religion is a real relationship with God; a relationship that makes demands on God's people but is also costly to God, who suffers when his love is rejected and his people are unfaithful. Hosea's marriage to Gomer, his adulterous wife, is utilized as a metaphor for the intimate covenant relationship between Israel and her God, characterized as a spiritual "marriage." Gomer's infidelities are then paralleled with Israel's idolatry, likewise characterized as "spiritual adultery."

Israel's unfaithfulness
Israel's turning away from God, paralleled with Gomer's adulterous betrayal of the prophet, Hosea, affected their religious, political, and moral lives.

The love of God
God loved Israel despite their sin. Hosea mentions different ways in which God's love is expressed, involving both blessing and judgement.

The need for knowledge
The heart of Israel's problem lay in their failure to understand God. If they really knew him, then their behavior would be transformed.

Joel

Author
Joel.

Date
c. 835 BC.

Outline
National disaster 1:1-20
The Day of the Lord 2:1-32
The future foretold 3:1-21

Major themes in Joel

The outpouring of God's Spirit
Joel expects a great outpouring of God's Spirit "on all people" (2:28), which will take place "before the coming of the great and dreadful day of the Lord" (2:31). Peter said Joel's prophecy was fulfilled on the day of Pentecost (ACTS 2:1–21).

God's judgment—the "Day of the LORD"
When God disciplined his people he used famine or plagues (like Joel's locusts) and other nations. But sometimes those nations got the wrong idea: they became proud, boastful—and, in turn, had to be punished.

Joel.

Amos

Author
Amos.

Date
Probably 760–753 BC.

Outline
Judgment against Israel and its neighbors 1:1–6:14
Israel's punishment and reward 7:1–9:15

Major themes in Amos

Breaking the law of God
The nations are condemned for their sin, their rebellion against God's law. Breaking God's law lies at the root of sin. These transgressions were both personal and national.

The punishment of God
When people sin, punishment is inevitable. Punishment is greater for those who have the privilege of being in a special relationship with God (3:2). Punishment is carried out by God only with great reluctance (7:1–6).

The voice of God
One of the worst fates is to endure a period when God is silent (8:11–12).

An ordinary man
Amos was not a professional prophet but a man called from an ordinary job—a sheep herder, with a burning desire to speak God's word.

Obadiah

Author
Obadiah.

Date
Either c. 840 BC or between 586 and 539 BC.

Outline
Destruction of Edom 1–9
Reasons for the destruction 10–14
Terrible Day of God 15–16
Israel restored 17–21

Major themes in Obadiah

The light and shade of God's character
The sternness of our God, reflected in the punishment of his enemies, along with his mercy and grace, as seen in the restoration and redemption of his people

The kingdom will be the Lord's
God's "kingship" or "kingdom," centered in Christ.

Jonah

Author
Jonah.

Date
c. 782–753 BC.

Outline
Runaway prophet 1:1–17
Grateful prophet 2:1–10
Obedient prophet 3:1–10
Harsh prophet 4:1–11

Major themes in Jonah

Grace

Jonah knew that God was "gracious and compassionate…slow to anger and abounding in love" (4:2 NIV) because God had been gracious to him. This makes Jonah's harsh dealing with others harder to take.

Unfulfilled prophecy

God's promise of judgement on Nineveh (the principal city of the Assyrian Empire) through Jonah never happened (3:10), because the Ninevites repented upon hearing the prophet's preaching. Not all prophecy needs to be fulfilled. Although God cannot be manipulated, he does respond to human repentance and is able to fulfil his purpose by different means.

Jonah and Jesus

Jesus used Jonah's experience as an illustration of his own (see MATTHEW 12:39–41; 16:4). Just as Jonah was marked out as God's servant by his miraculous deliverance, Jesus' claims and message would be endorsed by his resurrection from the dead (see ROMANS 1:3–4).

Jonah and the great fish.

Micah

Author
Micah.

Date
735–710 BC.

Outline
Judgments against Israel and Judah 1:1–3:12
Hope for God's people 4:1–5:15
Israel on trial 6:1–7:7
Forgiveness for those who confess their sins 7:8–20

Major themes in Micah

Judgment

The crimes of the people of Judah involved every aspect of their lives. Notice how the punishment fits the crime.

Justice

God is a God of justice and he expects justice from his people. Justice in Micah is seen in practical ways, not as a mere abstract concept. Perhaps the most powerful metaphor employed by Micah is that of the prophets of the LORD as his "divine prosecuting attorneys," indicting the people of God in his divine courtroom for the violation of his covenant statutes.

Hope

Micah envisages the future for Jerusalem (4:1–3, 8, 13); for the remnant (2:12; 4:6–7, 10; 5:7–8); and for all nations (4:2–4).

Forgiveness

Micah ends with a description of God's gracious forgiveness. These verses are read by Jews on the Day of Atonement, as they seek cleansing from the sins of the past year.

Nahum

Author
Nahum "the Elkoshite."

Date
Possibly 663–654 BC.

Outline
God portrayed 1:1-8
Destruction of Nineveh 1:9-15
Assault on Nineveh 2:1–3:4
God versus Nineveh 3:5-19

Major theme in Nahum

Man's accountability to God
Because of their crimes, Edom and Assyria must face God's judgment.

Habakkuk

Author
Habakkuk.

Date
Probably 609–605 BC.

Outline
Suffering and injustice 1:1–2:1
God in control 2:2–3:19

Major themes in Habakkuk

The prophet's crisis of faith
For a brief time, Habakkuk was dismayed at God's *apparent* lack of concern over his people's injustice, violence, and callous indifference to the poor, along with the fact that God would use such a wicked nation as Babylon to bring judgment against his people. God's response, however, restores the prophet's trust in him.

God
In spite of these initial misgivings, Habakkuk ends up describing God as holy, just, sovereign, unchanging, merciful, saving, judging, and revealing truth.

Faith
"The righteous man will live by faith" (2:4), that is, his loyalty to God, despite the godlessness of others.

Habakkuk.

Zephaniah

Author
Zephaniah.

Date
c. 635–625 BC.

Outline
God's judgment 1:1-18
Message to Judah 2:1–3:8
God's mighty promises 3:9-20

Major themes in Zephaniah

God's rule
God receiving the homage of all men.

A new lifestyle
God brings about a radical change in his people.

Haggai

Author
Haggai.

Date
520 BC.

Outline
Introduction 1:1
Put first things first: take care of God's house before your own dwellings 1:2-15
Look to the future: the glory of the rebuilt Temple will be greater than that of Solomon's Temple 2:1-9
Promise for the future: God will bless his people 2:10-19
Safety in the storm 2:20-23

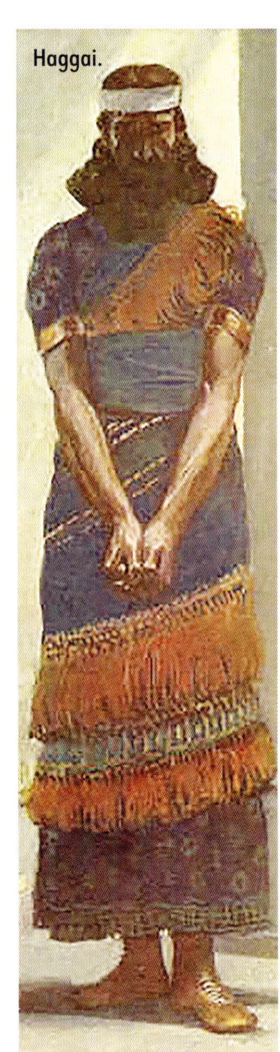
Haggai.

Major themes in Haggai

About the wrong priority of money
"Why are you living in luxurious houses while my house lies in ruins?" (1:4, NLT).

About life's achievements
"Give careful thought to your ways" (1:5, 7, NIV).

About the future of God's world
"The glory of this present house will be greater than the glory of the former house" (2:9, NIV).

About God's loving purpose
"I will take you…and I will make you…for I have chosen you" (2:23, NIV).

Zechariah

Author
Zechariah.

Date
480–470 BC.

Outline
Eight visions 1:1–6:8
Crowning of Joshua the High Priest 6:9-15
Exhortation to true worship: Justice and mercy—not fasting 7:1-14
Divine promise to bless Jerusalem 8:1-23
"Day of the LORD" oracles: divine judgment on Israel's enemies, and eternal salvation through the Messiah and his everlasting kingdom 9:1–14:21

Major themes in Zechariah

Encouragement for God's people
This theme dominates the entire prophecy. The eight night visions (1:1—6:8) encapsulate this theme via the expression of glorious hope for the people of God, symbolized by the reconstruction of the Second Temple. And the two figures of Joshua the High Priest, and Zerubbabel the governor are central to the reestablishing of this renewed Temple (cf. 6:9–15)

The Day of the LORD
In the second half of the book (chs. 9—14), there is a series of judgment and salvation oracles that focus, respectively, on the destruction of the enemies of God and his people, and the coming of the Messiah and the glorious consummation of his heavenly kingdom.

Malachi

Author
Malachi.

Date
Probably 432–425 BC.

Outline
God's love for Israel 1:1-5
Unfaithful priests and broken promises 1:6–2:16
Judgment—and rewards 2:17–4:6

Major themes in Malachi

Divine love
God reminds his people he had a special love for them, which is why he dealt with them as he did (1:2–5).

Divine displeasure
God was displeased with his people: they lacked reverence for him and for his house (1:6–14), and lacked sound teaching (2:7–9). They were unfaithful (2:10–16), cynical (2:17; 3:14–15), indifferent to human need (3:5), and withheld God's rightful dues (3:8–9).

Divine promises
God promises to intervene and bless.

Divine remembrance
God knows those who are his (3:16–18). and will vindicate them (4:2–3).

Rulers of the Babylonian Empire

Nabopolassar 626–605 BC
Nabopolassar was the founder and first king of the Neo-Babylonian Empire. Prior to his coronation, Nabopolassar had led an uprising against the Assyrian Empire, which led to the complete destruction of that world power.

Nebuchadnezzar II 605–562 BC
Nebuchadnezzar II enjoys the reputation of being the Babylonian Empire's greatest king. His rule lasted 43 years, and constituted the longest reign of the Babylonian dynasty. He is renowned in the Old Testament as the invader and destroyer of the kingdom of Judah, leading to four deportations of the Judean population between 605 and 581 BC. The largest and most significant of these was in 587 BC, when the city of Jerusalem was captured and destroyed, and its population exiled to Babylon. The people were brought back from captivity in 539 BC, at the outset of the (Medo-) Persian Empire.

Evil-Merodach 562–560 BC
Evil-Merodach was the third king of the Neo-Babylonian Empire. He succeeded his father, Nebuchadnezzar II, in 562 BC, ruling until 560 BC, when he was overthrown and murdered. Evil-Merodach is best remembered for releasing Jeconiah (Jehoiachin)—the penultimate king of Judah—after 37 years of imprisonment (2 KINGS 25:27).

Neriglissar 560–556 BC
Neriglissar was the fourth king of the Neo-Babylonian Empire, who ruled from his seizing of the throne in 560 BC, until he died in 556 BC.

Labashi-Marduk 556 BC
Labashi-Marduk was the fifth and second last king of the Neo-Babylonian Empire. He succeeded his father, Neriglissar; but his reign was very short, lasting only a few months. Labashi-Marduk was deposed and murdered by Belshazzar, the son of Nabonidus. Belshazzar then proclaimed Nabonidus as king.

Nabonidus 556–539 BC
Nabonidus was the last king of the Neo-Babylonian Empire, ruling from 556 BC to the end of the Babylonian Kingdom in 539 BC, when Cyrus the Persian came to power as head of the (Medo-) Persian Empire.

All dates are approximate

Rulers of the Persian Empire

Cyrus II "the Great" 550–530 BC
The conqueror of Babylon, Cyrus II reversed previous policy and returned exiled peoples to their homelands. By his decree, the Jews returned to Judea.
2 CHRONICLES 36:22–23; EZRA 1–6; ISAIAH 44:28; 45:1; DANIEL 10:1

Cambyses II 530–522 BC

Darius I 530–486 BC
A strong ruler, confirmed the decree of Cyrus II and ordered the Jerusalem Temple to be completed at Persian expense.
EZRA 5:3–6:15; NEHEMIAH 12:22; HAGGAI 1:1; ZECHARIAH 1:1

Xerxes I 486–465 BC
Xerxes was the Greek name for this Persian ruler, who was most likely the same king as Ahasuerus (Hebrew name) in the book of Esther. He failed in two attempts to invade Greece.
ESTHER

Artaxerxes I 464–423 BC
Nehemiah was cupbearer to Artaxerxes I, who granted his request and made him governor of Judea. During his rule, the walls of Jerusalem were rebuilt.
EZRA 7:1, 21-26; NEHEMIAH 2:1-8

Xerxes II 425–424 BC

Darius II 423–404 BC

Artaxerxes II 404–359 BC

Artaxerxes III 359–338 BC

Arses (Artaxerxes IV) 338–336 BC

Darius III 336–331 BC

Palace of Xerxes, Persepolis.

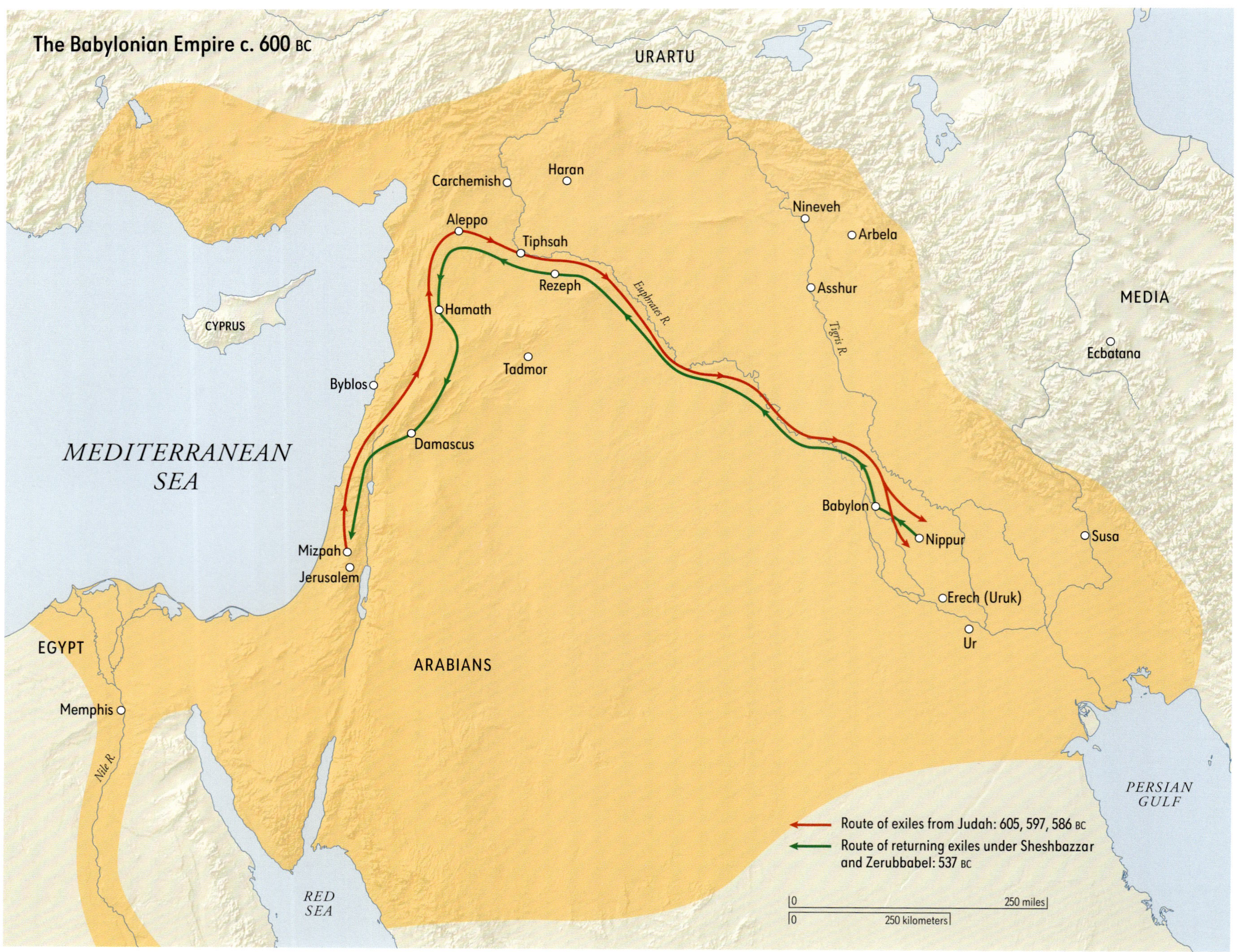
The Babylonian Empire c. 600 BC
URARTU
Carchemish
Haran
Aleppo
Tiphsah
Rezeph
Euphrates R.
Nineveh
Arbela
Asshur
Tigris R.
MEDIA
Ecbatana
CYPRUS
Hamath
Tadmor
Byblos
Damascus
MEDITERRANEAN SEA
Babylon
Nippur
Susa
Mizpah
Jerusalem
Erech (Uruk)
Ur
EGYPT
ARABIANS
Memphis
Nile R.
PERSIAN GULF
RED SEA
Route of exiles from Judah: 605, 597, 586 BC
Route of returning exiles under Sheshbazzar and Zerubbabel: 537 BC
0 250 miles
0 250 kilometers

The Persian Empire c. 450 BC
THRACE
MACEDONIA
Sardis
ARMENIA
CASPIAN SEA
Oxus R.
Araxes R.
Carchemish
Haran
Nineveh
Asshur
MEDIA
Ecbatana
PARTHIA
Euphrates R.
Tigris R.
Byblos
MEDITERRANEAN SEA
Damascus
Babylon
Susa
Taxila
Samaria
Jerusalem
Memphis
ARABIANS
Persepolis
EGYPT
PERSIA
Pura
Nile R.
Thebes
PERSIAN GULF
RED SEA
Route of returning exiles under Ezra and Nehemiah: 458, 445 BC
0 600 miles
0 600 kilometers

Between the Testaments

From the Persians to the Greeks

The Old Testament era ends with Ezra and Nehemiah; we know very little in detail about Jewish affairs after that until about 200 BC.

The major event in this period was the fall of the Persian Empire to Alexander the Great (336–323 BC), who inaugurated an era of Greek rule throughout the eastern Mediterranean region and far beyond. Both Egypt and the former Babylonia came under Alexander's control, as did the whole of Palestine.

Greek culture became dominant throughout the eastern Mediterranean—shown by the fact that the New Testament is written in Greek. Greek ideas, philosophy, and customs were soon widespread, a process known as Hellenization. Many Greek ways of thinking were absorbed by subject peoples, such as the Jews.

After Alexander's death in 323 BC, his empire broke up into several smaller empires. The Greek general Ptolemy became king of Egypt, and his Ptolemaic Empire governed Judea for the following century. The neighboring Greek Empire to the north of Judea centered on Syria, and is known as the Seleucid kingdom, after its first ruler, Seleucus. The two empires quarreled over Palestine, and a Seleucid king, Antiochus III, defeated the armies of Egypt in 198 BC and took possession of Palestine.

The Maccabean Revolt

When Antiochus III conquered Judea in 198 BC, the high priest was Simon II. After the Babylonian Exile, the high priest became the most important political figure in Judea, under the foreign governor.

A generation later, the Seleucid king Antiochus IV decided to appoint the high priest. Devout Jews were outraged by his interference in religious affairs. Then, in 168 BC, angered by unrest in Jerusalem, Antiochus attacked Jewish practices. He plundered the temple, erected in it an altar to a pagan god, and banned Jewish customs. His pagan altar was called "the Abomination of Desolation" by the Jews (DANIEL 11:31).

An elderly priest named Mattathias sparked a revolt. One of his five sons, Judas Maccabeus, led the rebels (1 MACCABEES 2). He died in battle in 160 BC, but his brothers Jonathan (until 142 BC) and Simon (until 135 BC) continued the struggle. In 164 BC, following its defilement by the Seleucids, the Temple was purified and restored, and sacrifices began to be offered again, inaugurating the Jewish festival of Hanukkah.

When the Seleucid Empire was temporarily weakened by internal divisions, the Jews gained virtual independence. Alexander Jannaeus (103–76 BC) completed the conquest of most of Israel and founded a new dynasty, the Hasmoneans. While one influential Jewish party favored Hellenization, this was opposed by the Hasidim, "the devout," who supported Judas in his struggle to cleanse the temple. Various groupings appeared among the Jews, which resulted in the parties and sects known in New Testament times—such as the Pharisees, Sadducees and others.

Judas Maccabeus' brother Jonathan was made high priest in 152 BC. His family was not Zadokite, and this breach of sacred tradition scandalized some Jews. Simon not only held the high priesthood but also ensured it stayed in his family, his successors adding the title of king to high priest.

Whilst the early Hasmoneans were patriots, their successors were worldly, violent men—especially Alexander Jannaeus (103–76 BC), who quarreled with the pious Pharisees and executed hundreds of them. This period ended in civil war. The Romans intervened, and in 63 BC took control of the entire region. The Roman general Pompey marched into Judea: from now on the Romans were to oversee affairs in Judea.

Mosaic of Alexander the Great.

The Old Testament Apocrypha

The Apocrypha is a collection of books and additions to Old Testament books, written between 300 BC and AD 100. These books were not accepted by the Jews as part of the Hebrew Scriptures, but were included in the Septuagint (the Greek translation of the Hebrew Bible).

1 Esdras
An historical account of the return of the Jews from Babylonian captivity, paralleling Chronicles, Ezra, and Nehemiah.

2 Esdras (4 Ezra)
Visions and revelations of early Jewish rabbis.

Tobit
A didactic fiction about Tobit's trials in eighth century BC Nineveh.

Judith
The fictional exploits of a Jewish heroine, Judith, who assassinated the Assyrian general Holofernes.

Additions to Esther (also known as The Rest of Esther)
Five additions that give a more religious emphasis to the book of Esther.

The Wisdom of Solomon
A first-century BC call to wisdom.

Ecclesiasticus (also known as The Wisdom of Sirach/Ben Sira)
A collection of writings by Joshua ben-Sira (c. 180 BC) giving his advice for a successful life—combining personal piety with practical wisdom.

Baruch
This book was allegedly written by Baruch, a friend of Jeremiah, and meant as an encouragement to Jews during the Babylonian Exile of 597 BC

The Letter of Jeremiah
An attack on idolatry, in the form of a letter from the prophet Jeremiah, often added to the book of Baruch.

The Song of the Three Holy Children
A hymn of praise sung by Shadrach, Meshach, and Abednego in the fiery furnace, as described in the book of Daniel.

The Story of Susanna
The story of a virtuous woman who was falsely accused of adultery and defended by Daniel.

Bel and the Dragon
A folkloric story written to ridicule idolatry.

The Prayer of Manasseh
Prayer of the idolatrous king Manasseh, begging for forgiveness, referred to in 2 Chronicles 33:11–19.

1 Maccabees
The struggle of Jews against Hellenistic rulers (175–134 BC), particularly the battle with Antiochus Epiphanes.

2 Maccabees
A narrative of the Maccabean revolt.

3 Maccabees
An account of Jewish life under Ptolemy IV (221–204 BC).

4 Maccabees
About the rule of reason over passion.

Judas Maccabeus.

New Testament

Who wrote the New Testament?

Name	Nationality	Occupation	Writings	How he died
Matthew	Jewish	Tax-collector	Matthew	By tradition martyred in Ethiopia
Mark	Jewish		Mark	By tradition martyred
Luke	Greek	Physician	Luke, Acts	By tradition martyred in Greece
John	Jewish	Fisherman	John, 1-3 John, Revelation	Banished to Patmos; died naturally
Paul	Jewish	Tentmaker	Romans, 1 and 2 Corinthians, Galatians, Ephesians, Philippians, Colossians, 1 and 2 Thessalonians, 1 and 2 Timothy, Titus, Philemon	By tradition martyred in Rome by Nero
James	Jewish		James	By tradition martyred
Peter	Jewish	Fisherman	1 and 2 Peter	By tradition crucified upside-down in Rome by Nero
Jude	Jewish		Jude	By tradition martyred
Unknown	Jewish		Hebrews	

The Message of the New Testament book-by-book

Matthew
Life of Jesus, stressing how it fulfilled God's covenant with Israel and the importance of Jesus' teachings.

Mark
Life of Jesus, emphasizing his last week in Jerusalem, crucifixion, and resurrection.

Luke
Life of Jesus, underlining his humanity and the people he affected—including both Jews and Gentiles, but with a major emphasis on the latter.

John
Life of Jesus, written to reveal him as Christ, the Son of God.

Acts
The coming of the Holy Spirit, initiating the new Covenant age, and empowering the growth and spread of Christianity.

Romans
Paul sets out the doctrine of justification by faith in Jesus Christ in all its complexity, and—more broadly—righteousness from God. Paul also expresses a deep concern for Israel.

1 Corinthians
Paul's letter to the Christians of Corinth, rebuking and correcting their sin, and calling on them to love, and to work on developing holiness of character.

2 Corinthians
Paul writes with concern to the Corinthians, explaining the reason for his change of itinerary, encouraging them to live in love and unity, and to complete the collection of money for the relief of those in need. He also stresses his authenticity as an apostle.

Galatians
Paul's proclamation of Christian liberty—opposing the claims of the heretical, legalistic Judaizers—stating that justification by God's grace is through faith alone, not by works of the Law.

Ephesians
Paul writes about Christ and the church, by which means the wisdom and grace of God are revealed, via the bestowing of spiritual gifts from the indwelling Holy Spirit, in order to facilitate the expression of genuine, godly ministry.

The Message of the New Testament continued

Philippians
Paul reveals the joy and beauty of Christian living, coupled with a hymn of praise to Christ, celebrating both his humility and his exaltation. He also encourages them to stand firm in the face of persecution; and warns the Philippians against the Judaizers (legalists) and antinomians (libertines) among them.

Colossians
Paul attacks errors in the church, presenting Jesus Christ as the only antidote for these false teachings, and presents him alone as adequate for the salvation of all people.

1 Thessalonians
Paul calls Christians to be faithful, pure, and holy, and to wait expectantly for Jesus' return. His message was directed at new converts, as well as mature Christians.

2 Thessalonians
Paul writes about Christ's second coming, and enjoins the Thessalonians to pray, and seek to avoid undisciplined lives in relation to the Gospel.

1 and 2 Timothy
Paul writes to Timothy about the church in Ephesus, urging him to actively refute false teaching, which had taken hold there, and also to give instructions for worship and administration, including the qualifications and duties of church leaders.

Titus
Paul writes to Titus, emphasizing the importance of maintaining church order, and of eliminating false teaching, to be followed by the promotion of sound doctrine.

Philemon
Paul asks his friend Philemon to receive back his runaway slave, Onesimus, as a brother in Christ.

Hebrews
Defends the Christian faith as superseding the Mosaic covenant, emphasizing that Christ is superior to the angels, to Moses, and to the Aaronic priesthood. He is our great, heavenly High Priest, and is all-sufficient for our salvation.

James
James emphasizes that genuine Christian faith is characterized not only by doctrinal purity, but also by the "fruit" of good works, as evidence of the genuineness of our faith. He also warns his readers of the dangers of worldliness.

1 Peter
Peter's letter calls God's chosen people to purity and spirituality, including dedication to Christ alone; perseverance in the face of persecution; submission to divinely-instituted civil authority; the roles of husbands and wives; and living godly lives.

2 Peter
Peter warns believers to remain in the truth, opposing false teachers and their heresies, and holding fast to the certainty of Christ's second coming.

1 John
John exhorts his readers to hold fast to the fundamentals of the faith, revealed in Jesus Christ, in the light of the dangerous heresy associated with the philosophy of Gnosticism—a pagan worldview that grew and plagued the early church in the 2nd century AD.

2 John
The importance of love in Christian fellowship; warnings against false teaching, especially that of traveling Gnostic heretics.

3 John
John writes here primarily about providing hospitality for traveling Christian teachers, and commends several church leaders for doing so.

Jude
Jude condemns false teachers and calls believers to remain faithful to Christ.

Revelation
A record of apocalyptic visions granted to John the Apostle, in exile on the island of Patmos. The visions are preceded by the content of letters written to seven churches suffering severe persecution during the latter part of the 1st century AD. The book stresses the lordship of Christ, the sovereignty of God, and his final victory over sin and evil.

The Old City, Jerusalem.

Jesus' birth and infancy: what happened and when...

6–5 BC	An angel announces to Zechariah the birth of John to his wife, Elizabeth.	Luke 1:5-25
Six months later	Angel Gabriel announces the birth of Jesus to Mary. Mary visits Elizabeth.	Luke 1:26–38 Luke 1:39–56
Three months later	Mary returns to Nazareth. Joseph has a dream. John is born.	Luke 1:56 Matthew 1:18–24 Luke 1:57–80
5 BC	Jesus is born in Bethlehem.	Matthew 1:25; Luke 2:1-7
Eight days later	Jesus is circumcised.	Luke 2:21
Thirty-three days later	Jesus is presented at the Temple.	Luke 2:22-38
4 BC	The wise men visit baby Jesus. The holy family flees to Egypt Massacre of the innocents—infants of Bethlehem murdered.	Matthew 2:1–12 Matthew 2:13–15 Matthew 2:16–18
3 or 2 BC	The holy family return to Nazareth	Luke 2:39; Matthew 2:19–23

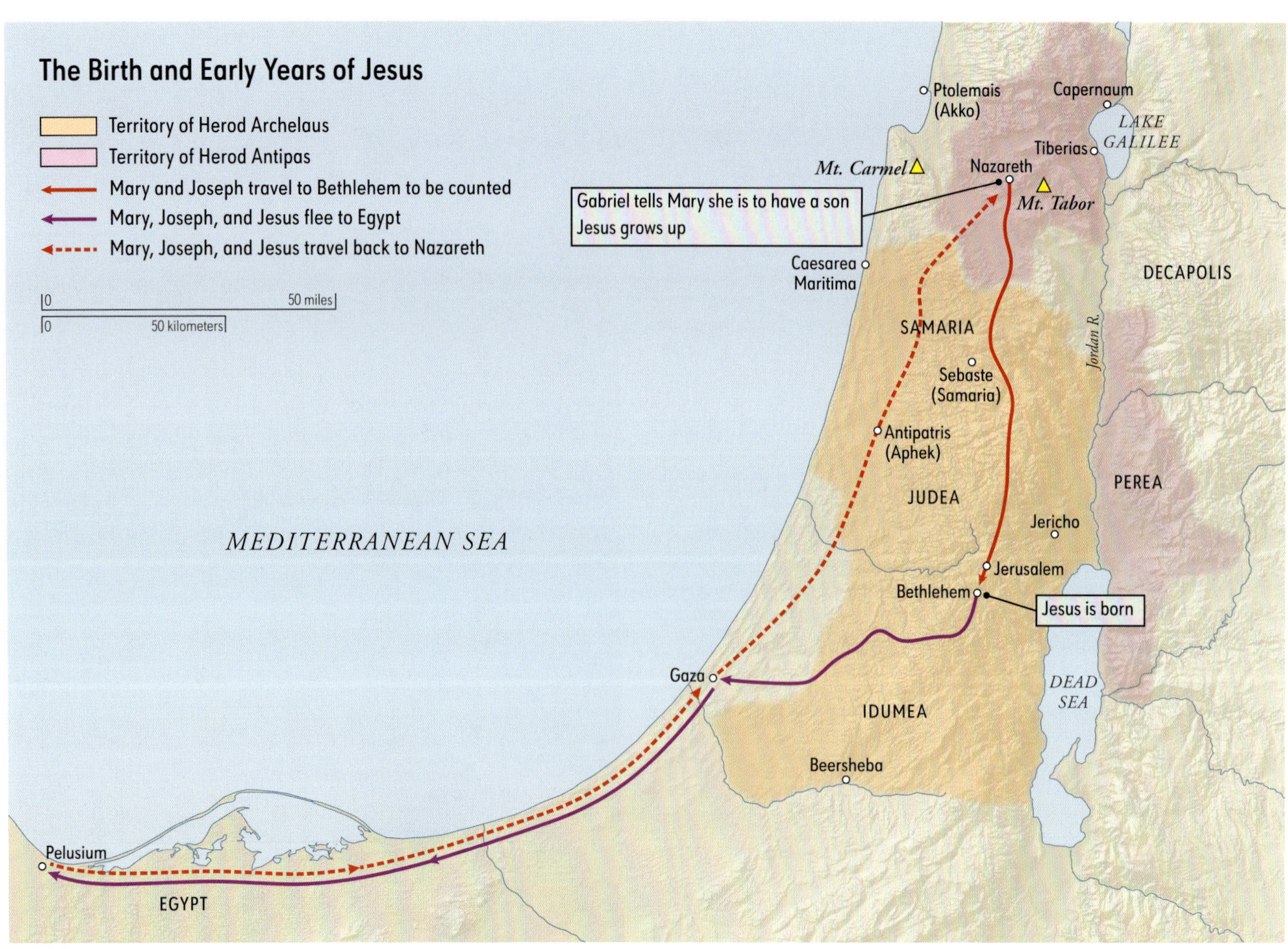

The Magi

Numerous myths and legends have arisen around the "wise men" of Matthew 2. By tradition known as the "Magi," they are also referred to as "Three Wise Men" and "Three Kings," bringing gifts to the baby Jesus and alerting King Herod to his birth.

"Magi" is the plural of "magus," a member of a Persian priestly caste.

The Bible never names the Magi, nor does it say how many there were. Matthew's Gospel lists three gifts—gold, frankincense, and myrrh—so it is often assumed there were three Magi.

The Magi are often popularly named as Caspar, Melchior, and Balthasar. Other names include Larvandad, Hormisdad, and Gushnasaph.

The gifts of the Magi are often interpreted symbolically: gold representing Christ's kingship; frankincense—the purest incense—his divinity; myrrh—a medicine—his humanity.

The Magi.

The Magi followed the Star of Bethlehem to find Jesus. Some believe this to have been a comet; others, a conjunction of the planets Jupiter and Saturn.

Angels

The word "angel" (Greek, "*angelos*") literally means "messenger." In the Bible, it applies mostly to supernatural beings of the unseen world, used as messengers in the service of God—or Satan.

Angels played an important role in the life of Jesus

An angel announced the birth of John. LUKE 1:11–17
An angel said Elizabeth's son should be called John. LUKE 1:13
An angel foretold the birth of Jesus to Mary. LUKE 1:26–37
An angel foretold the birth of Jesus to Joseph. MATTHEW 1:20–21
An angel said Mary's son should be called Jesus. MATTHEW 1:21
Angels announced to shepherds the birth of Jesus. LUKE 2:8–15
Angels sang hallelujahs. LUKE 2:13–14
An angel directed Jesus' flight into Egypt. MATTHEW 2:13, 20
Angels ministered to Jesus at his temptation. MATTHEW 4:11
An angel came to Jesus in Gethsemane. LUKE 22:43
An angel rolled away the stone of Jesus' tomb. MATTHEW 28:2
An angel announced Jesus' resurrection to the women. MATTHEW 28:5–7
Two angels presented Jesus to Mary Magdalene. JOHN 20:11–14

Medieval painting of the Annunciation.

Harmony of the Gospels

Where to find the same events and teachings in the different Gospels

	Matthew	Mark	Luke	John
Jesus' birth and childhood 5/4 BC				
Jesus' genealogy	1:1-17		3:23-38	
Jesus' birth foretold	1:18-25		1:26-38	
Jesus is born	2:1-12		2:1-39	
Jesus' childhood and visit to the Temple			2:40-52	
Jesus prepares for his public ministry AD 29				
Jesus is baptized	3:13-17	1:9-11	3:21-22	1:31-34
Jesus is tempted in the wilderness	4:1-11	1:12-13	4:1-13	
Jesus' ministry begins				
John points to Jesus				1:19-34
John's disciples follow Jesus				1:35-51
Jesus' first miracle: water into wine				2:1-11
"You must be born again"				3:1-21
Jesus in Galilee				
Jesus arrives in Galilee	4:12-17	1:14	4:14	4:43-45
Jesus calls the first of the Twelve	4:18-22	1:16-20	5:1-11	1:35-42
Many miracles	8:1-17, 23-27	1:40–2:12	5:12-26	
The Sermon on the Mount	5:1–7:29		6:20-49	
Jesus speaks in parables	13:1-53	4:1-34	8:4-18	
A series of miracles	8:23–9:8	4:35–5:43	8:22-56	
Jesus recognized as Christ and Son of God	16:13-26	8:27–9:1	9:18-27	
Jesus is transfigured	16:27–17:13	9:2-13	9:28-36	
Jesus predicts his death and resurrection	17:22-23	9:31-32	9:43-45	
Jesus' last ministry in Galilee	17:24–18:35	9:33-50	9:46-50	7:1-9

Harmony of the Gospels continued

	Matthew	Mark	Luke	John
Jesus in Judea and Perea				
Jesus' journey to Jerusalem	19:1-2	10:1	9:51-62	7:10
Jesus claims deity				8:12-59
Jesus the good shepherd				10:1-21
Parable of the Good Samaritan			10:25-37	
Jesus in Mary and Martha's home			10:38-42	
Jesus teaches a prayer	6:5-13		11:1-13	
Jesus raises Lazarus				11:1-44
Jesus travels towards Jerusalem				
The rich young ruler	19:16-30	10:17-31	18:18-30	
Jesus predicts his death	20:17-19	10:32-34	18:31-34	
Jesus arrives at Bethany				11:55–12:11

For chronology of Jesus' last week, death, and resurrection see pp. 96ff.

The Beatitudes

Taught to Jesus' followers at the Sermon on the Mount.

God blesses those who realize their need for him, for the Kingdom of Heaven is given to them.

God blesses those who mourn, for they will be comforted.

God blesses those who are gentle and lowly, for the whole earth will belong to them.

God blesses those who are hungry and thirsty for justice, for they will receive it in full.

God blesses those who are merciful, for they will be shown mercy.

God blesses those whose hearts are pure, for they will see God.

God blesses those who work for peace, for they will be called the children of God.

God blesses those who are persecuted because they live for God, for the Kingdom of Heaven is theirs.

God blesses you when you are mocked and persecuted and lied about because you are my followers.

Be happy about it! Be very glad! For a great reward awaits you in heaven.

MATTHEW 5:3–11, NLT

The Mount of Beatitudes, Galilee.

All the Miracles of Jesus—and where to find them

Healing of individuals	Matthew	Mark	Luke	John
Son of government official				4:46-54
Sick man at a pool				5:1-18
Man in synagogue		1:21-28	4:31-37	
Man with skin disease	8:1-4	1:40-45	5:12-14	
Roman officer's servant	8:5-13		7:1-10	
Dead son of a widow			7:11-15	
Peter's mother-in-law	8:14-15	1:29-31	4:38-39	
A demon-possessed man	8:28-34 (2 men)	5:1-20	8:26-39	
Paralyzed man	9:1-8	2:1-12	5:17-26	
Woman with severe bleeding	9:20-22	5:25-34	8:43-48	
Dead girl	9:18-26	5:21-43	8:40-56	
Dumb man	9:32-34			
Man with paralyzed hand	12:9-14	3:1-6	6:6-11	
Blind and dumb man	12:22-23		11:14	
Canaanite woman's daughter (Syro-phoenician)	15:21-28	7:24-30		
Deaf and dumb man		7:31-37		
Blind man at Bethsaida		8:22-26		
Boy with epilepsy/demoniac	17:14-20	9:14-29	9:37-43	
Blind Bartimaeus	20:29-34	10:46-52	18:35-43	
Woman with bad back/demoniac			13:10-17	
Sick man with dropsy			14:1-6	
Man born blind				9:1-41
Dead friend named Lazarus				11:1-44
Slave's ear			22:49-51	

Healing of groups	Matthew	Mark	Luke	John
Crowd in Capernaum	8:16-17	1:32-34	4:40-41	
Two blind men	9:27-31			
Crowd by Sea of Galilee	12:15-16	3:7-12	6:17-19	
Crowd on hillside by Sea of Galilee	15:29-31			
Ten men—lepers			17:11-19	
Control over nature				
Water changed to wine				2:1-11
Catch of fish			5:1-11	
Jesus calms storm	8:23-27	4:35-41	8:22-25	
More than 5,000 people fed	14:14-21	6:30-44	9:10-17	6:1-13
Jesus walks on the water	14:22-33	6:45-52		6:15-21
More than 4,000 people fed	15:32-39	8:1-10		
Fish and the payment of taxes	17:24-27			
Fig tree withers	21:18-22	11:12-14, 20-24		
Another catch of fish				21:1-11

Jesus' resurrection appearances

The Gospels do not record details of the actual process of the resurrection, but leave their readers in no doubt that it actually did occur. And the Gospel writers also recount many people meeting with the risen Christ.

Jesus walks on the Sea of Galilee.

1. Mary Magdalene (JOHN 20:11–18)
2. Simon Peter (LUKE 24:34)
3. Two disciples on the road to Emmaus (LUKE 24:13–22)
4. The disciples, apart from Thomas (JOHN 20:19–23)
5. The disciples, including Thomas (JOHN 20:24–29)
6. Mary Magdalene and "the other Mary" (MATTHEW 28:1–10)
7. The apostles in Galilee (MATTHEW 28:16–17)
8. Seven disciples by the Sea of Galilee (JOHN 21:1–14)
9. More than five hundred of Jesus' followers (1 CORINTHIANS 15:6)
10. James (1 CORINTHIANS 15:7)
11. Jesus' disciples (ACTS 1:4–9)
12. Saul/Paul (ACTS 9:1–9) The risen Lord Jesus appears to Saul in a vision, shortly after the resurrection.

The Life of Jesus

6 BC	John the Baptist's birth foretold
5 BC	Annunciation to Mary of Jesus' birth Birth of John the Baptist Birth of Jesus (Late 5 BC/early 4 BC)
4 BC	Jesus presented in the Temple Visit of wise men/Magi; flight into Egypt Return from Egypt to Nazareth
AD 8	Jesus visits the Temple, aged twelve
AD 27	Baptism of Jesus and temptation in wilderness First miracle, Cana First Passover, Jerusalem Jesus preaches in Judea Jesus returns to Galilee via Samaria
AD 28	Beginning of Jesus' public ministry, Galilee First disciples called Return of Jesus to Jerusalem for second Passover Sermon on the Mount Healing and preaching in Galilee Teaching of parables: sower, tares, pearl Sending of the Twelve John the Baptist beheaded
AD 29	Syrophoenician girl and others healed Jesus foretells his death Sending of the Seventy Jesus departs for Judea Jesus visits Mary and Martha in Bethany
AD 30	Jesus ministers beyond Jordan Jesus raises Lazarus from the dead

For breakdown of events of Easter Week see pp. 96ff.

Jesus and his family

Jesus of Nazareth

Jesus' mother, Mary, laid her baby in a manger at his birth in Bethlehem, where shepherds visited him. Jesus was presented in the Temple, and Mary and Joseph fled to Egypt with Jesus after the wise men visited. They later returned to Nazareth, where Joseph worked as a carpenter. Apart from Jesus' visit to the Temple aged twelve, when he listened to the teachers and asked them questions, nothing else is known of his childhood.

When Jesus was about 30, John baptized him in the Jordan River, after which Jesus went into the wilderness and was tempted by Satan. Jesus then started his public ministry, choosing twelve apostles to be with him. Jesus performed many miracles, such as changing water into wine at Cana, and many healings, such as Jairus' daughter being brought back to life. He also preached often, as in the Sermon on the Mount, and told numerous memorable parables, such as the Good Samaritan and the Prodigal Son.

The four Gospel-writers concentrate on the last seven days of Jesus' life. On the Sunday before his death, Jesus entered Jerusalem on a donkey, to the cheers of the crowds. The following Thursday, Jesus ate the Last Supper with his disciples, before going to the Garden of Gethsemane to pray, where Judas betrayed him. Jesus was arrested, tried unfairly, unjustly condemned to death, crucified like a criminal and buried. But the following Sunday his tomb was found empty: he had been raised from the dead. Forty days later, after many resurrection appearances, Jesus ascended to heaven, promising he would one day return.
MATTHEW, MARK, LUKE, JOHN

Mary

Mary, a young Jewish virgin who was betrothed to a carpenter called Joseph, was chosen by God to conceive and bear his Son, Jesus Christ. The angel Gabriel announced this to her, and she responded with humility and trust. Her Magnificat, or song of praise to God, shows her love and devotion for God. Jesus' first sign, when he changed water into wine, was performed at the instigation of Mary. Mary stood at the foot of the cross as Jesus died; she was also in the upper room on the day of Pentecost.

MATTHEW 1; MARK 6:3; LUKE 1—2; JOHN 2:1–11; 19:25–27; ACTS 1

Joseph

Joseph was betrothed to Mary when they discovered she was pregnant through the action of the Holy Spirit. Joseph married Mary and became legal father to Jesus. Warned in a dream, Joseph took Mary and Jesus from Bethlehem to Egypt to escape Herod's massacre of baby boys in Bethlehem. After Herod's death, Joseph returned to his home town, Nazareth, where he was a carpenter. After Jesus' visit to the Jerusalem Temple, aged twelve, Joseph is not heard of again; it is assumed he died while Jesus was still young.

MATTHEW 1—2; LUKE 1:27—2:52

Elizabeth

Elizabeth, wife of the priest Zechariah, was visited by her cousin Mary when they were both pregnant. Elizabeth greeted Mary, "Blessed are you among women, and blessed is the child you shall bear." Elizabeth's son was John the Baptist.

LUKE 1

John the Baptist

John the Baptist, son of Elizabeth and Zechariah, lived in the Judean wilderness. John wore clothes made from camels' hair, as the prophet Elijah had centuries earlier. He boldly preached repentance, preparing the way for his cousin, Jesus Christ, whom he baptized in the Jordan River. John said, "Jesus must become greater; I must become less" (John 3:30). He was imprisoned, and later beheaded for speaking out against Herod Antipas' marriage to his brother Philip's wife, Herodias.

MATTHEW 3; 11:1–19; 14:1–12; MARK 1:1–8; LUKE 1; JOHN 1:1–34

Zechariah

Zechariah, a godly priest and husband of Elizabeth, was told by an angel they would have a son who must be called John, and who would bring many people back to God. Elizabeth was advanced in years and childless, so Zechariah greeted the news with incredulity. For this he was struck dumb, unable to speak until the baby was born and named John.

LUKE 1

Temptation.

Jesus raises Jairus' daughter.

New Testament Timeline

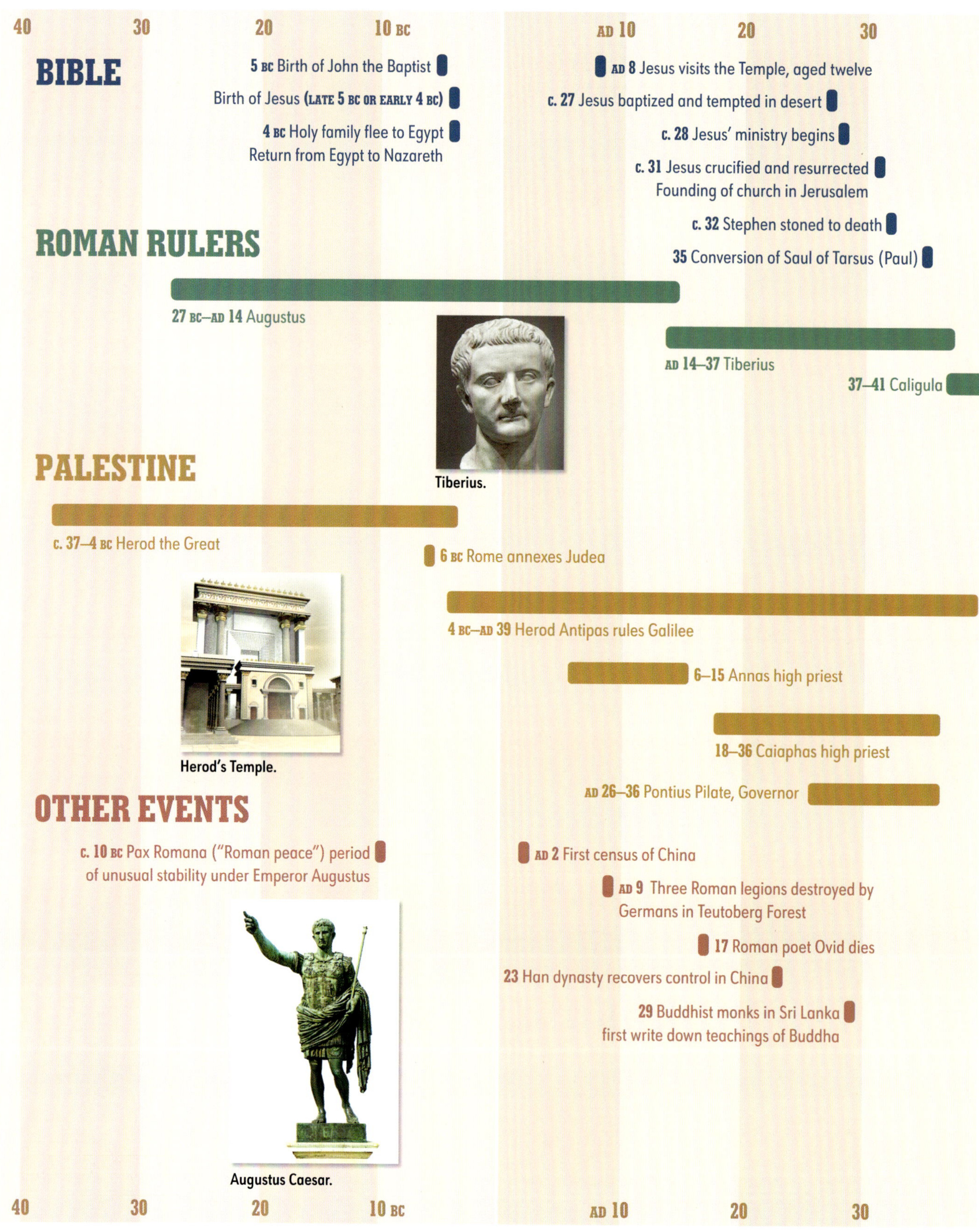

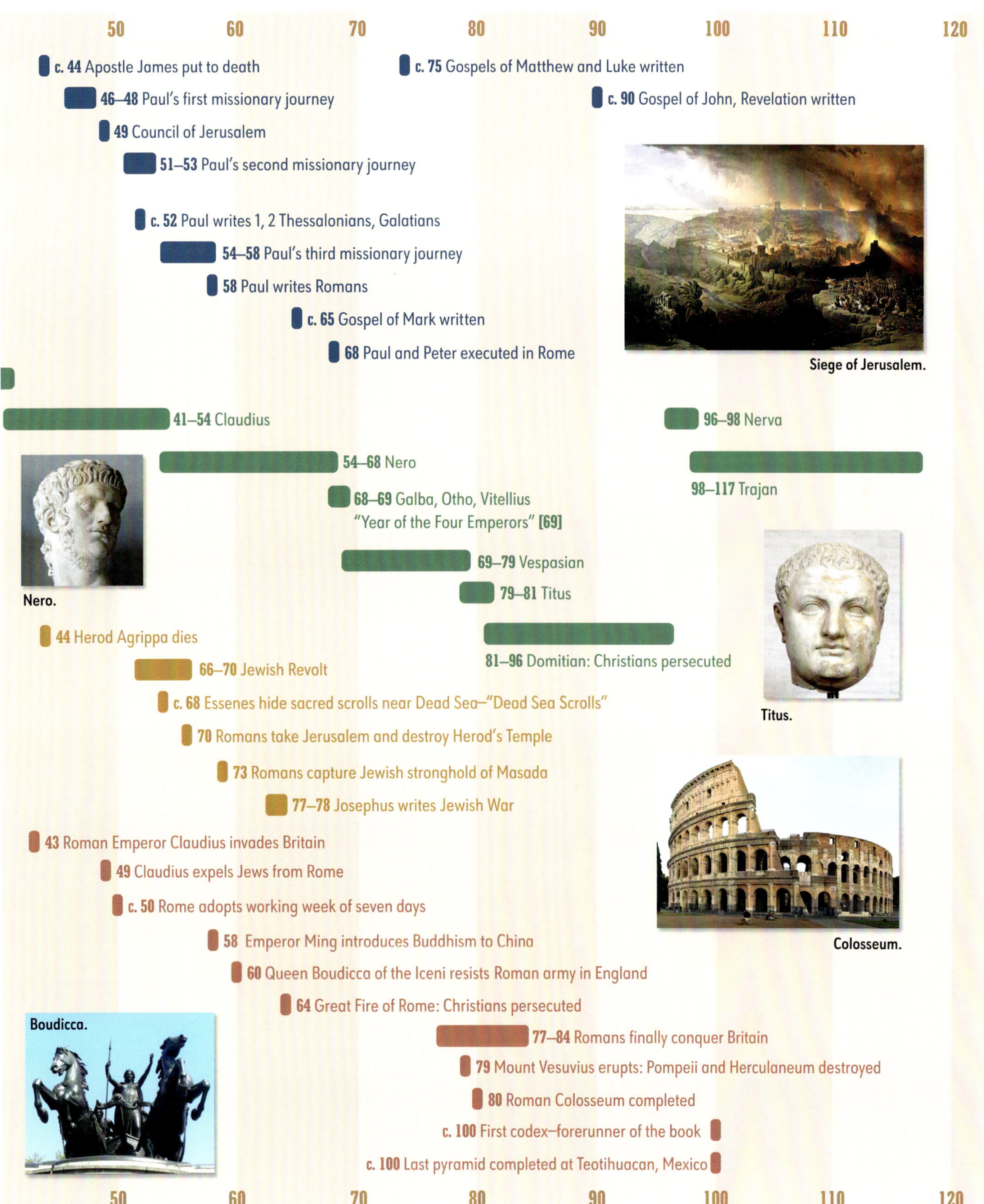

Siege of Jerusalem.

Nero.

Titus.

Colosseum.

Boudicca.

The Twelve Apostles

Jesus chose twelve men to be with him during his three years' preaching and teaching. He called them his "apostles" meaning "those who are sent." Although the core group—Andrew, Peter, James, and John—is clear, some apostles are given different names in different Gospels and others—for instance, Thaddaeus and Nathanael—are little mentioned. There are lists of the apostles in MATTHEW 10:2–4; MARK 3:16–19; LUKE 6:14–16; and ACTS 1:13.

Andrew

Andrew introduced his brother, Peter, to Jesus when they were both following John the Baptist. Andrew and Peter were fishermen on the Sea of Galilee. Andrew brought to Jesus a boy who had two fish and five loaves, which Jesus used in a miracle to feed 5,000 men, plus women and children.

MATTHEW 4:18-20; MARK 1:16-18; JOHN 1:35-42; 6:8-9

Bartholomew

Nothing is known about Bartholomew; the only time his name appears is in the list of Jesus' apostles. He is probably the same person as Nathanael.

MATTHEW 10:3; JOHN 1:45

James, later called "the elder"

James was a fisherman, working with his brother, John, and father, Zebedee. Jesus nicknamed John and James "sons of thunder" because of their stormy nature. James was beheaded for his faith about ten years after the death of Jesus.

MATTHEW 4:21-22; 10:2; 17:1-13; 26:37; MARK 5:37; 10:35-45; LUKE 9:51-56; ACTS 12:2

James, later called "the less" or "the younger"

James was the son of Alphaeus; nothing else is known about him.

MATTHEW 10:3; ACTS 1:13

John

John, a fisherman and son of Zebedee, was one of Jesus' inner group of three apostles. John leaned on Jesus at the Last Supper and was Jesus' closest friend. When Jesus was dying, he asked John to look after his mother, Mary. John wrote one Gospel, the book of Revelation during exile on the island of Patmos, and three letters. In his Gospel, John never mentions himself by name, but calls himself "the disciple Jesus loved." John became a leader in the early church.

MATTHEW 4:21-22; 10:2; 20:20-23; JOHN 13:23-25; 19:25-27; ACTS 1:13; 3–4; GALATIANS 2:9; 1, 2, AND 3 JOHN; REVELATION 1:1

Judas or Jude, "the Zealot" or "Zelotes"

The Judas who did not betray Jesus is also called "son of James" or "Judas, not Iscariot." Probably the same person as Thaddaeus.

LUKE 6:16; JOHN 14:22; ACTS 1:13

Judas Iscariot (that is, "from Kerioth")

Judas, son of Simon Iscariot, was treasurer for the apostles. For 30 pieces of silver he betrayed Jesus in the Garden of Gethsemane. When Judas saw that Jesus had been condemned to death, he returned the silver to the elders, saying, "I have sinned for I have betrayed innocent blood." He then hanged himself.

MATTHEW 10:4; 26:1–27:10; JOHN 6:71; ACTS 1:15-26

Matthew

Also known as Levi, Matthew was a tax-collector when Jesus asked him to follow him. He wrote the first Gospel.

MATTHEW 9:9-10; MARK 2:14

Nathanael

Probably the same person as Bartholomew. Jesus said of him, "Here is a true Israelite, in whom there is nothing false."

JOHN 1:43-51

Thomas ("the twin"–"Didymus" in Greek)

Remembered as "doubting" Thomas because he said he would not believe in Jesus' resurrection unless he saw Jesus and touched his wounds. When the risen Jesus appeared to him, he worshiped him and called him Lord and God.

MATTHEW 10:3; JOHN 11:16; 14:5-6; 20:24-28

Simon the Zealot, or "Canaanean"

Known as "the Zealot," probably because he belonged to a Jewish revolutionary group trying to drive the Romans out of Israel.

MATTHEW 10:4; LUKE 6:15

Philip

Philip, like Andrew and Peter, came from Bethsaida, near the Sea of Galilee. At the Last Supper, when Philip asked Jesus to show them the Father, Jesus replied, "I am in the Father and the Father is in me."

MARK 3:18; JOHN 1:43-51; 6:5-7; 12:20-22; 14:8-9

The Twelve Apostles continued

Simon Peter "bar Jonah"

Peter, the outspoken leader of the twelve, always heads lists of the apostles. With his brother, Andrew, Peter left his fishing to become one of Jesus' three closest disciples. At Caesarea Philippi, Peter told Jesus he was "the Christ, the Son of the living God" (MATTHEW 16:16, KJV). Peter boasted he would die for Jesus, but denied him three times. After Jesus' resurrection, Jesus told Peter to be a shepherd and "feed his sheep."

Peter led the first Christians, preaching boldly on the day of Pentecost. John and Peter healed a man in Jerusalem, but were imprisoned for teaching the resurrection of the dead through Jesus. Peter wrote two short letters, and much of Mark's Gospel is seen as summarizing his teaching. Jesus predicted Peter would be martyred, and it is thought he was executed in Rome by Nero.

MATTHEW 4:18-20; 10:2; 14:25-31; 16:13-23; 17:1-13; 26:31-35, 69-75; 1 AND 2 PETER

Also

Matthias

After Judas betrayed Christ, the remaining disciples chose Matthias to replace him.

ACTS 1:26

Saul, later, Paul—after his conversion

The Apostle to the Gentiles, chosen by Jesus.

ACTS 9:3-6; ROMANS 11:13

Old Testament Prophecies fulfilled in Matthew's Gospel

Prophecy	Reference in Matthew	Reference in Old Testament
Jesus' virgin birth	1:23	Isaiah 7:14
Jesus' birthplace	2:6	Micah 5:2
Jesus' return from Egypt	2:15	Hosea 11:1
Jesus' healing ministry	8:17	Isaiah 53:4
Jesus the Servant	12:18-21	Isaiah 42:1-4
Jesus' parables	13:34	Psalm 78:2
Jesus enters Jerusalem	21:5	Zechariah 9:9
Jesus is rejected	21:42	Psalm 118:22
Jesus is God	22:44	Psalm 110:1
Jesus is deserted	26:31	Zechariah 13:7
Jesus will return	26:64	Daniel 7:13
Jesus and the cross	27:34, 48	Psalm 69:21
Jesus and the cross	27:35	Psalm 22:18
Jesus and the cross	27:39-40	Psalm 22:7
Jesus and the cross	27:43	Psalm 22:8
Jesus and the cross	27:46	Psalm 22:1
Jesus' burial	27:57-60	Isaiah 53:9

Jesus is crucified between two thieves.

Ten people raised from the dead

Old Testament

Widow's son
1 KINGS 17:17–24

Shunammite woman's son
2 KINGS 4:32–37

Man who touched Elisha's bones
2 KINGS 13:20–21

New Testament

Son of a widow
LUKE 7:11–15

Jairus' daughter
LUKE 8:41–42, 49–55

Lazarus
JOHN 11:1–44

Holy people who had died, after Jesus died
MATTHEW 27:52-53

Jesus
MATTHEW 28:1–8

Tabitha
ACTS 9:36–43

Eutychus
ACTS 20:9–10

Elijah raises Shunammite woman's son from the dead.

Women of the New Testament

Bernice
Sister of Agrippa, before whom Paul defended himself.
ACTS 25:13

Candace
Queen of Ethiopia.
ACTS 8:27–39

Chloe
Woman who knew about divisions in the church at Corinth.
1 CORINTHIANS 1:11

Claudia
Christian of Rome.
2 TIMOTHY 4:21

Damaris
Athenian woman converted by Paul.
ACTS 17:34

Dorcas (Tabitha)
Believer at Joppa, raised from the dead by Peter.
ACTS 9:36–41

Drusilla
Wife of Felix, Governor of Judea.
ACTS 24:24

Elizabeth
Mother of John the Baptist.
LUKE 1:5, 13

Eunice
Mother of Timothy.
2 TIMOTHY 1:5

Herodias
Queen who demanded the execution of John the Baptist.
MATTHEW 14:3–10

Joanna
Provided for the needs of Jesus and his disciples.
LUKE 8:3

Lois
Grandmother of Timothy.
2 TIMOTHY 1:5

Lydia
Converted by Paul at Philippi.
ACTS 16:14

Martha
Sister of Lazarus; friend of Jesus.
LUKE 10:38–42

Mary
Sister of Lazarus; friend of Jesus.
LUKE 10:38–42

Mary Magdalene
Woman from whom Jesus cast out demons.
MATTHEW 27:56–61; MARK 16:9

Phoebe
Servant in church at Cenchrea.
ROMANS 16:1–2

Priscilla (Wife of Aquila)
Co-worker of Paul at Corinth and Ephesus.
ACTS 18:2, 18–19

Salome
Mother of James and John.
MATTHEW 20:20–24

Sapphira
Held back goods from early church.
ACTS 5:1

Susanna
Provided for the needs of Jesus and his disciples.
LUKE 8:3

Jewish Sects and Parties

In New Testament times there were many different Jewish political, religious, and social groups in Palestine/Judea.

Religious groups

Pharisees

This group accepted and studied both the written Law and the oral, or traditional, Law. They believed their strict observance of the Law made them the only righteous Jews. They held religious power in Jerusalem during Jesus' ministry (MATTHEW 5:20; LUKE 11:42), and some of them were Jesus' fiercest enemies.

Sadducees

A small Jewish sect, mainly made up of priests and members of the Sanhedrin council (ACTS 4:1; 5:17). They hated change, wanting to keep things as they were, which led to many disputes with the Pharisees. Their Bible was limited to the Pentateuch, and they rejected any doctrines not found there. Unlike the Pharisees, they did not believe in a resurrection, angels, or spirits (MARK 12:18; ACTS 23:8). The Sadducees kept on good terms with the Romans occupying the land.

Essenes

A Jewish sect who lived like monks in isolated communities such as Qumran. They strove for purity and communion with God through self–denial and contemplation.

Political groups

Herodians

Jewish sect who agreed to subject themselves to Roman rule. They believed that the Roman-backed Herod and his descendants offered the final chancc for Isracl to havc its own government, and helped plot Jesus' death (MARK 12:13; MATTHEW 22:16).

Zealots

Strongly nationalist Jewish sect. They combined the religious practices of the Pharisees with hatred for any non-Jewish government, believing it was God's will for Jews to take up arms against Rome (MATTHEW 10:4).

Galileans

Sect that believed foreign control of Israel was contrary to Scripture, so refused to acknowledge foreign rulers. They were eventually absorbed into the similar Zealots sect (ACTS 5:37).

Social groups

Scribes

Jewish men who copied out, taught, and explained the Law. Many were Pharisees, believing that oral traditions were authoritative (LUKE 20:46). They were important in Jewish society as teachers of the Law, and often served as judges or lawyers.

Nazirites

Jews who took a vow of separation for a set time—sometimes for life. Easy to recognize because they vowed never to cut their hair, Nazirites separated themselves by their lifestyle to get close to God (NUMBERS 6:2, 4–6; JUDGES 13:5; 1 SAMUEL 1:11; ACTS 18:18; 21:23–24).

Proselytes

Non-Jewish converts to Judaism. After being circumcised, a convert was seen as having joined the family of Abraham, and was expected to follow the Law.

Publicans

Jews who collected taxes for the Roman government. They were seen as disloyal to Israel (LUKE 19:1–9), and often cheated those being taxed.

Priests plot to kill Jesus.

Jesus' Friends and Enemies

As well as the twelve apostles, Jesus had many followers, helpers, and friends—but some of the religious leaders opposed him.

Anna

Anna, an old, widowed prophetess, spent her life worshiping God in the Temple. She recognized the baby Jesus as the Messiah when he was brought to the Temple.

LUKE 2:36-38

Annas

After Jesus was arrested, he was taken before Annas for questioning. Annas had been high priest. After Jesus' ascension, Peter and John were questioned by Annas because of their preaching.

JOHN 18:12-14, 19-24; ACTS 4:6

Augustus

One of the more enlightened ancient rulers. The Roman Empire enjoyed a period of unparalleled peace and prosperity during his rule. Jesus was born during his reign, probably around the time of the second or third census (6 BC and AD 4).

LUKE 2:1

Barabbas

Barabbas had been condemned to death. At the feast of Passover, it was customary to release one prisoner chosen by the crowd. The crowd demanded Barabbas' release—and that Jesus be executed.

MATTHEW 27:11-26; MARK 15:1-15; LUKE 23:18-25; JOHN 18:40

Bartimaeus

As Jesus passed through Jericho, a blind beggar shouted to him. Jesus healed him of his blindness. Bartimaeus then followed Jesus.

MARK 10:46-52

Caiaphas

Caiaphas, Annas' son-in-law, was a leader of the Sadducees and high priest, AD 18 through 36. He presided over the trial of Jesus, declaring him guilty of blasphemy. He sent Jesus to Pilate to be sentenced to death. Caiaphas is referred to as "the high priest" in Acts and persecuted the first Christians.

MATTHEW 26:3-5, 57-68; MARK 14:53-55; LUKE 3:2; JOHN 11:49-51; 18:12-14, 19-24; ACTS 5:27

Herod the Great

Herod, the evil king of Judah from 34 BC to about 4 BC, was visited by the wise men, and ordered the slaughter of all male babies in Bethlehem under two years of age. He was called "the Great" because the country prospered during his long reign and he built many splendid buildings, including the magnificent Temple in Jerusalem. But he was loathed for his cruelty, and retained power by sucking up to the Romans and killing all rivals.

MATTHEW 2; LUKE 1:5

Herodias

While Herodias' husband, Herod Philip, was still alive, she married his brother-in-law. Herodias detested John the Baptist because he denounced her marriage. She had him thrown in prison, and was responsible for his execution.

MATTHEW 14:1-12; MARK 6:14-29

Jairus

Jairus, a ruler of the synagogue at Capernaum, asked Jesus to heal his sick young daughter. On their way to the house, news came that the daughter had died. Yet Jesus went to Jairus' home and healed her.

MARK 5:21-43

Joseph of Arimathea

Joseph of Arimathea, a wealthy member of the Jewish Sanhedrin council, secretly followed Jesus. When Jesus died on the cross, he took Jesus' body for burial.

MATTHEW 27:57-61; MARK 15:42-44; LUKE 23:50-55; JOHN 19:38-42

Lazarus

Jesus loved Lazarus, brother of Mary and Martha. When Lazarus died, Jesus brought him back to life, claiming to be the resurrection and the life.

JOHN 11:1–12:11

Martha

The sister of Mary and Lazarus, Martha entertained Jesus at her home in Bethany, just outside Jerusalem. Martha once complained that Mary just sat listening to Jesus while she did all the work. Jesus said Mary had made the better choice.

LUKE 10:38-42; JOHN 11:1–12:8

Mary
Mary, sister of Martha and Lazarus, loved sitting listening to Jesus' teaching. Before Jesus died, Mary anointed his feet with expensive perfume.
LUKE 10:38-42; JOHN 11:1–12:8

Mary, mother of James and Joseph
Galilean woman who followed Jesus after being healed.
MATTHEW 27:56; 28:1; MARK 15:40, 41, 47

Mary Magdalene
Mary was named for Magdala, the Galilee town she came from. Jesus expelled seven demons from her and she became his follower, standing near his cross when he died. She was the first person the risen Jesus appeared to.
MATTHEW 27:55-56; 28:1-10; MARK 15:40; 16:1-8; LUKE 8:2; JOHN 19:25; 20:1-18

Nicodemus
Nicodemus, a leading Pharisee, visited Jesus by night. Jesus told him he needed to be born again.
JOHN 3:1-21; 7:45-52; 19:39

Pilate
Pontius Pilate was the Roman governor of Judea (AD 26-36), and the only person who could pass the death sentence. When the crowd shouted that he would be opposing Caesar if he let Jesus go, he handed him over to be crucified.
MATTHEW 27:11-26; MARK 15:1-15; LUKE 23:1-25; JOHN 18:28–19:22

Salome
Salome was Herodias' daughter and Herod's stepdaughter. At a feast on Herod's birthday, she danced, and Herod promised her any gift she wished. She asked for John the Baptist's head on a plate.
MATTHEW 14:6-11; MARK 6:21-28

Simeon
A devout Jew who lived in Jerusalem. When Mary and Joseph brought baby Jesus to the Temple, Simeon took him in his arms and praised God. His song of joy, called the Nunc Dimittis, is sung regularly in many churches.
LUKE 2:25-35

Simon
On his way into Jerusalem, Simon of Cyrene was made to carry Jesus' cross as Jesus was taken to Golgotha.
MATTHEW 27:32; MARK 15:21; LUKE 23:26

Tiberius
Tiberius was Roman emperor from AD 14 to AD 37 and ruled during most of Jesus' lifetime.
LUKE 3:1

Zacchaeus
Zacchaeus, a wealthy, dishonest tax-collector, climbed a tree to get a good view of Jesus when he visited Jericho. Jesus told him to come down and then visited his house; Zacchaeus said he would give half his money to the poor.
LUKE 19

Roman officials in New Testament times

Caesar
Family name of Julius Caesar taken by Augustus. From his time, used as title for the emperor.
LUKE 2:1; 3:1

Proconsul
Governor of a province administered by the Roman Senate.
ACTS 13:7; 18:12

Procurator
Imperial agent in a province, or governor of a minor province.
MATTHEW 27.11; ACTS 23.24; 24:27

Tribune
High-ranking military officer, in charge of up to 1,000 men.
ACTS 21:31

Centurion
Officer in charge of, nominally, 100 men.
MARK 15:39; ACTS 10:1

Jesus' Last Week

	Matthew	Mark	Luke	John
Sunday (Palm Sunday)				
Jesus enters Jerusalem in triumph	21:1-11	11:1-10	19:28-44	12:12-19
Jesus visits the Temple and returns to Bethany	21:12-17	11:11	19:45-46	
Monday				
Jesus curses an unfruitful fig tree	21:18-19	11:12-14		
Jesus cleanses the Temple court		11:15-19	19:45-48	
Tuesday				
Jesus explains the withered fig tree	21:20-22	11:20-26		
Jesus' authority questioned	21:23-27	11:27-33	20:1-8	
Jesus teaches in the Temple	21:28–22:45	12:1-37	20:9-44	
Jesus condemns the scribes and Pharisees	23:1-36	12:38-40	20:45-47	
Jesus points out the widow's gift		12:41-44	21:1-4	
Jesus predicts the destruction of the Temple—and end of the world	24:1-44	13:1-37	21:5-36	
Wednesday				
Jewish leaders plot against Jesus	26:1-5	14:1-2	22:1-2	
Jesus is anointed at Bethany	26:6-13	14:3-9		
Judas agrees to betray Jesus	26:14-16	14:10-11	22:3-6	
Thursday (Maundy Thursday)				
Jesus prepares to celebrate Passover	26:17-19	14:12-16	22:7-13	
The Last Supper	26:20-29	14:17-25	22:14-38	13:1-38
Jesus and disciples withdraw to Gethsemane	26:30-46	14:26-42	22:39-46	18:1
Jesus is betrayed and arrested	26:47-56	14:43-52	22:47-53	
Jesus is tried before Annas				18:12-14, 19-23
Jesus before Caiaphas and the Sanhedrin and Peter's denial	26:57-75	14:53-72	22:54-71	18:15-18, 24-27
Friday (Good Friday)				
Jesus tried before Pilate; Judas' suicide	27:1-14	15:1-5	23:1-5	18:28-38
Jesus sent before Herod			23:6-16	
Pilate imposes death sentence	27:15-26	15:6-15	23:17-25	18:39–19:16
Jesus scourged and led to Golgotha	27:27-32	15:15-21		19:16, 17

Jesus' Last Week continued

Friday (Good Friday)	Matthew	Mark	Luke	John
Jesus' crucifixion and death	27:33-56	15:22-41	23:33-49	19:18-30
Jesus is buried	27:57-61	15:42-47	23:50-56	19:31-42
Saturday (Low Saturday)				
Jesus' tomb guarded	27:62-66			
Sunday (Easter Day)				
The empty tomb and the risen Christ	28:1-20	16:1-8	24:1-53	20:1-21:25

The Events of the Crucifixion and Jesus' Seven Last Cries from the Cross

Jesus comes to Golgotha (Calvary). MATTHEW 27:33; MARK 15:22; LUKE 23:33; JOHN 19:17

He is offered a numbing drink. MATTHEW 27:34

Jesus is nailed to the cross. MATTHEW 27:35

Jesus' **first cry** from the cross: "Father, forgive these people, because they don't know what they are doing" LUKE 23:34, refers to those crucifying him.

Jesus' garments are divided up between the Roman soldiers. MATTHEW 27:35

Jesus is mocked by the soldiers. MATTHEW 27:39–44; MARK 15:29

The crucified thieves turn on Jesus—but one believes. MATTHEW 27:38–44

Jesus' **second cry** from the cross: "I assure you, today you will be with me in paradise." LUKE 23:43, spoken to the penitent thief crucified next to him.

Jesus' **third cry** from the cross: "Woman, here is your son." … "Here is your mother." JOHN 19:26, 27—Jesus to his mother, Mary, and to his disciple John

Darkness falls at midday. MATTHEW 27:45; MARK 15:33

Jesus' **fourth cry** from the cross: "*Eli, Eli, lama sabachthani*?"—Aramaic for "My God, my God, why have you abandoned me?" MATTHEW 27:46; MARK 15:34, QUOTING PSALM 22:1

Jesus' **fifth cry** from the cross "I am thirsty." JOHN 19:28, probably referencing PSALM 69:21 "they offer me sour wine for my thirst."

Jesus' **sixth cry** from the cross: "It is finished!" JOHN 19:30

Jesus' **seventh cry** from the cross, "Father, I entrust my spirit into your hands!" LUKE 23:46, referencing PSALM 31:5: "I entrust my spirit into your hand."

ALL QUOTES FROM NLT.

"The Last Supper" by Leonardo da Vinci.

Herod's Temple

Wonder of the ancient world

Solomon's Temple suffered neglect, plunder, misuse, and looting and destruction by the Babylonian King Nebuchadnezzar in 587 BC. The Ark of the Covenant disappeared—and was never recovered or replaced.

Under the leadership of King Zerubbabel and the high priest Joshua, the Israelites rebuilt Solomon's Temple on an inferior scale. Prophets encouraged the returned Jewish exiles to complete the restoration of the Temple. The Second Temple was probably improved during the third and second centuries BC, but we know little about this period. In 167 BC Antiochus IV, the Seleucid king, set up a pagan altar in the Temple, polluting it for the Jews. When the Jewish heroes, the Maccabees, defeated the Seleucids, they cleansed the Temple and rededicated it (1 MACCABEES 4:36–59). In 63 BC the Roman general Pompey captured Jerusalem.

Herod's Temple.

Herod rebuilds

With Roman backing, King Herod started to rebuild the Temple, to curry favor with the Jews, whom he needed to keep happy to remain puppet king under the Romans. Herod loved grand building projects. His stronghold of Herodium, situated near Bethlehem, is one of the largest fortresses ever built to protect one man; Masada, Herod's other palace/fortress, overlooked the Dead Sea. Virtually impregnable, Jewish zealots made their last stand against Rome there in AD 73.

Herod started dismantling the Second Temple around 21 BC to prepare for his massive Temple. The Temple platform was greatly enlarged; part of it, known today as the Western Wall, is still faced with huge stones dating from Herod's time. Herod surrounded the Temple enclosure with magnificent porches. Through the Huldah gates—its arches are still visible—worshippers emerged through tunnels into the Court of the Gentiles. Women were not allowed beyond the Court of the Women, where four huge lampstands stood, lit only on special occasions such as the Festival of Lights. At the center of the innermost court—the Court of the Priests—stood the Temple itself.

Jesus and the Temple

The Temple is the focus of many important events. The birth of John the Baptist was announced here (LUKE 1:11–20); Simeon and Anna greeted baby Jesus here (2:22–38). Jesus came to the Temple as a boy of twelve (2:42–51), and taught here during his ministry (JOHN 7:14).

Herod's Temple continued

Jesus used the Temple to illustrate his resurrection, saying, "Destroy this temple, and I will raise it again in three days," to which the Jews objected, "It has taken forty-six years to build this temple" (JOHN 2:19–20, NIV). Jesus' cleansing of the Temple helped bring about his death. After the resurrection, Christians continued to worship at the Temple; Paul was arrested there when attacked by a mob (ACTS 3; 21:27–33).

The Temple destroyed

In AD 66 the Jews rebelled against Rome. Herod's Temple was the center of resistance, where the Jews held out against the Roman siege. By August AD 70, except for the Temple, Jerusalem was entirely occupied by the Romans. Led by Titus, they torched the Temple, seizing some of its priceless furnishings. The Titus Arch in Rome depicts soldiers carrying off treasures such as the seven-branched golden lampstand and the table of the showbread. All that remained was the platform the Temple had been built on.

Jesus cleanses Temple.

Bible Weights and Measures

	Imperial	Metric
Measures of length—Old Testament		
finger	0.72 inches	1.8 cm
handbreadth (4 fingers)	2.91 inches	7.4 cm
span (3 handbreadths)	8.74 inches	22.2 cm
cubit (2 spans)	17.49 inches	44.4 cm
Ezekiel's cubit (7 handbreadths)	20.37 inches	51.7 cm
Measures of length—New Testament		
cubit	about 1.5 feet	about 30.5 cm
fathom	about 6 feet	about 1.83 m
furlong	660 feet	201 m
(Roman) mile	about 4,879 feet	about 1.49 km
Sabbath day's journey	about 3/5 mile	about 1 km

	Imperial	Metric
Measures of capacity: Dry Measures—Old Testament		
kab	1.159 quarts	1.1 kg
omer (1 4/5 kabs)	2.087 quarts	1.97 kg
seah (3 1/3 omers)	6.959 quarts	6.58 kg
ephah (3 seahs)	20.878 quarts	19.75 kg
lethech (5 ephahs)	3.262 bushels	97.9 kg
kor/homer (30 seahs)	6.524 bushels	195.9 kg
Measures of Capacity: Dry Measures—New Testament		
choinix	0.98 quarts	0. 92 kg
modios	7.68 quarts	7.26 kg
saton (Hebrew: seah)	6.95 quarts	6.58 kg
koros (Hebrew: kor)	6.52 bushels	195.9 kg

The Parables of Jesus

	Matthew	Mark	Luke	John
Nature and farming				
Birds and flowers	6:25–34		12:22–31	
A tree and its fruit	7:15–20		6:43–45	
The sower	13:1–9, 18–23	4:1–9, 13–20	8:4–8, 11–15	
Growing seed		4:26–29		
The unfruitful fig tree			13:6–9	
Weeds	13:24–30, 36–43			
Mustard seed	13:31–32	4:30–32	13:18–19	
Lost sheep	18:10–14		15:1–7	
Workers in the vineyard	20:1–16			
Tenants in the vineyard	21:33–46	12:1–12	20:9–19	
Fig tree	24:32–35	13:28–31	21:29–33	
Sheep and goats	25:31–46			
Harvest time				4:35–38
The shepherd				10:1–18
Grain of wheat				12:20–26
The vine				15:1–17
Everyday things of Bible times				
Water				4:5–14; 7:37–39
Salt	5:13			
Light	5:14–16	4:21–22	8:16–18	12:35–36
Bread				6:25–35
Builders	7:24–27		6:46–49	
Mending clothes	9:16	2:21	5:36	
New wine	9:17	2:22	5:37–39	
Yeast	13:33		13:20–21	
The pearl	13:45–46			
The fishing net	13:47–50			
Lost coin			15:8–10	

The Parables of Jesus continued

Daily life	Matthew	Mark	Luke	John
Unwilling children	11:16-19		7:31-35	
New truths and old	13:51-52			
Forgiveness	18:21-35			
Two sons	21:28-32			
The wedding feast	22:1-14		14:15-24	
Ten bridesmaids	25:1-13			
Servants	25:14-30		19:11-27	
Debts and debtors			7:41-47	
Good Samaritan			10:25-37	
Friend in need			11:5-13	
Rich fool			12:16-21	
Watchful servants		13:33-37	12:35-40	
Humility and hospitality			14:7-14	
Cost of discipleship			14:25-33	
Lost son			15:11-32	
Shrewd manager			16:1-13	
Rich man and Lazarus			16:19-31	
A servant's duty			17:7-10	
The persistent widow			18:1-8	
Pharisee and tax-collector		18:9-14		

Parable of the sower.

What is a parable?

Parables are short stories that are told to teach a lesson. Sometimes they are just short sayings comparing something people do with something in nature or a shared human experience. For example, Proverbs 6:7–8 compares an ant, which collects its own food and plans for the future, with humans, who ought to be dependable and responsible. Isaiah the prophet compared the people of Israel of his day with a vineyard that produced no grapes (ISAIAH 5:1–5), so that the owner gave up tending the vineyard. Similarly, Isaiah says, God will not continue to care for the people of Israel if they do not produce good fruit, by doing what is right.

In Matthew, Mark, and Luke, Jesus uses parables to describe God and explain how he expects people to live in the kingdom. Some are just short sayings, such as the blind leading the blind (MATTHEW 15:14), a family that fights and destroys itself (MATTHEW 12:25), throwing pearls before pigs (MATTHEW 7:6), and the eye as the window of the soul (MATTHEW 6:22, 23). More than forty parables are in the form of short stories, such as Jesus comparing the kingdom of heaven with a farmer planting seed (MATTHEW 13.3–9) and with buried treasure (MATTHEW 13:44). In some cases, an explanation of the parable followed the story, to help followers of Jesus better understand his message.

Matthew

Author
Matthew, the former Jewish tax-collector and disciple of Jesus.

Audience
Originally, the Jewish Christian church and Jewish people.

Date
c. AD 55–80.

Outline
Jesus' birth and preparation for ministry 1:1–4:11

Jesus teaches about his kingdom 4:12–7:29

Jesus demonstrates his kingdom 8:1–11:1

Jesus meets opposition 11:2–13:53

Jesus trains his disciples 13:54–18:35

Jesus approaches the cross 19:1–26:13

Jesus dies and rises, Lord of all 26:14–28:20

Purpose
Matthew is a natural bridge between the Old Testament and the New because it has the most Jewish character of all four Gospels. From the first verse to the last, Matthew establishes Jesus as a descendant of King David, preserving and fulfilling his royal line, as well as a descendant of Abraham, the father of Israel. Matthew shows that Jesus is king of a heavenly kingdom, focusing on how people behave as citizens, with Jesus as their loving king.

Author and audience
Matthew may have been the first apostle to write a gospel, and possibly wrote in Hebrew (Aramaic)—although this view is disputed by the overwhelming majority of NT scholars, who maintain the traditional view that the entire New Testament was written initially in Koine (common) Greek. Matthew was a wealthy tax-collector, who, prior to his conversion and calling as an apostle, profited from representing Rome.

Major themes in Matthew

Old Testament
Matthew connects the past with the present and future. He quotes 60 times from the Old Testament, showing us the New Testament is the Old Testament unfolded and explained. The Old Testament is more central in Matthew than in any other Gospel, both in frequency and emphasis.

Parables
Matthew records many of Jesus' parables. Twelve are detailed by Matthew, nine of them unique to his Gospel. He gives us two miracles found nowhere else: the healing of two blind men (9:27ff.) and the coin miraculously found in a fish's mouth (17:24–27). Through these simple stories the nature of God's kingdom comes to life.

Heavenly kingdom
The phrase "kingdom of heaven" is used nearly 40 times, as Jesus offers it to us—while Jesus is described as king 14 times. This is the Gospel of the king and his kingdom—a different kingdom than his followers expected. The kingdom Jesus ushered in would not liberate the Jewish people from the oppression of the Roman government as they expected. Instead, he offers not only Jews, but everyone, access to an eternal, heavenly kingdom, free from the consequences of sin.

Kingdom living
Matthew's Gospel is also about his subjects, living in his kingdom. The church is the community of Christ's heavenly kingdom, and Jesus' Sermon on the Mount (chs. 5–7) is the law of the kingdom. The Gospel of Matthew presents the power and majesty of our loving king.

What is a Gospel?

The four Gospels—Matthew, Mark, Luke, and John—all give an account of the life and teachings of Jesus. The word "Gospel" comes from an Old English word meaning "good news."

The Gospels were probably written down in their present form between thirty and sixty years after Jesus' death on the cross. Jesus left no writings, but the Gospels record stories and eyewitness descriptions that had been passed on by word of mouth. As Jesus' first followers grew older and died, it became important to have a written record of what Jesus did and said, and to describe his death and resurrection.

Matthew, Mark, and Luke have much material in common and follow the same outline and are often called the "Synoptic" Gospels, from a Greek word meaning "seeing together." These three Gospels are more similar to each other than any of them is like John's Gospel. They concentrate on Jesus' teachings and miracles in Galilee, but also include information about Jesus' early work in Judea. John contains some of Jesus' sayings not found in the other Gospels, including the "I am" sayings.

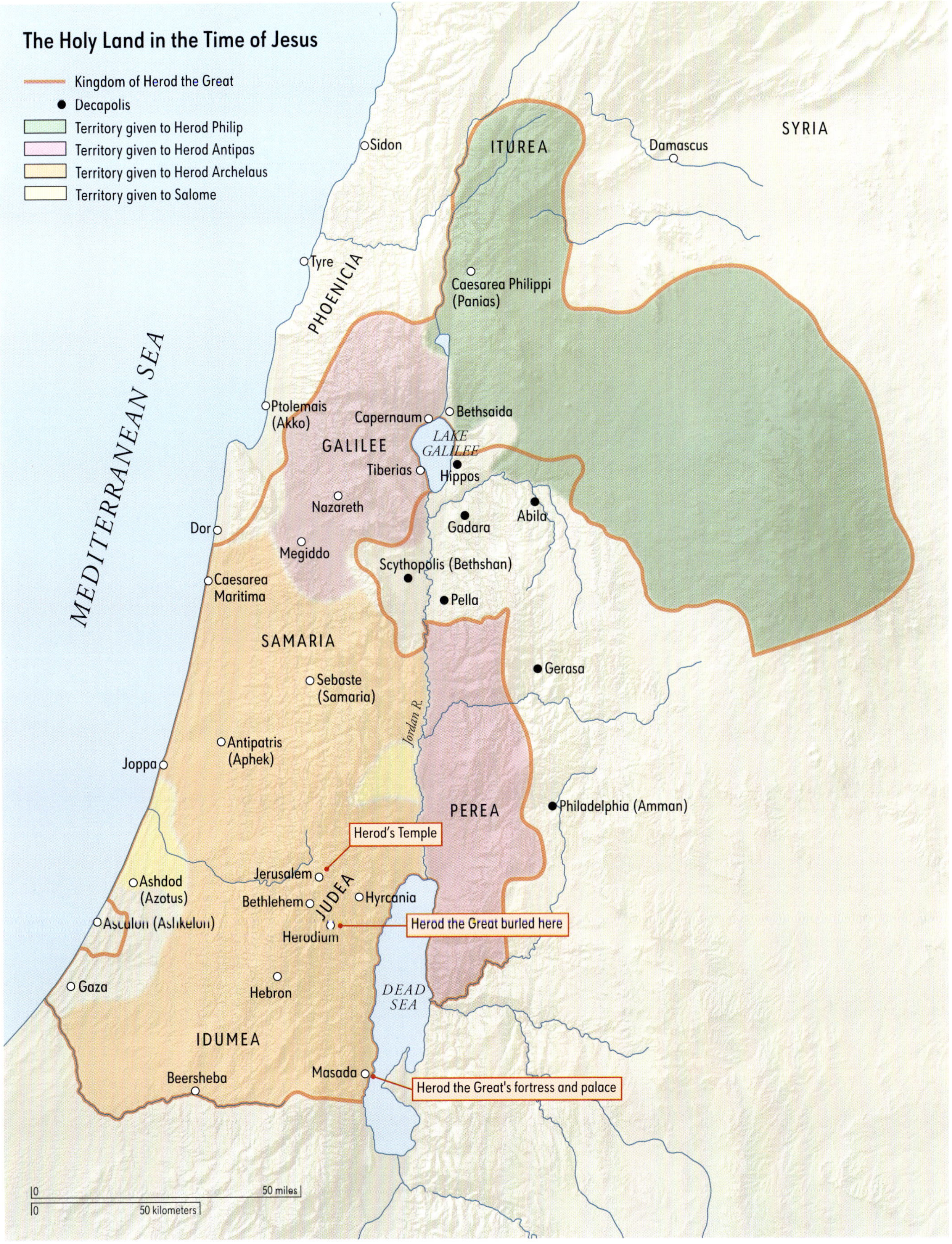

The Holy Land in the Time of Jesus
Kingdom of Herod the Great
Decapolis
Territory given to Herod Philip
Territory given to Herod Antipas
Territory given to Herod Archelaus
Territory given to Salome
SYRIA
Damascus
ITUREA
Sidon
Tyre
PHOENICIA
Caesarea Philippi (Panias)
MEDITERRANEAN SEA
Ptolemais (Akko)
Capernaum
Bethsaida
LAKE GALILEE
GALILEE
Tiberias
Hippos
Nazareth
Gadara
Abila
Dor
Megiddo
Scythopolis (Bethshan)
Caesarea Maritima
Pella
SAMARIA
Gerasa
Sebaste (Samaria)
Jordan R.
Antipatris (Aphek)
Joppa
PEREA
Philadelphia (Amman)
Herod's Temple
Jerusalem
Ashdod (Azotus)
Bethlehem
JUDEA
Hyrcania
Ascalon (Ashkelon)
Herodium
Herod the Great buried here
Gaza
Hebron
DEAD SEA
IDUMEA
Beersheba
Masada
Herod the Great's fortress and palace
0 50 miles
0 50 kilometers

Mark

Author
John Mark, who was related to Barnabas and lived in Jerusalem. Many believe Mark received much of the material in his Gospel from Peter.

Audience
Roman Christians.

Date
c. AD 50–55.

Outline
Prologue 1:1-13
Jesus' Galilee ministry 1:14–6:13
Jesus leaves Galilee 6:14–8:21
Jesus journeys to Jerusalem 8:22–10:52
Jesus' transfiguration in the presence of Peter, James, and John 9:2–13
Jesus' Jerusalem ministry 11:1–13:37
Jesus' passion 14:1–15:47
Jesus' resurrection 16:1-8 (9-20*)

* The most reliable early manuscripts do not have Mark 16:9-20

Purpose
Two broad aims stand out: To confirm Jesus' messianic identity.

Israel expected a conquering hero Messiah—but Jesus is the Suffering Servant Messiah. Through the cross he achieves his full glory and full identity.

To call believers to follow Jesus' example. We are to pattern our lives after Jesus' faithful, cross-shaped life.

A woman carries water through fields.

Major themes in Mark

The person of Jesus

Mark wrote his Gospel to write Jesus' story, which reveals who he is. Two titles, "Messiah" and "Son of God," point to what Jesus came to do, the key to understanding who he is. He is the bearer of God's salvation, announced in words and deeds, teaching and miracles, and ultimately in his sacrificial death for our sins, and his resurrection from the dead.

Jesus' Messianic mission

A particular aspect of Mark's Gospel is the so-called "Messianic Secret." At various times Jesus commands his disciples not to reveal his true messianic identity. Though he demonstrated it through his miracles and teaching, his full identity as Israel's Messiah is not revealed until the end of Mark, when he rises from the dead.

The work of Jesus

Jesus' death plays a central role in this Gospel. Mark wrote to show that Jesus' death on the cross was God's plan from the beginning. Through the crucifixion we see Jesus was both the long-awaited Messiah and the Son of God.

Discipleship and faith

At every turn in Mark's Gospel, Jesus invites people to follow him. This kind of following involves three things: self-denial, cross bearing, and daily living.

Kingdom of God

"The Kingdom of God is near!" (NLT MARK 1:15) Jesus announced at the beginning of his ministry. For Mark, the kingdom is already dynamically in the present, yet fully experienced in the future.

Jesus crucified.

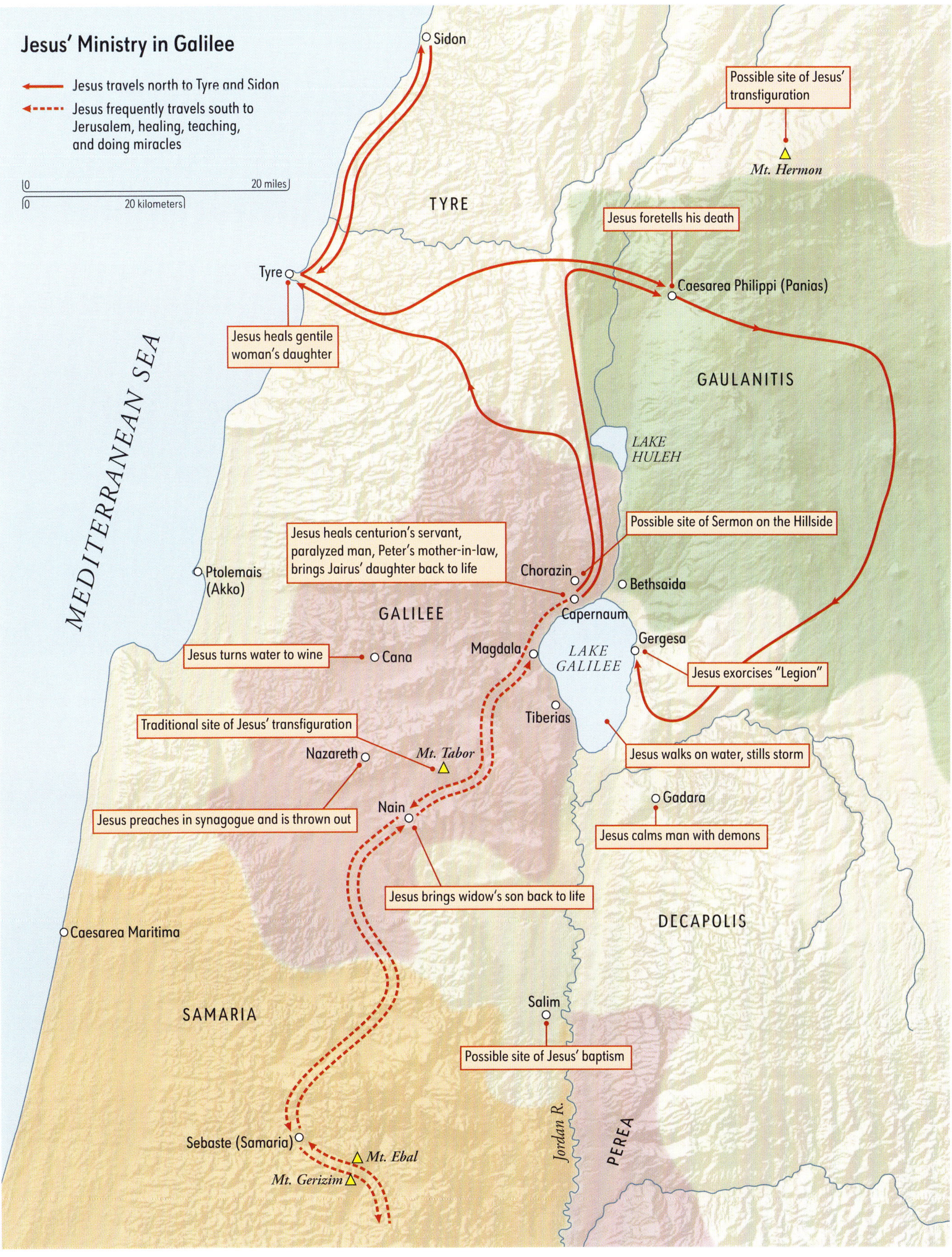

Jesus' Ministry in Galilee
Jesus travels north to Tyre and Sidon
Jesus frequently travels south to Jerusalem, healing, teaching, and doing miracles
0
20 miles
0
20 kilometers
Sidon
Possible site of Jesus' transfiguration
Mt. Hermon
TYRE
Jesus foretells his death
Tyre
Caesarea Philippi (Panias)
Jesus heals gentile woman's daughter
MEDITERRANEAN SEA
GAULANITIS
LAKE HULEH
Possible site of Sermon on the Hillside
Jesus heals centurion's servant, paralyzed man, Peter's mother-in-law, brings Jairus' daughter back to life
Chorazin
Ptolemais (Akko)
Bethsaida
GALILEE
Capernaum
Gergesa
Jesus turns water to wine
Cana
Magdala
LAKE GALILEE
Jesus exorcises "Legion"
Tiberias
Traditional site of Jesus' transfiguration
Nazareth
Mt. Tabor
Jesus walks on water, stills storm
Gadara
Nain
Jesus preaches in synagogue and is thrown out
Jesus calms man with demons
Jesus brings widow's son back to life
Caesarea Maritima
DECAPOLIS
Salim
SAMARIA
Possible site of Jesus' baptism
Jordan R.
PEREA
Sebaste (Samaria)
Mt. Ebal
Mt. Gerizim

Luke

Author
Luke, beloved physician, friend and companion of Paul.

Audience
Theophilus, and all "lovers of God."

Date
Late AD 60s, possibly AD 70–85.

Outline
Preface 1:1-4
Jesus' birth and childhood 1:5–2:52
Jesus prepares for ministry 3:1–4:13
Jesus' ministry in Galilee 4:14–9:50
Jesus heads to Jerusalem 9:51–19:44
Jesus teaches in Jerusalem 19:45–21:38
Jesus' suffering and death 22:1–23:56
Jesus' resurrection and exaltation 24:1–53

About Luke
Luke emphasizes the humanity of Jesus—the servant of all and sacrifice for all. Every barrier is broken down in Luke's Gospel: between Jew and gentile, man and woman, rich and poor.

In Luke we see Jesus as the Savior of all who come to him.

Luke shares Jesus' teachings on prayer, forgiveness, and our duty to show mercy and grace toward others.

Much of Luke's Gospel is not found in any other Gospel. If we did not have the book of Luke, we wouldn't know about the Prodigal Son, the Good Samaritan, the Wedding Banquet, and other amazing stories.

Purpose
Luke gives us a full picture of Jesus' life and ministry, ensuring that what we read is factual.

He shows how God has been faithful to Israel and to the promises he has made.

Author and audience
Luke was a companion of the Apostle Paul for some of his missionary journeys, and possibly one of his early converts. He wrote especially for non-Jewish lovers of God who may have felt out of place in what was originally a Jewish movement.

Major themes in Luke

The person and work of Jesus
Jesus is the sent one, both Lord and Messiah, anointed by the Spirit to bring in God's heavenly kingdom. His ultimate act was to bear the sins of the world on the cross, give up his life as a sacrificial offering, rise from the dead, and ascend into heaven.

The promised kingdom
In Jesus Christ, all of God's promises are fulfilled, chief among them God's promised kingdom, which is both present and coming.

Women and the poor
Women are a crucial part of Jesus' ministry. In Luke's Gospel they provide examples of deep piety and devotion. And throughout Luke the poor receive special attention, showing God reaches out to those society casts away.

The Holy Spirit
The Holy Spirit plays a major role in Luke's Gospel, and is referenced nearly twenty times. The Spirit is the driving force in Luke's portrayal of God's coming salvation. He is present from Jesus' conception and birth, baptism, and throughout his powerful miracle ministry.

The transfiguration.

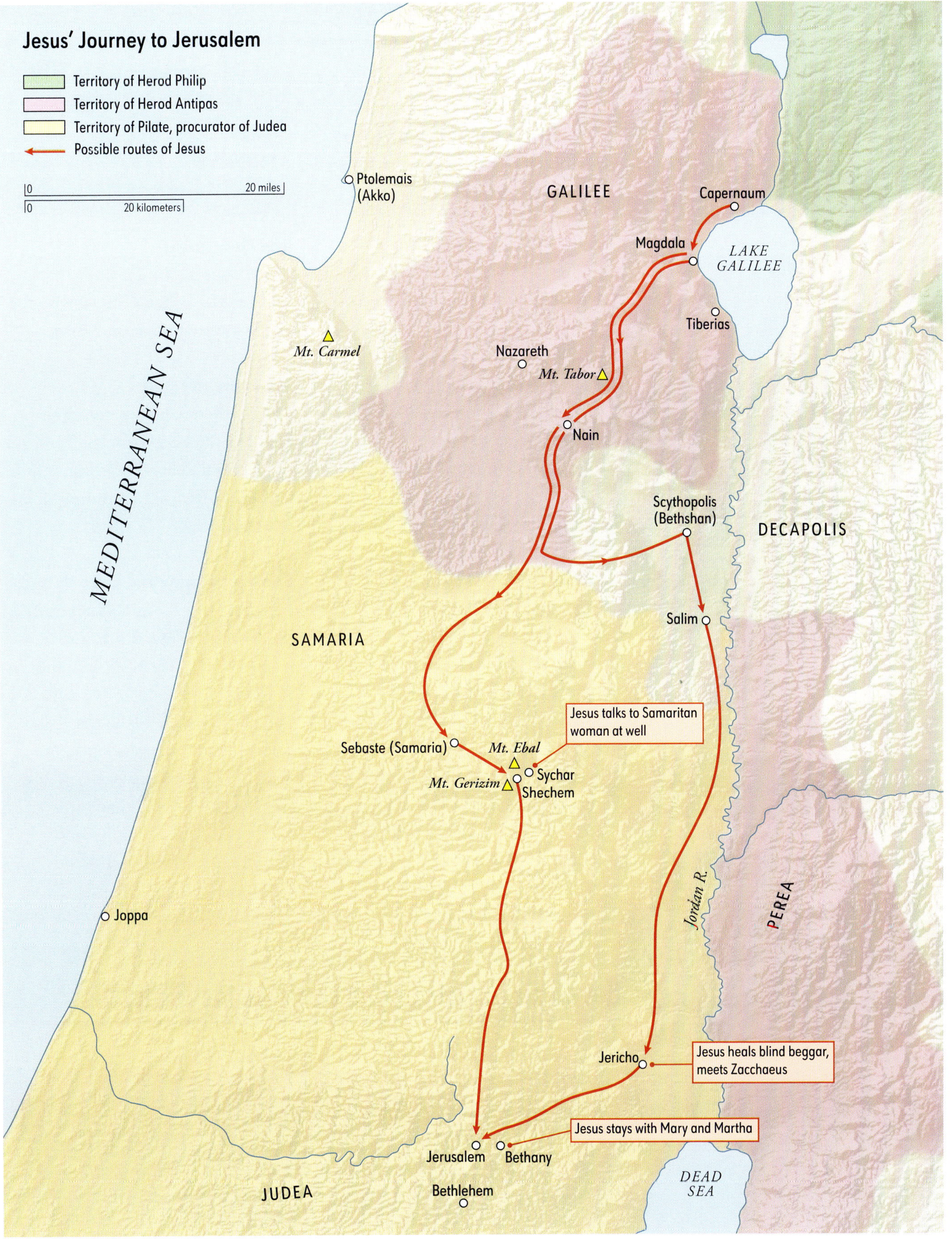
Jesus' Journey to Jerusalem
Territory of Herod Philip
Territory of Herod Antipas
Territory of Pilate, procurator of Judea
Possible routes of Jesus
0
20 miles
0
20 kilometers
MEDITERRANEAN SEA
Ptolemais
(Akko)
GALILEE
Capernaum
Magdala
LAKE
GALILEE
Tiberias
Mt. Carmel
Nazareth
Mt. Tabor
Nain
Scythopolis
(Bethshan)
DECAPOLIS
Salim
SAMARIA
Jesus talks to Samaritan
woman at well
Sebaste (Samaria)
Mt. Ebal
Sychar
Mt. Gerizim
Shechem
Jordan R.
PEREA
Joppa
Jericho
Jesus heals blind beggar,
meets Zacchaeus
Jesus stays with Mary and Martha
Jerusalem
Bethany
DEAD
SEA
JUDEA
Bethlehem

John

Author
The apostle John.

Audience
Diaspora Jews and believers.

Date
c. AD 80-85; although an earlier date of c. AD 50-55 is possible.

Outline
Prologue 1:1-18
Testimony of John the Baptist 1:19-51
The new order in Jesus 2:1–4:42
Jesus: mediator of life and judgment 4:43–5:47
Jesus: bread of life 6:1-71
Jesus: water and light of life 7:1–8:59
Jesus: light and shepherd 9:1–10:42
Jesus: resurrection and life—the raising of Lazarus 11:1-54
Jesus: triumphant king 11:55–12:50
Jesus' ministry to his disciples 13:1–17:26
Jesus' betrayal, trial, death, and resurrection 18:1–20:31
Epilogue 21:1-25

Purpose
John wrote to non-believers, mostly Jews but also gentiles—probably Greeks and Greek-thinkers for the most part—to persuade them to believe that Jesus is the One through whom they will find and experience eternal life. He is also writing to believers, that they would more fully believe, in order to experience the fullness of that life in Jesus' powerful name. The word "believe" is found nearly one hundred times in John: this is the Gospel of believing.

Author and audience
Many believe John penned this Gospel about AD 80-85. However, the Dead Sea Scrolls hint at a date as early as AD 50-55, as some verses in the Dead Sea Scrolls are almost the same as verses in John's Gospel.

Major themes in John

The other three Gospels give us the history of Christ, but John writes to unveil the mystery of Christ as the Son of God. Jesus is seen as the sacrificial Lamb of God, the good shepherd, the kind forgiver, the tender healer, the compassionate intercessor, and the great I AM. There are seven of these "self-descriptions" overall:

The "I ams" of John's Gospel
I am the bread of life. 6:35–48, 51
I am the light of the world. 8:12; 9:5
I am the gate for the sheep. 10:7
I am the good shepherd. 10:11, 14
I am the resurrection and the life. 11:25
I am the way, the truth, and the life. 14:6
I am the true grapevine. 15:1
ALL QUOTATIONS FROM NLT

The person of Jesus as God
The question "Who is Jesus?" lies at the heart of this Gospel. For John, Jesus is the Son of God.

The work of Jesus in salvation
John makes it clear that God the Father is the one who alone initiates human salvation. The one who bears the Father's salvation is the Son. Jesus is the Lamb of God, come to take away the sins of the world.

The Holy Spirit
John connects the gift of the Holy Spirit to the people of God, with the death and exaltation of the Son.

Believing in Jesus
The claims of Christ on our lives require us to believe in who he is and what he has done. John speaks of this "believing" 92 times. It means doing what Jesus says.

Eternal life now and later
Like the other Gospels, John oriented his around the life, death, and resurrection of Jesus, the purpose of which is that humanity might have life—eternal life in the age to come—while experiencing a taste of it now. John emphasizes the present enjoyment of this eternal life—but also makes it clear that Jesus will return to gather his own to the dwelling he has prepared for them (14:2–3).

Seven signs pointing to Jesus as the Messiah

In the first half of John's Gospel Jesus' demonstrates he is Messiah through seven signs:

Changing water into wine 2:1–11
Healing an official's son 4:46–54
Healing an invalid 5:1–15
Feeding a crowd 6:5–13
Walking on water 6:16–21
Healing a man born blind 9:1–7
Raising Lazarus 11:1–44

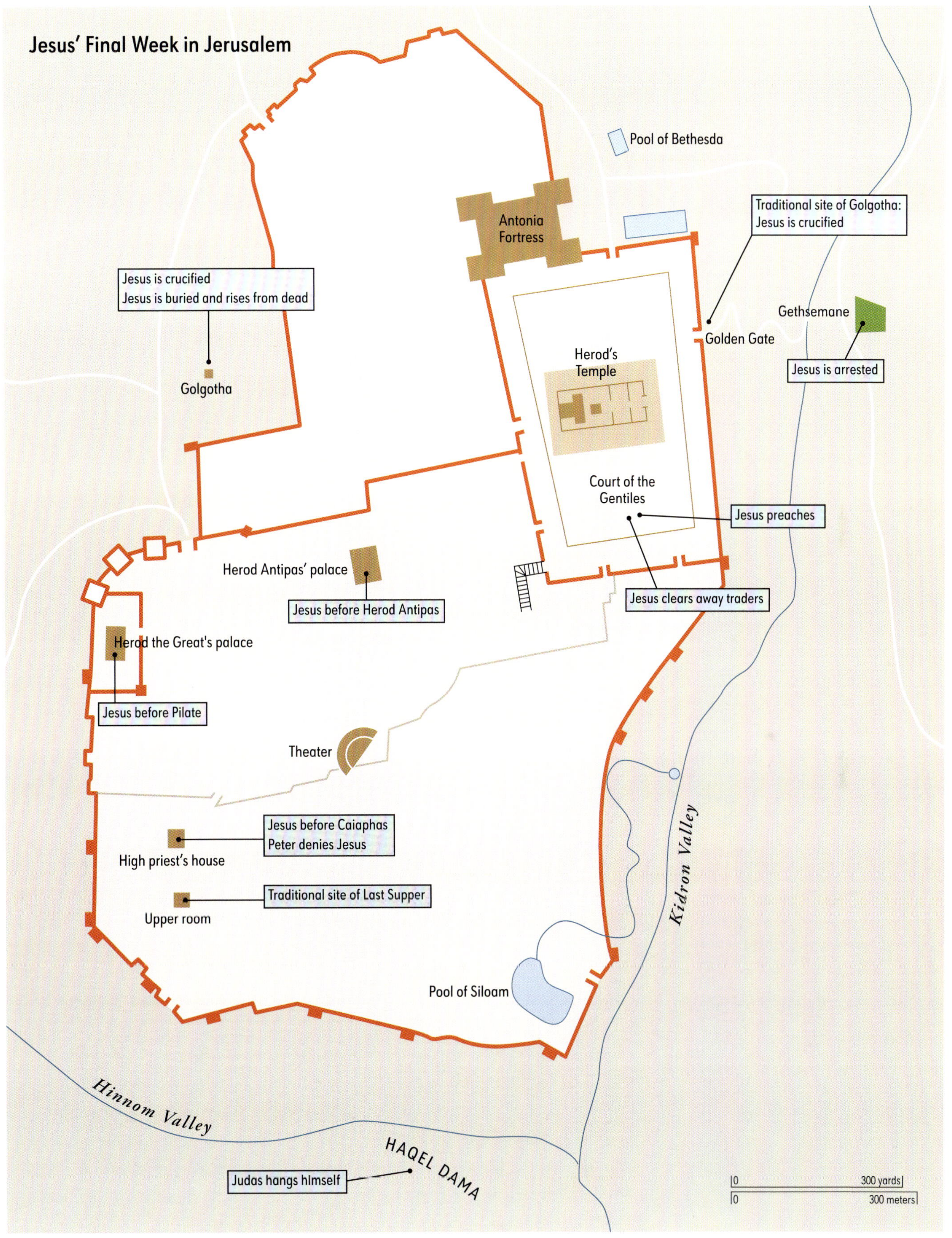
Jesus' Final Week in Jerusalem
Pool of Bethesda
Antonia Fortress
Traditional site of Golgotha: Jesus is crucified
Jesus is crucified
Jesus is buried and rises from dead
Golgotha
Golden Gate
Gethsemane
Jesus is arrested
Herod's Temple
Court of the Gentiles
Jesus preaches
Jesus clears away traders
Herod Antipas' palace
Jesus before Herod Antipas
Herod the Great's palace
Jesus before Pilate
Theater
Jesus before Caiaphas
Peter denies Jesus
High priest's house
Traditional site of Last Supper
Upper room
Kidron Valley
Pool of Siloam
Hinnom Valley
HAQEL DAMA
Judas hangs himself
0 300 yards
0 300 meters

Acts

Author
Luke, beloved physician, friend and companion to Paul.

Audience
Theophilus, and all lovers of God.

Date
Mid-to-late AD 60s, possibly AD 70-85.

Outline
The church is born 1:1–6:7
The church is persecuted and expands 6:8–9:31
The mission to the Gentiles 9:32–12:25
Paul's first missionary journey 13:1–15:35
Paul's second and third missionary journeys 15:36–21:16
Paul's arrest and journey to Rome 21:17–28:31

About Acts
The book of Acts tells how the church began. Although many call this book the "Acts of the Apostles" it would be more accurate to call it the "Acts of the Holy Spirit."

It begins with 120 disciples who had been in a ten-day prayer meeting, and the outpouring of the Holy Spirit that resulted in tongues, prophecy, miracles, and birthing of countless churches. Acts demonstrates the healing miracles of Peter, Paul, and the apostles, and the story of Paul's three missionary journeys, with many gentile nations hearing the gospel and believers added to the church.

Author and audience
Both Luke and Acts were written by a physician named Luke. Luke and Acts cover a period of about sixty years, from the birth of Christ to the birth of the church and the early years of the expansion of God's kingdom on the earth.

Major themes in Acts

Jesus, the exalted, exclusive Lord of salvation
Acts opens as Luke closes, with the ascension of Jesus to the right hand of the Father. The disciples pick up where Jesus left off in seeing the salvation of the world realized.

The Holy Spirit of power
The Holy Spirit takes center stage in Acts, as the promised gift dispensed to Christ's disciples. He enables the church to carry out its mission, empowers them to bear witness to the gospel, and anoints God's people to perform mighty wonders.

Salvation for the world
Salvation by grace through faith in Jesus is available to the entire world.

The church, mission, and persecution
For Luke, the church is a Spirit-fueled movement, guided by leaders who apply the power of the gospel. Like most movements, it faces opposition and persecution, yet triumphs and expands through the power of the Holy Spirit.

Discipleship and ethics in the church
After Pentecost, believers are able to follow Jesus in ways they were unable to before they received the Spirit. They become an active community, on a mission to bear witness to the risen Christ. Through their love for neighbors and God, prayer, perseverance in suffering, watchfulness, faith, joy, and commitment to the lost, we find passionate disciples of Jesus at every turn.

Women and the poor
Luke continues the emphasis in his Gospel, insisting that women are fully included in Jesus' work. They receive the Spirit of power. In some contexts, women teach and prophesy. We also find the church pooling its resources to care for the poor in their city, and sending food to other cities in need.

Religion in Roman Times

At the time when Christianity was starting to spread through the Roman Empire, most Romans believed many different gods and goddesses controlled every aspect of their lives and of nature. People also believed a particular god or goddess protected their town or city. The Roman god Jupiter was considered the greatest god, controlling the forces of nature as well as human history. In the first century AD, worship of the Roman Emperor became common.

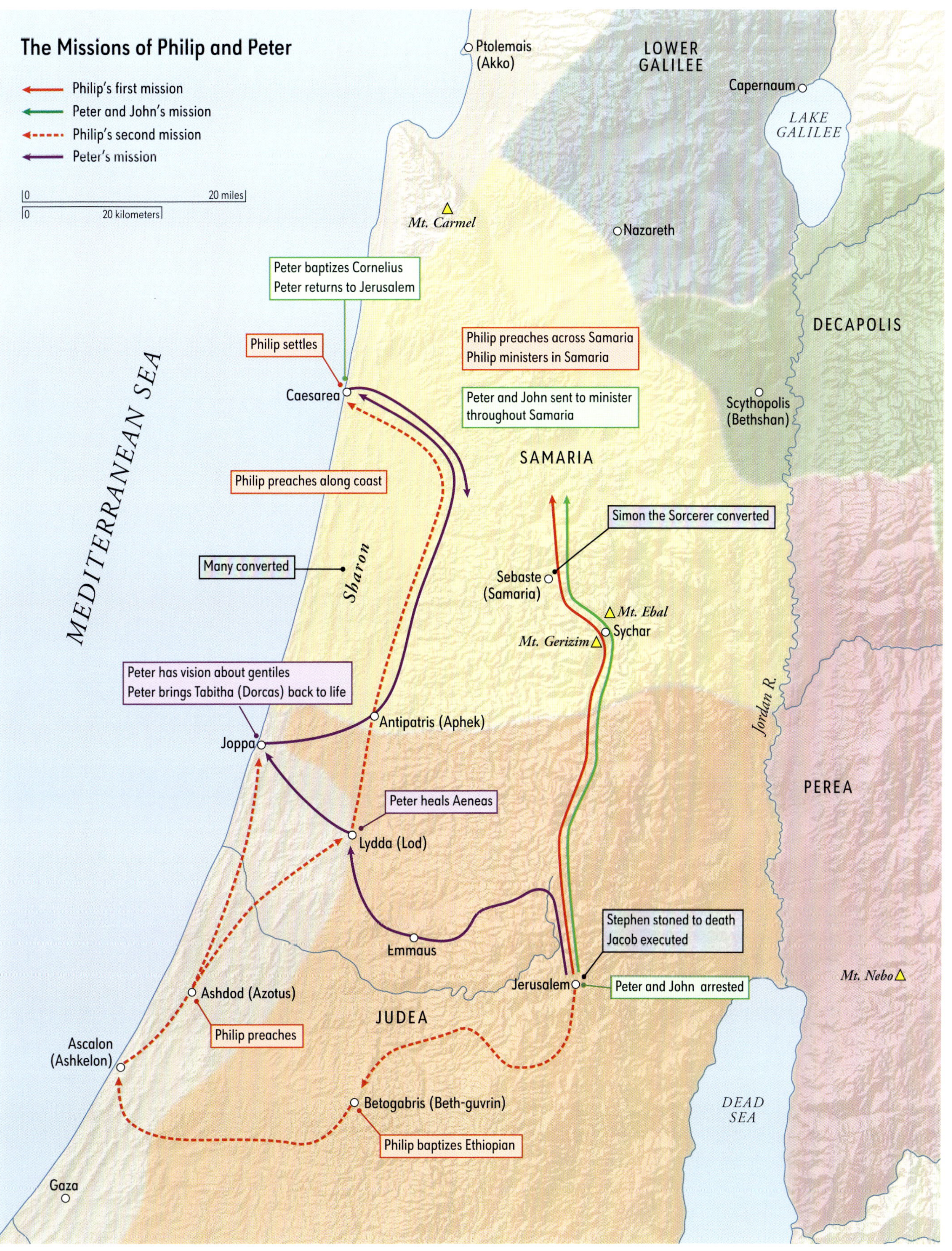
The Missions of Philip and Peter
Philip's first mission
Peter and John's mission
Philip's second mission
Peter's mission
0
20 miles
0
20 kilometers
Ptolemais
(Akko)
LOWER
GALILEE
Capernaum
LAKE
GALILEE
Mt. Carmel
Nazareth
Peter baptizes Cornelius
Peter returns to Jerusalem
DECAPOLIS
Philip settles
Philip preaches across Samaria
Philip ministers in Samaria
MEDITERRANEAN SEA
Caesarea
Peter and John sent to minister
throughout Samaria
Scythopolis
(Bethshan)
SAMARIA
Philip preaches along coast
Simon the Sorcerer converted
Many converted
Sharon
Sebaste
(Samaria)
Mt. Ebal
Sychar
Mt. Gerizim
Peter has vision about gentiles
Peter brings Tabitha (Dorcas) back to life
Jordan R.
Antipatris (Aphek)
Joppa
PEREA
Peter heals Aeneas
Lydda (Lod)
Stephen stoned to death
Jacob executed
Emmaus
Mt. Nebo
Jerusalem
Peter and John arrested
Ashdod (Azotus)
JUDEA
Philip preaches
Ascalon
(Ashkelon)
Betogabris (Beth-guvrin)
DEAD
SEA
Philip baptizes Ethiopian
Gaza

The Jewish festivals

Passover (Pesach) and Unleavened Bread

Commemorating Israel's deliverance from Egypt.

Each family celebrated the deliverance of the Hebrews from slavery in Egypt, and symbolically re-enacted the first Passover as they ate their own special meal. The celebration continued for seven days, as they commemorated the Exodus and wilderness wanderings by eating unleavened bread, recalling the haste with which they left Egypt, when they did not have time to let the bread rise.

EXODUS 12:11–30; LEVITICUS 23:4–8; NUMBERS 28:16–25; MATTHEW 26:17

Firstfruits

A barley harvest feast, at the end of the seven-day Passover festival.

LEVITICUS 23:9–14; NUMBERS 28:26–31

Second Passover

For those unable to keep the first Passover.

NUMBERS 9:9–13; 2 CHRONICLES 30:2–3

Pentecost (Shavuot, Weeks, Firstfruits, Harvest)

A celebration of harvest. At Pentecost, seven weeks after Passover, the Jews celebrated the gathering in of the wheat harvest. The priests offered symbolically two loaves made from the new flour. This feast also celebrated the giving of the Law to Moses at Mount Sinai.

LEVITICUS 23:9–22; DEUTERONOMY 16:9–12; ACTS 2:1

Trumpets (Rosh Hashanah, New Year, Judgment, Memorial)

A time of reckoning with God. This two-day celebration was marked by the blowing of trumpets to greet the civil new year, and was also the beginning of the most solemn month in the year. The Israelites prepared themselves for Yom Kippur, which comes ten days later, by praising God, whose standard they had failed to meet, and recounting his greatness, love, and mercy.

LEVITICUS 23:23–25; NUMBERS 29:1–6

Day of Atonement (Yom Kippur)

The most holy day in the Jewish year. On Yom Kippur Israel confessed the nation's sins, and asked forgiveness and cleansing. A scapegoat was sent into the desert, symbolically carrying the people's sin. The high priest entered the most holy place of the Temple on this day alone, to present the blood of a sacrifice for the people's sins. The people fasted, neither eating nor drinking for 24 hours.

LEVITICUS 16; 23:26–32; NUMBERS 29:7–11

Tabernacles (Succoth, Booths, Ingathering)

A festival that commemorated Israel's wanderings in the wilderness. A joyful harvest festival celebrating the gathering in of the grapes. During the seven-day celebration, the people thanked God for protecting them in the wilderness and for the harvest. For seven days they lived in shelters made of branches, to remind them of their time living in tents in the wilderness.

LEVITICUS 23:33–44; NUMBERS 29:12–39; JOHN 7:2

Simchat Torah (Rejoicing in the Law)

Marked the end of the annual reading of the entire cycle of the Law. A joyful celebration, giving thanks for the Pentateuch—the first five books of the Hebrew Bible.

Dedication (Hanukkah, Lights, Maccabees)

At Hanukkah, the Jews celebrated the expulsion of the Syrians by Judas Maccabeus in 164 BC, and the cleansing and rededication of the Jerusalem Temple, which the Syrians had desecrated. Lighting a new candle each day for eight days, the Jews commemorated the miracle of the Temple's holy candelabrum: for the rededication they had only one day's worth of consecrated oil, but it burned for eight full days, the time required to consecrate more oil.

1 MACCABEES 4:41–49; JOHN 10:22

Purim (Lots)

Celebrated the failure of Haman's plot to destroy the Jews. A time of feasting and joy, when the people celebrated the deliverance of the Jews from death through the bravery of Queen Esther of Persia.

ESTHER 9:21, 27–28

The Hebrews escape from Egypt.

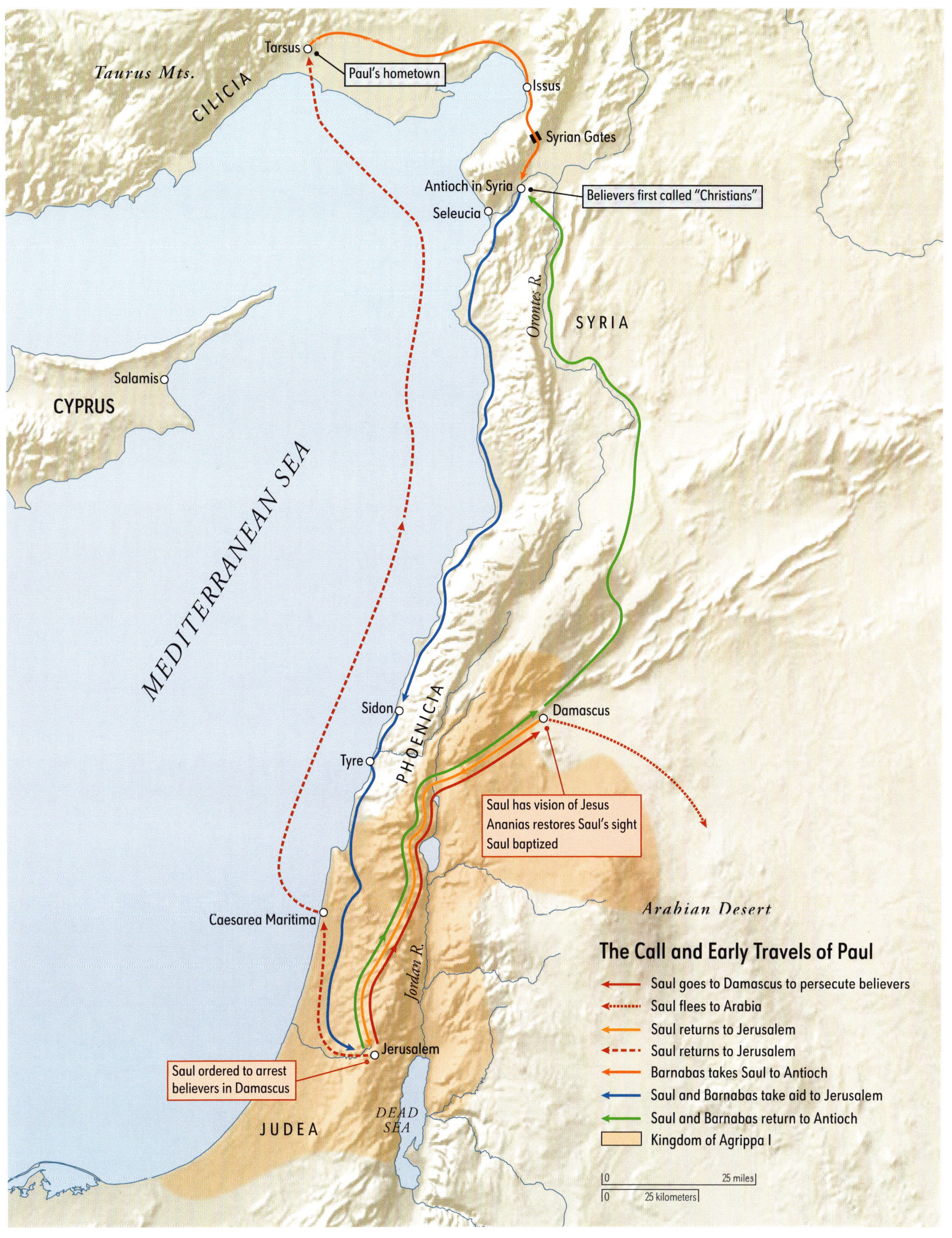
Tarsus
Paul's hometown
Taurus Mts.
CILICIA
Issus
Syrian Gates
Antioch in Syria
Believers first called "Christians"
Seleucia
Orontes R.
SYRIA
Salamis
CYPRUS
MEDITERRANEAN SEA
Sidon
PHOENICIA
Tyre
Damascus
Saul has vision of Jesus
Ananias restores Saul's sight
Saul baptized
Arabian Desert
Caesarea Maritima
Jordan R.
Jerusalem
Saul ordered to arrest believers in Damascus
JUDEA
DEAD SEA
The Call and Early Travels of Paul
Saul goes to Damascus to persecute believers
Saul flees to Arabia
Saul returns to Jerusalem
Saul returns to Jerusalem
Barnabas takes Saul to Antioch
Saul and Barnabas take aid to Jerusalem
Saul and Barnabas return to Antioch
Kingdom of Agrippa I
0 25 miles
0 25 kilometers

Some of the first Christians

The Acts of the Apostles describes people who became followers of Christ in the first days of the church.

Stephen

Stephen was the leading deacon of seven in the Jerusalem church. He was brought before the Sanhedrin council when some Jews objected to his preaching. When he accused them of killing "the Righteous One," they dragged him from the city and stoned him to death. The first Christian martyr, Stephen prayed forgiveness for those who stoned him. His death was witnessed by Saul (Paul).

ACTS 6:1–8:2

Ananias

Ananias, with his wife, Sapphira, sold property and gave some of the money to the apostles, but pretended that they gave all of it. Peter accused Ananias of lying to the Holy Spirit, at which Ananias fell dead.

ACTS 5:1-11

Mary, mother of John Mark

A relative of Barnabas; her home was a gathering place for the Jerusalem church.

ACTS 12:12-13; COLOSSIANS 4:10

Cleopas

One of two disciples who talked with the risen Christ on their way from Jerusalem to Emmaus. Only as Jesus broke bread with them did they recognize him. The two friends returned to Jerusalem to share their experience with the apostles.

LUKE 24:13-49

Cornelius

Roman centurion known to be a generous and devout man of prayer. As a result of Peter's preaching, Cornelius and his household believed in Christ, the first known Gentiles to follow Jesus.

ACTS 10

Matthias

After Judas Iscariot's suicide, the remaining eleven apostles drew lots to decide who would replace him. Matthias was chosen.

ACTS 1:15-26

Rhoda

Servant in the house of Mary, mother of John Mark. When Peter was miraculously delivered from prison and knocked at Mary's door, Rhoda ran to tell the praying Christians that Peter was outside. In her excitement, she forgot to open the door.

ACTS 12:1-19

James, brother of Jesus

One of Jesus' brothers. After Jesus' resurrection, James became leader of the church in Jerusalem, and probably wrote the letter of James.

MATTHEW 13:55; MARK 6:3; ACTS 12:2; 15:13-21; 21:18; GALATIANS 1:19; 2:9

Agabus

Prophet from Jerusalem who prophesied at Antioch about a famine across the Roman Empire. He also predicted Paul would be bound if he went to Jerusalem.

ACTS 11:27-30; 21:10-11

Simon (Magus)

Magus from Samaria who astonished people with his magic. After hearing Philip preach about Jesus, Simon believed and was baptized. When he saw that the Spirit had been given to believers after the apostles laid their hands on them, he tried to buy this power from Peter and John. Peter told Simon to repent of his sin.

ACTS 8:9-25

Jude

One of Jesus' brothers, sometimes called Judas, who believed in Jesus only after his resurrection. Probably the writer of the letter of Jude.

MATTHEW 13:55; MARK 6:3; JUDE 1

Stephen is stoned to death.

Some of the first Christians continued

Crippled beggar
Each day a man crippled from birth was carried to the temple gate called Beautiful, where he begged. Peter and John did not give money, but healed him. He entered the temple, walking and praising God.
ACTS 3:1-10

Aeneas
Disabled man who lived in Lydda, unable to get out of bed for eight years. Peter said, "Jesus Christ heals you." Immediately he was able to walk again.
ACTS 9:32-35

Dorcas (Tabitha)
Christian widow in Joppa who helped the poor. When she fell ill and died, Peter prayed and brought her back to life.
ACTS 9:36-43

Sergius Paulus
Paul and Barnabas visited Cyprus, where Sergius Paulus was Roman proconsul. He believed after the sorcerer Elymas was struck blind by Paul.
ACTS 13:4-12

Philippian jailer
Paul and Silas were thrown into prison in the town of Philippi. After an earthquake shook the prison, the jailer was going to kill himself, fearing the prisoners had escaped. Paul reassured him, and he asked, "What must I do to be saved?" The jailer and his family believed and were baptized.
ACTS 16:22-40

Philip
One of seven deacons appointed by the Jerusalem church, Philip became a leading evangelist to the Samaritans and Gentiles. He told a traveling Ethiopian official the good news about Jesus, and the man was immediately baptized.
ACTS 6:5; 8:4-13, 26-40; 21:8

Ethiopian official
Queen Candace's chief officer, returning from Jerusalem, was reading Isaiah 53 when Philip joined him and explained that Isaiah's prophecies applied to Christ. The Ethiopian believed and Philip baptized him.
ACTS 8:26-39

Great sermons in Acts

Speech	Theme	Reference
Peter at Pentecost to crowds	Peter explains the significance of events	Acts 2:14-40
Peter at the temple to crowds	The Jews need to repent for crucifying Messiah	Acts 3:12-26
Peter to the Sanhedrin	A lame man is healed by Jesus' power	Acts 4:5-12
Stephen to the Sanhedrin	Account of the history of the Jews, whom Stephen accuses of killing Messiah	Acts 7
Peter to Gentiles	Gentiles, like Jews, can be saved	Acts 10:28-47
Peter to the church in Jerusalem	Peter defends ministry to Gentiles	Acts 11:4-18
Paul in Antioch synagogue	Jesus the Messiah fulfils Old Testament prophecy	Acts 13:16-41
Peter to Jerusalem council	Salvation is by grace, and freely available to all	Acts 15:7-11
James to Jerusalem council	Gentile believers need not be circumcised	Acts 15:13-21
Paul to Ephesian elders	Keep the faith—despite false teaching and persecution	Acts 20:17-35
Paul to Jerusalem crowd	Paul recounts his conversion and mission to non-Jews	Acts 22:1-21
Paul to Sanhedrin council	Paul's defense as both Pharisee and Roman citizen	Acts 23:1-6
Paul to Agrippa	Paul recounts his conversion	Acts 26
Paul to Jewish leaders in Rome	Paul describes his heritage as a Jew	Acts 28:17-20

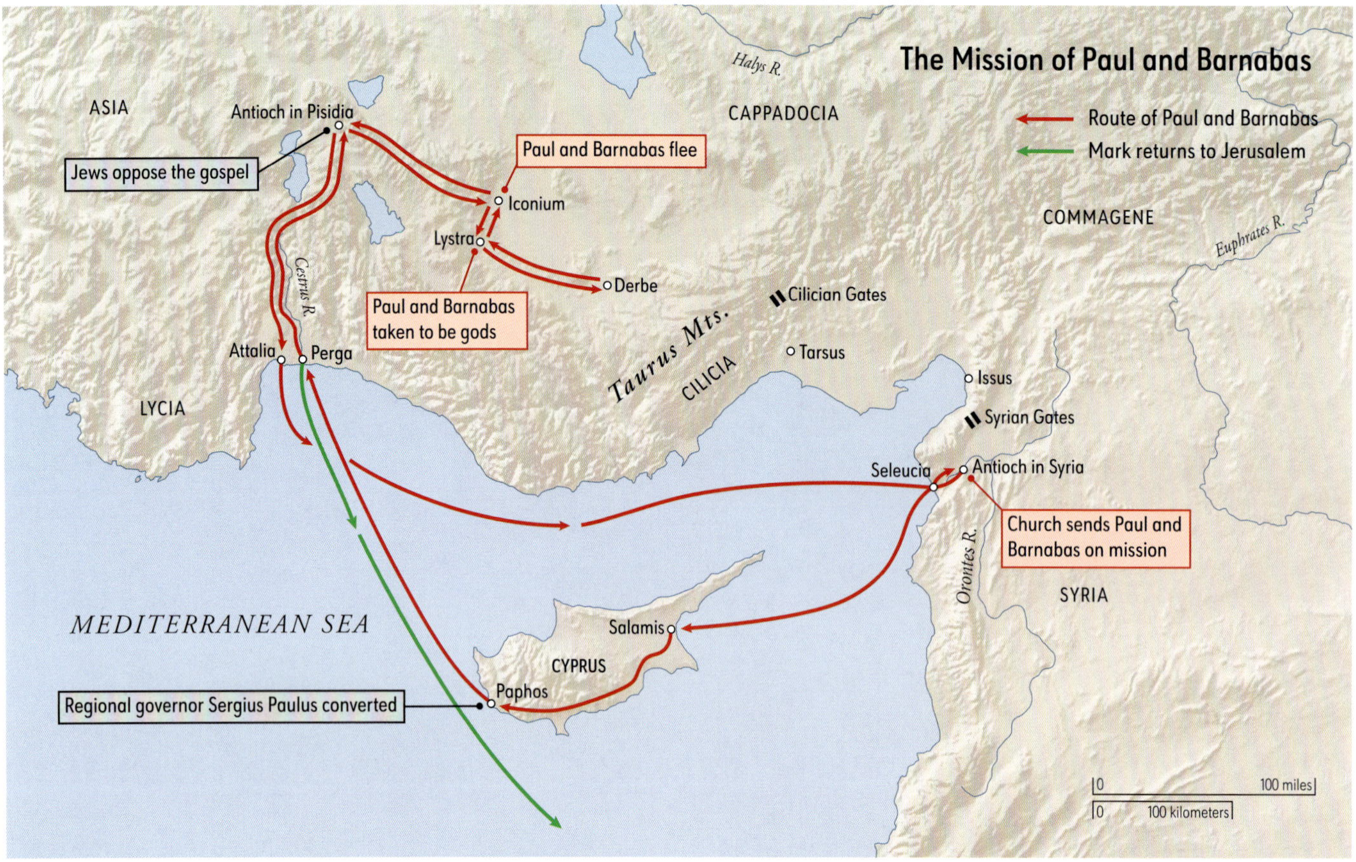

The Mission of Paul and Barnabas

Route of Paul and Barnabas
Mark returns to Jerusalem

ASIA
Antioch in Pisidia
Jews oppose the gospel
Paul and Barnabas flee
Iconium
Lystra
Derbe
Paul and Barnabas taken to be gods
Halys R.
CAPPADOCIA
COMMAGENE
Euphrates R.
Cestrus R.
Cilician Gates
Taurus Mts.
CILICIA
Tarsus
Attalia
Perga
LYCIA
Issus
Syrian Gates
Seleucia
Antioch in Syria
Church sends Paul and Barnabas on mission
Orontes R.
SYRIA
MEDITERRANEAN SEA
Salamis
CYPRUS
Paphos
Regional governor Sergius Paulus converted
0 100 miles
0 100 kilometers

Paul's Second Missionary Journey

Route of Paul and Silas

MACEDONIA
Philippi
THRACE
BLACK SEA
Amphipolis
Neapolis
Via Egnatia
Thessalonica
Berea
Apollonia
Paul and Silas in jail
SAMOTHRACE
Troas
MYSIA
AEGEAN SEA
Paul has vision calling him to Macedonia
GALATIA
Halys R.
ASIA
Paul speaks at Areopagus
ACHAIA
Corinth
Athens
Ephesus
Antioch in Pisidia
Iconium
Lystra
Derbe
Taurus Mts.
Cilician Gates
Cenchrea
Paul stays with Aquila and Priscilla
LYCIA
CILICIA
Tarsus
Issus
Syrian Gates
Antioch in Syria
RHODES
Paul and Silas joined by Timothy
Seleucia
Paul and Silas leave on second mission
SYRIA
CYPRUS
Damascus
MEDITERRANEAN SEA
Conference AD 49
Paul returns to Antioch
CYRENAICA
Caesarea Maritima
JUDEA
Jerusalem
0 200 miles
0 200 kilometers

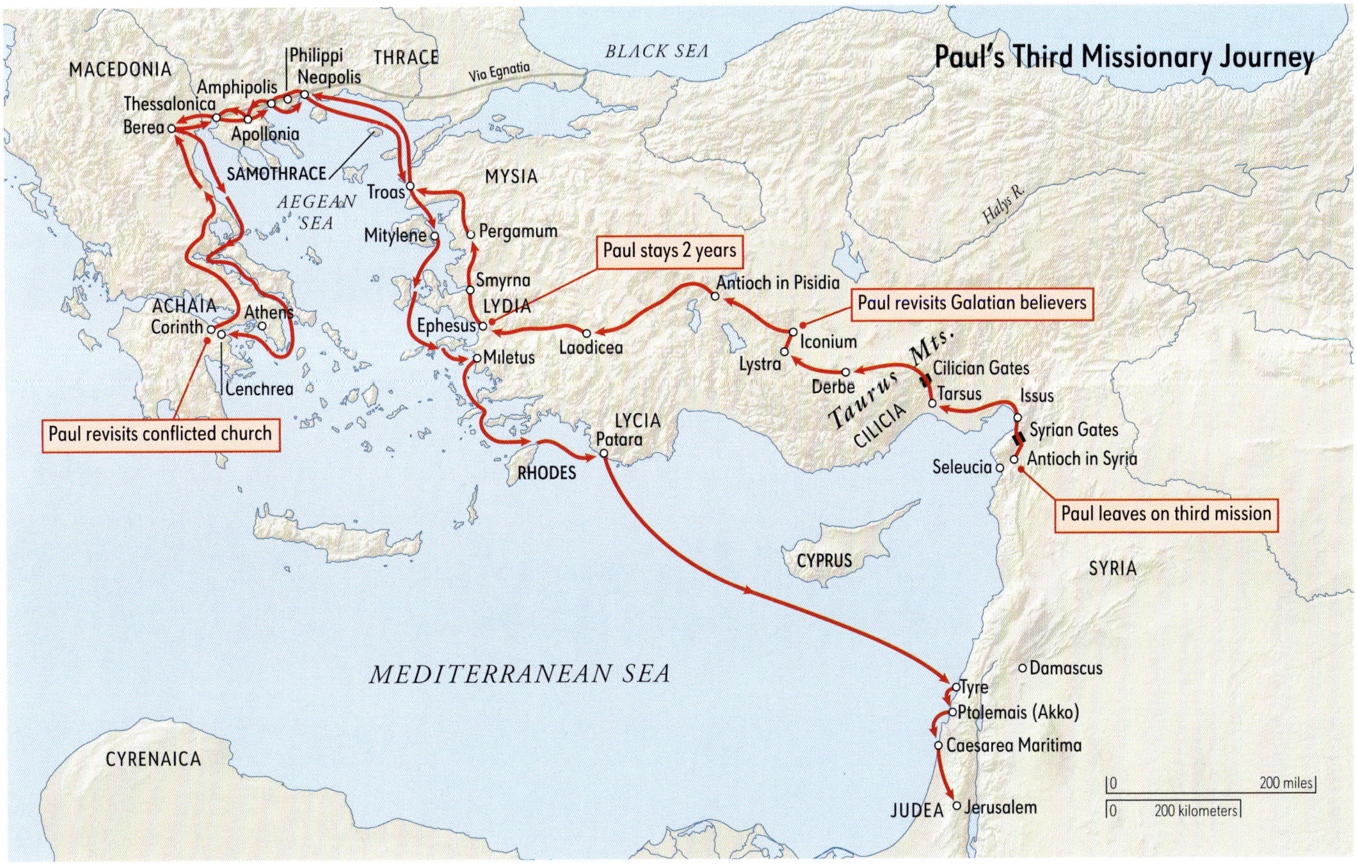

Paul's Third Missionary Journey

MACEDONIA
THRACE
BLACK SEA
Philippi
Neapolis
Amphipolis
Thessalonica
Berea
Apollonia
Via Egnatia
SAMOTHRACE
AEGEAN SEA
Troas
MYSIA
Halys R.
Mitylene
Pergamum
Paul stays 2 years
Smyrna
LYDIA
Antioch in Pisidia
Paul revisits Galatian believers
ACHAIA
Corinth
Athens
Ephesus
Laodicea
Iconium
Miletus
Lystra
Taurus Mts.
Cilician Gates
Derbe
Tarsus
Issus
Cenchrea
CILICIA
Paul revisits conflicted church
LYCIA
Patara
Syrian Gates
Antioch in Syria
RHODES
Seleucia
Paul leaves on third mission
CYPRUS
SYRIA
MEDITERRANEAN SEA
Damascus
Tyre
Ptolemais (Akko)
CYRENAICA
Caesarea Maritima
0 200 miles
0 200 kilometers
JUDEA
Jerusalem

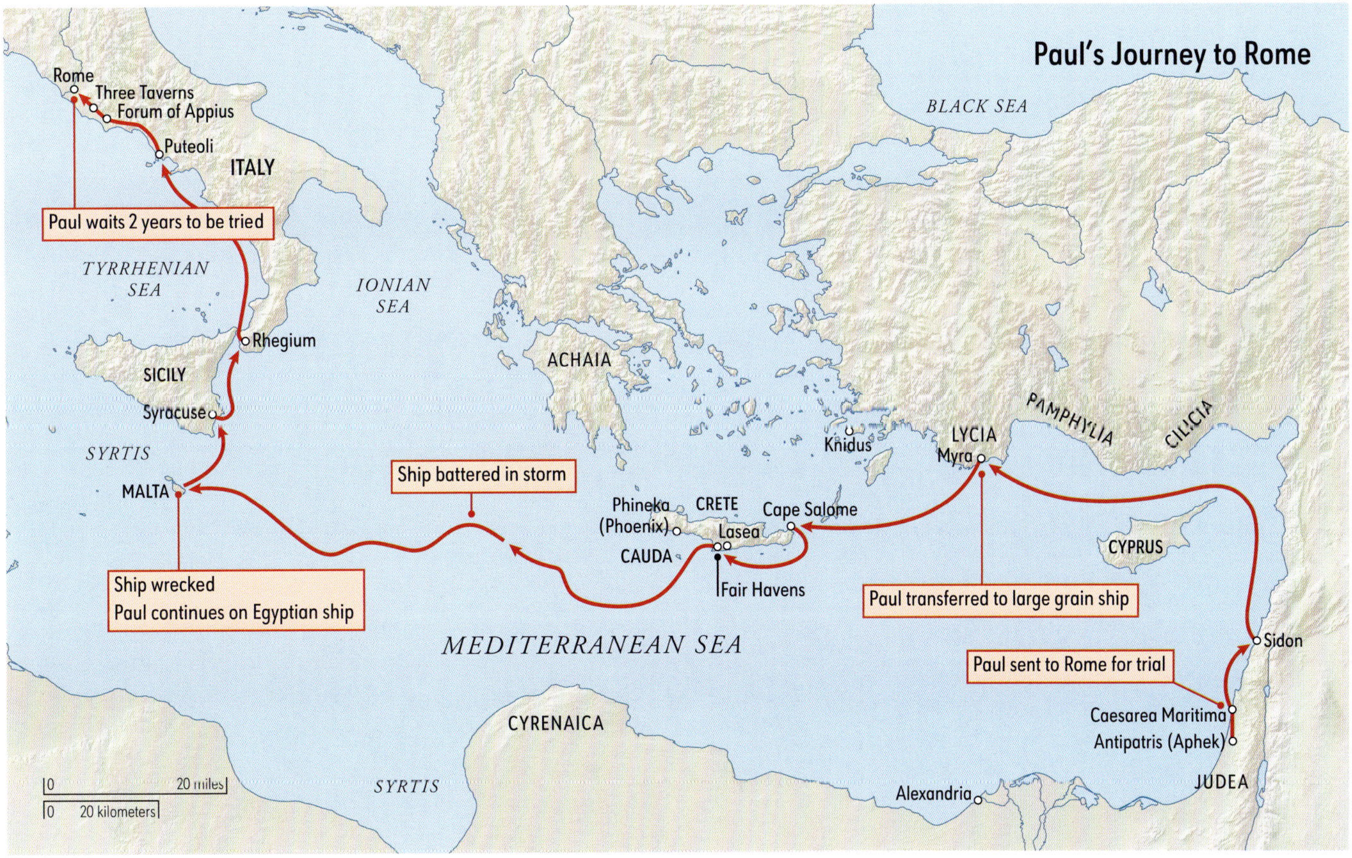

Paul's Journey to Rome

Rome
Three Taverns
Forum of Appius
BLACK SEA
Puteoli
ITALY
Paul waits 2 years to be tried
TYRRHENIAN SEA
IONIAN SEA
Rhegium
SICILY
ACHAIA
Syracuse
PAMPHYLIA
CILICIA
SYRTIS
Knidus
LYCIA
Myra
MALTA
Ship battered in storm
Phineka (Phoenix)
CRETE
Cape Salome
Lasea
CYPRUS
CAUDA
Fair Havens
Paul transferred to large grain ship
Ship wrecked
Paul continues on Egyptian ship
Sidon
MEDITERRANEAN SEA
Paul sent to Rome for trial
Caesarea Maritima
Antipatris (Aphek)
CYRENAICA
JUDEA
0 20 miles
0 20 kilometers
SYRTIS
Alexandria

Roman Emperors of Bible times

Name	Reign	Christian	Bible reference
Julius	49–44 BC		
Augustus	31 BC–AD 14	Birth of Jesus	Luke 2:1
Tiberius	AD 14–37	Ministry and death of Jesus	Luke 4ff
Caligula	AD 37–41		
Claudius	AD 41–54	Jews expelled from Rome	Acts 11:28; 18:2
Nero	AD 54–68	Trial of Paul Persecution at Rome	Acts 25:10–12; 27:24
Galba	AD 68–69		
Otho	AD 69		
Vitellius	AD 69		
Vespasian	AD 69–79	Jerusalem destroyed	
Titus	AD 79–81		
Domitian	AD 81–96	Persecution	
Nerva	AD 96–98		
Trajan	AD 98–117		
Hadrian	AD 117–138		

Nero.

Augustus Caesar.

Paul and his friends

Silas

A leader of the church in Jerusalem, Silas traveled with Paul on his second missionary journey and was jailed with him at Philippi. He is probably the "Silvanus" mentioned in Paul's letters.

ACTS 15–18; 2 CORINTHIANS 1; 1 THESSALONIANS 1; 1 PETER 5

Titus

A Gentile Christian and helper of Paul, Titus worked in Corinth, breaking down bad feelings between the Christians there and Paul. He delivered Paul's second letter to the Corinthians, and helped collect money in Corinth for poor Christians in Judea. Paul wrote his letter to Titus while Titus was working in Crete.

2 CORINTHIANS 7–8; GALATIANS 2; TITUS

Tychicus

Friend of Paul, probably from Ephesus, Tychicus was chosen by the churches of Asia Minor to take the money they collected to poor Christians in Judea. He was with Paul in prison in Rome and delivered Paul's letters to the churches at Colossae and Ephesus.

EPHESIANS 6; COLOSSIANS 4; 2 TIMOTHY 4; TITUS 3

John Mark

Writer of the second Gospel, Mark lived in Jerusalem, where the first Christians met in his mother's house. Cousin of Barnabas, he accompanied Paul and Barnabas on their first missionary journey, but left half-way. Paul refused to take him on his second trip. Later Mark joined Paul in Rome, and was described by him as "my son Mark."

ACTS 12–15; 2 TIMOTHY 4; PHILEMON

Barnabas

Native of Cyprus and member of the Jerusalem church, Barnabas befriended Paul when others were suspicious of him after the apostle came to Jerusalem following his conversion. The Jerusalem church sent Barnabas to Antioch to build up the church, and asked Paul to join him. Barnabas accompanied Paul on his first missionary journey from Antioch, but on the second trip they disagreed about taking John Mark with them.

ACTS 4, 9, 11, 12, 15; GALATIANS 2

Erastus

An assistant of Paul, Erastus joined Timothy to work in Macedonia when Paul stayed in Asia Minor.

ACTS 19; 2 TIMOTHY 4

Timothy

Friend and aide of Paul, Timothy helped on Paul's second missionary journey, staying in Thessalonica to assist persecuted believers. Paul sent Timothy to teach the church at Corinth. Paul's two letters to him are full of advice to leaders in the church.

ACTS 16, 17; 1 AND 2 TIMOTHY

Gaius

Macedonian Christian who joined Paul on his third missionary journey. During the silversmiths' riot at Ephesus, he was dragged into the amphitheater.

ACTS 19

Luke

Greek-speaking doctor and friend of Paul who wrote the third Gospel. Luke accompanied the apostle on some of his journeys, and wrote up his experiences in Acts. Luke sailed to Rome with Paul, and stayed with him while he was a prisoner there.

COLOSSIANS 4; 2 TIMOTHY 4; LUKE-ACTS

Paul writes to encourage Christians.

Paul

The great apostle and pioneering missionary whose letters form a major part of the New Testament, Paul was a Jew and a Roman citizen. Born in Tarsus, Cilicia, he was named Saul, and educated by the rabbi Gamaliel in Jerusalem. He belonged to the Pharisee sect, strongly opposed to the Christians, and watched the stoning of Stephen.

On his way to Damascus to arrest Christians, Saul was blinded by light and heard Jesus ask, "Why do you persecute me?" He was led into Damascus, where Ananias restored his sight. After Saul had been baptized, he started preaching the gospel. Jews in Damascus plotted to kill him, so he fled to Jerusalem, where the Christians were afraid of him. Barnabas befriended him and introduced him to the apostles. After another plot to kill him, Saul returned to Tarsus.

Some years later, Barnabas fetched Saul to help the church at Antioch in Syria. This church later sent them to Asia Minor to spread the gospel. After their visit to Cyprus, Saul was known as Paul, the Greek form of his Hebrew name. Paul helped Jewish Christians in Jerusalem to accept Jesus as the Savior of all, not solely of the Jews.

On his second missionary journey, Paul was accompanied by Silas, first visiting Christian converts in Galatia. They were joined in Lystra by Timothy and sailed to Greece from Troas, where Luke joined them. They started a new church in Philippi, but Paul and Silas were beaten and jailed. After their release, they traveled on through Greece, Paul preaching in Athens and settling in Corinth for eighteen months. Paul then returned to Jerusalem, taking gifts for poor Christians from believers in Greece and Asia Minor. Paul stayed a period in Syria before leaving again for Ephesus, where he worked and preached for nearly three years, then revisited Corinth before returning to Jerusalem. Arriving back in Jerusalem, Paul was arrested again and sent to Caesarea for trial. Following two years in jail, Paul appealed to be tried before Caesar and was sent to Rome, but was shipwrecked off the coast of Malta. He eventually reached Rome, where he was under house arrest for two years, writing many of his letters from jail. Paul was probably released following his trial, but rearrested and executed by the Emperor Nero around AD 67.

ACTS 9–28; PAUL'S LETTERS

Romans

Author
The apostle Paul.

Audience
The church of Rome.

Date
c. AD 55–57.

Outline
Opening 1:1–17
The human condition 1:18–3:20
The gospel solution 3:21–5:21
Gospel freedom 6:1–8:39
The gospel and Israel 9:1–11:36
The gospel and our new life 12:1–15:13
Letter closing 15:14–16:27

Purpose
Paul wrote Romans to set out the grand themes of God's grace and glory encapsulated in the gospel. No one comes into glory except by the grace of God, which fills believers with his righteousness. Neither our attempts to please God nor our works of religion are able to make us holy. But God is so compassionate and gracious that he shares his righteousness with all who receive his Son, Jesus Christ. He causes his faith-filled people to be made holy by his grace and glory. Paul wrote his letter to explain this message, why he preached it, and how it should impact Christians in their daily life and community.

Author and audience
Rome was the center of the known world when Paul penned this letter. Paul had not yet been there.

Major themes in Romans

The gospel
The Greek word for gospel is *euangelion*, which means "good news"—the amazing, joyful message of God's saving work in Jesus Christ. The gospel is the message of how God has acted in the world to rescue humanity from sin and death through the life, death, and resurrection of Jesus.

Salvation
God's salvation is presented to us in this letter—salvation not of works or religious efforts, but the gift that comes to all who believe the good news of Jesus Christ, who has come to save us and set us free.

The love of God
Paul sings of God's love throughout the book of Romans.

Justification
This legal term means "to acquit." While we were all under God's wrath because of our sin, because Jesus paid the price of our sin in our place, we have been acquitted of all charges against us, and declared "not guilty" in heaven's court.

The righteousness of God
We are actually made right by God when we believe in Jesus.

The law
Through Christ, God achieved what we could not: Christ perfectly fulfilled every requirement of the law so that now we "no longer follow our sinful nature but instead follow the Spirit." (8:4, NLT).

The flesh versus the Spirit
Paul compares our old life in the flesh with our new life in the life-giving Spirit, exhorting us to live in the new way as true children of God, moved by the impulse of the Holy Spirit.

The destiny of Israel/the Church
Although Jews have fallen into unbelief, Paul makes it clear that God will bring "all Israel" to salvation. There are differing opinions as to whether "all Israel" here, refers to ethnic Israel or the Church—or even both (11:25–32).

Paul's letters

Each of Paul's letters focuses on two major themes: the importance of right doctrine and the importance of right living. For example, Romans chapters 1—11 contains instructions and teachings on the proper belief system about sin, salvation, the work of the cross in our lives, God's endless love for us, and the place of Israel in the plan of God.

Only after Paul has instructed the church does he encourage Christians to live holy lives. Right understanding of truth is vital for having a right understanding of how we are to live to the glory of God.

Although each of Paul's letters was addressed to a specific church, person, or group, they were circular letters intended to be read by all the churches. Scholars believe they were all written in less than fourteen years.

Paul's converts and opponents

As a traveling missionary, Paul made numerous friends—and many enemies.

Aquila
Jewish Christian, husband of Priscilla, and friend and supporter of Paul. Aquila was born in Pontus and expelled from Rome by the Emperor Claudius. A tentmaker, he met Paul in Corinth, where Paul worked and stayed with him. Aquila and Priscilla traveled with Paul to Ephesus and later returned to Rome. In Ephesus and Rome, the church met in their home.
ACTS 18; ROMANS 16:3; 1 CORINTHIANS 16:19

Priscilla
Wife of Aquila.
ACTS 18; ROMANS 16:3; 1 CORINTHIANS 16:19; 2 TIMOTHY 4:19

Apollos
Jewish Christian from Alexandria. Priscilla and Aquila taught Apollos more about God. He encouraged the Christians of southern Greece, and refuted the Jews in public debate.
ACTS 18:24–19:1; 1 CORINTHIANS 16:12

Crescens
Companion of Paul during his imprisonment in Rome.
2 TIMOTHY 4:10

Crispus
Crispus and his household believed as a result of Paul's preaching in Corinth.
ACTS 18:7–11; 1 CORINTHIANS 1:14

Demetrius
Silversmith in Ephesus who made silver shrines of the local goddess, Artemis (Diana). When Paul's preaching threatened his trade, Demetrius organized a riot.
ACTS 19:23–20:1

Demas
One of Paul's helpers, Demas deserted Paul during his imprisonment in Rome.
COLOSSIANS 4:14; PHILEMON 24

Dionysius
Member of the Areopagus council in Athens who became a follower of Paul and believed.
ACTS 17:34

Elymas
Nicknamed Bar-Jesus, Elymas was a Jewish sorcerer who opposed Paul and Barnabas at Paphos, and attempted to turn the proconsul, Sergius Paulus, from the faith. Because of this, Paul struck him temporarily blind.
ACTS 13:4–12

Epaphras
Leader of the church at Colossae, Epaphras visited Paul while a prisoner in Rome. Paul wrote his letter to the Colossians in response to what Epaphras told him about the church.
COLOSSIANS 1:7; 4:12; PHILEMON 23

Onesimus
Runaway slave who, after meeting Paul in prison in Rome, became a Christian. Paul sent him back to his master, Philemon, with a letter asking for Onesimus to be accepted back as a Christian brother.
PHILEMON

Philemon
The only surviving personal letter of Paul is to Philemon. Paul begs Philemon to receive back his runaway slave, Onesimus, as a fellow Christian.
PHILEMON

Epaphroditus
Member of the Philippian church who was sent to take a gift from them to Paul, imprisoned in Rome.
PHILIPPIANS 2:19–30; 4:18

Eutychus
Young man who fell asleep as Paul preached in Troas until midnight. He fell to his death from a window, but Paul brought him back to life.
ACTS 20:7–12

Jason
Jason looked after Paul and Silas during their stay in Thessalonica.
ACTS 17:1–9

Lydia
Business woman from Thyatira who traded in purple cloth, and believed in the Lord through Paul's preaching.
ACTS 16:11–15

Claudius
Roman emperor, AD 41–54, who expelled the Jews from Rome for rioting.
ACTS 11:28; 18:2

Nero
Although Nero is not named, he was the emperor responsible for persecuting Christians in Rome. Tradition has it that Peter and Paul suffered martyrdom at his hands.

Felix
Roman governor of Judea who tried Paul, keeping him in prison for two years.
ACTS 23:23–24:27

Festus
Succeeded Felix as Roman governor of Judea and continued Paul's trial.
ACTS 25–26

Agrippa
King Herod Agrippa II, ruler of Galilee, had Paul brought before him by Festus, and listened sympathetically to his defense.
ACTS 25

1 Corinthians

Author
The apostle Paul.

Audience
The church of Corinth.

Date
c. AD 53–55.

Outline
Opening 1:1-9
Causes and cures of division 1:10–4:21
Moral issues and marriage 5:1–7:40
Idolatry condemned 8:1–11:1
Worship and gifts 11:2–14:40
The resurrection of the dead 15:1-58
Closing 16:1-24

About 1 Corinthians
The influential seaport city of Corinth was strategically located at the crossroads of the world. Prosperous, powerful, and decadent, God sent the apostle Paul there on his third missionary journey, to establish a church in a city that desperately needed love and truth. Paul spent a year and a half in Corinth and saw the church grow. He wrote this letter to encourage them to carry on in their faith and remain steadfast to the gospel.

Written while Paul was in Ephesus, this letter had a powerful effect on the Corinthian believers. This book is remembered for the so-called love chapter—1 Corinthians 13—the masterpiece of love in the New Testament.

Purpose
Many errors had crept into the church of Corinth. Corinth was a modern, cosmopolitan, polytheistic city and believers had accommodated the gospel to make it palatable to that culture.

Paul needed to address such issues as living godly in a corrupt culture; being united in one body; maintaining sexual and moral purity in the church; understanding more completely the role of spiritual gifts in the church; embracing love as the greatest virtue in our hearts; maintaining orderly worship; and maintaining the hope of the resurrection.

Author and audience
Paul wrote to the church of Corinth as a founding father (see ACTS 18), responding to problems in the Corinthian church. Apparently, a delegation from Corinth had told Paul what was happening and asked for his advice. 1 Corinthians is his response.

Major themes in 1 Corinthians

The nature of the gospel
Paul identifies Jesus as the divine Son of God, particularly in relation to his resurrection from the dead. He is the *risen* Lord Jesus Christ, and his resurrection becomes the "template" for all believers—past, present, and future—who will all experience that same miraculous resuscitation from death to life, and spend eternity with their risen Lord, Redeemer, and King. Paul shared the core message: "Christ died for our sins … He was buried, and he was raised from the dead on the third day, just as the Scriptures said" (15:4, NLT).

The church of Christ
Paul set out the nature of church leadership and pastoral ministry, and discussed the nature of worship, particularly God's supernatural gifts, imparted to every believer.

Holy and ethical living
We may be saved by grace, but as Christians we are to live lives that glorify and honor God (10:31).

The importance of spiritual gifts
Paul spends some three chapters in his book (12—14), talking about the importance of spiritual gifts in the life of all believers—gifts that are uniquely and explicitly bestowed, for the purpose of building up the spiritual vitality of the church, as the New Covenant people of God. Every single believer has been given a variety of gifts for that purpose.

Love, the motivation of our lives
The love chapter (13) lays out the virtue of loving God and our neighbor, as Christ commanded.

The end
Our personal end, at death—and our world's end, when Christ returns. Our ultimate Christian hope is in the resurrection. Jesus' resurrection from the dead paved the way for our own resurrection. Because Jesus is alive, we have bright hope for tomorrow.

The Love chapter

A favorite for weddings. Yet the author, the apostle Paul, was actually arguing that love is more important and lasting than spiritual gifts such as speaking in tongues, asceticism, and prophesying.

If I speak in the tongues of men and of
angels, but have not love, I am only a
resounding gong or a clanging cymbal. 2If
I have the gift of prophecy and can fathom
all mysteries and all knowledge, and if I
have a faith that can move mountains,
but have not love, I am nothing. 3If I give
all I possess to the poor and surrender
my body to the flames, but have not love,
I gain nothing.
4Love is patient, love is kind. It does
not envy, it does not boast, it is not
proud. 5It is not rude, it is not self-
seeking, it is not easily angered, it keeps
no record of wrongs. 6Love does not
delight in evil but rejoices with the truth.
7It always protects, always trusts, always
hopes, always perseveres.
8Love never fails. But where there are
prophecies, they will cease; where there
are tongues, they will be stilled; where
there is knowledge, it will pass away. 9For
we know in part and we prophesy in
part, 10but when perfection comes, the
imperfect disappears. 11When I was a child,
I talked like a child, I thought like a child,
I reasoned like a child. When I became
a man, I put childish ways behind me.
12Now we see but a poor reflection as in a
mirror; then we shall see face to face. Now
I know in part; then I shall know fully,
even as I am fully known.
13And now these three remain: faith,
hope and love. But the greatest of these
is love.

1 CORINTHIANS 13, NIV

2 Corinthians

Author
The apostle Paul.

Audience
The church of Corinth.

Date
c. AD 56–57.

Outline
Opening 1:1-11
Paul's rift with the Corinthians 1:12–2:13
Paul's apostolic ministry 2:14–7:16
Paul's collection effort 8:1–9:15
Paul's ministry defense 10:1-18
Paul speaks as a fool 11:1–12:10
Paul's final warning 12:11–13:14

About 2 Corinthians
1 Corinthians was in fact Paul's second letter to Corinth, making 2 Corinthians his third. The church had received Paul's rebuke in his earlier letters; now they were ready to receive all that their spiritual father had to impart.

Purpose
Paul's letter to the church of Corinth is one of his most personal. He wrote to defend his apostleship against rival "super-apostles"—as he called them—who were threatening the spiritual ground Paul had prepared. He explained how the gospel should impact every aspect of their lives, encouraging them to stay faithful to the truth and love deposited in their hearts.

The Corinthians had not yet fully embraced the scandal of the cross and self-suffering nature of the cross-centered life, so Paul pointed to the glory that lies ahead, encouraging them to keep their eyes on the prize.

Author and audience
Paul wrote this letter to Corinth to bring them comfort, wisdom, and insight. Paul opens his heart in this book, sharing his deep emotions.

Major themes in 2 Corinthians

The incarnation and crucifixion of Christ
Jesus, who knew no sin, became sin for us, "so that we could be made right with God through Christ" (5:21, NLT).

The call of the gospel
The mystery of our being made right with God through the finished work of Christ on the cross. Our motivation is to honor God and love Christ, while persuading people to turn back to God and be made new.

Christian ministry
Paul outlines a theology of pastoral service that should be modeled and adopted by all ministers of the gospel.

Christian life
A powerful call to live a life of holiness.

Christian generosity
A challenge to generous giving.

Galatians

Author
The apostle Paul.

Audience
The church of Galatia.

Date
c. AD 47–48, or early AD 50s.

Outline
Opening 1:1-10
Paul defends his ministry and message 1:11–2:21
Paul defends his theology and gospel 3:1–4:31
Paul applies his message 5:1–6:10
Closing 6:11-18

Purpose
The first converts among the non-Jewish people needed clarity about the Jewishness of the gospel. Was the gospel based on grace or upon keeping the Law of Moses? Galatians answers these questions.

Major themes in Galatians

Grace
How people can become right with God—and not be condemned for their rebellion against him.

The law and legalism
Christ's redemptive work on the cross prevents Jews and non-Jews alike from trying to become right with God through religious works. Through God's grace, we are freed from the religious bondage that comes from laws and rituals.

Freedom and behavior
While Christians are free from the law, we are not free to live as we please. Instead, we are called to use that freedom to produce the fruit of the Spirit.

Jesus Christ
Jesus Christ stands at the center of this letter. He is fully divine and should alone be worshiped.

Descriptions of the church in the Bible

Believers
ACTS 2:44

Body of Christ
1 CORINTHIANS 12:27

Bride
EPHESIANS 5:27

Called
ROMANS 8:30; 1 CORINTHIANS 1:2

Children of light
EPHESIANS 5:8

Chosen people
1 PETER 2:9

Christians
ACTS 11:26

Church
MATTHEW 16:18; 18:17; 1 CORINTHIANS 1:2

Citizens of heaven
PHILIPPIANS 3:20

Disciples
ACTS 6:1; 11:26

God's building, God's field
1 CORINTHIANS 3:9

God's children
JOHN 1:12; ROMANS 8:14-23

God's elect
1 PETER 1:1

God's fellow-workers
1 CORINTHIANS 3:9

God's household
EPHESIANS 2:19

God's temple
1 CORINTHIANS 3:16

Heirs of God
ROMANS 8:17

Holy city
REVELATION 21:10-27

Holy nation
1 PETER 2:9

Israel of God
GALATIANS 6:16

Light of the world
MATTHEW 5:14

Living stones
1 PETER 2:5

People belonging to God
1 PETER 2:9

Pillar and foundation of the truth
1 TIMOTHY 3:15

Royal priesthood
1 PETER 2:9

Sanctified
1 CORINTHIANS 1:2

Saints
EPHESIANS 1:1, 15, 18; 3:18

Salt of the earth
MATTHEW 5:13

Sheep
JOHN 10:3

Soldiers of Christ
2 TIMOTHY 2:3-4

Strangers in the world
1 PETER 1:1

Ephesians

Author
The apostle Paul.

Audience
The church of Ephesus, and churches in the surrounding area.

Date
c. AD 60–62.

Outline
Opening 1:1-2
The church's heavenly calling 1:3–3:21
The church's earthly conduct 4:1–6:20
Closing 6:21-24

About Ephesians
God will one day submit everything to the leadership of Jesus Christ.

Purpose
This is a general, theologically reflective letter, meant to ground, shape, and challenge believers in their faith.

Author
Paul wrote this letter about AD 60, while in a prison cell in Rome.

Major themes in Ephesians

Salvation by grace through faith
God's undeserved favor from beginning to end.

Power of God over all
God's power trumps all other principalities, powers, and authorities in this world.

Christian unity
Jews and non-Jews share unity in Christ. Jesus' work unites all believers in one community.

Christian conduct
Chapters 3—6 focus on how new believers should live, cultivating a lifestyle consistent with their new life in Christ.

Christian identity
Believers are now in Christ. We exist in a personal, energizing relationship of unity with the risen Christ.

The theater, Ephesus.

The fruit of the Spirit

Love
Joy
Peace
Patience
Kindness
Generosity
Faithfulness
Gentleness
Self-control

GALATIANS 5:22

The full armor of God

The belt of truth
The breastplate of righteousness
Shoes of the gospel of peace
The shield of faith
The helmet of salvation
The sword of the Spirit

EPHESIANS 6:10-18

Roman centurion.

Philippians

Author
The apostle Paul.

Audience
The church of Philippi.

Date
c. AD 60–62.

Outline
- Opening 1:1-11
- Paul's gospel priority 1:12-26
- Gospel-living conduct 1:27–2:18
- Examples of gospel living 2:19-30
- Paul's gospel experience, including warnings against legalists and libertines 3:1-21
- Final encouragement 4:1-9
- Closing 4:10-23

Purpose
A letter written to friends.

Author and audience
Written by Paul about AD 60, while Timothy was visiting him in prison, to believers in Philippi. He had concerns about their disunity, suffering, and opponents.

Major themes in Philippians

The joyous gospel of Christ
The words "gospel," "joy," and "gladness" are found frequently in Philippians.

The lordship of Christ
At the heart of this letter is the "Christ Hymn" (2:6–11), which expresses lyrically the story of Jesus from his preexistent glory to the universal praise of him as Lord, paved by his obedience to death on the cross.

The conduct of Christ
Those who believe the gospel are called to live according to the gospel.

The community of Christ—the new people of God
Paul contrasts this new people with those in the old community, who tried to take non-Jewish Christians into Judaism.

Colossians

Author
The apostle Paul.

Audience
The church of Colossae.

Date
c. AD 60–61.

Outline
Opening 1:1-2
Thanksgiving and prayer 1:3-14
The supremacy of Christ 1:15-23
The letter's theme: Christ-centered living 2:6-7
Threats to Christ-centered living 2:8-23
Living a Christ-centered life 3:1–4:6
Closing 4:7-18

Purpose
Paul wrote to equip the Colossian church to fend off false teaching and help them resist false teachers in the community.

Author and audience
Paul had never visited Colossae, but heard of the believers there and began to pray for them.

Major themes in Colossians

The supremacy and centrality of Christ
In reigning supreme, Jesus is seated at God's right hand. As the glorified, risen, King of kings, he reigns over all creation alongside his Father. Jesus is all sufficient for our spiritual life, and should reign supreme at its center.

The body of Christ
Paul presents Christ as the church's ruler. He has authority over her and sustains her. As Christ's body, we are the continuing presence of Christ on the earth.

The true gospel
Paul confronts false teachers, who were adding Jewish legalism, human tradition, and angel worship to the true gospel.

The Christian life
Using the metaphor of the body, Paul teaches that our life as Christians must be rooted in Christ. He is the one who empowers and renews us.

1 Thessalonians

Author
The apostle Paul.

Audience
The church of Thessalonica.

Date
c. AD 50–51.

Outline
Opening 1:1
Thanksgiving for faith 1:2-10
Ministry explained, thanksgiving renewed 2:1–3:13
Call to Christian living 4:1–5:11
Closing 5:12-28

Purpose
To remind believers in Thessalonica what he had previously taught them and reinforce what they already knew.

Author and audience
Sent to the Christian community at Thessalonica, from Paul, Silas, and Timothy.

Major themes in 1 Thessalonians

Faith and the gospel explained and personalized
Paul speaks of the gospel as a power and as the Lord's message. Paul commends the believers' faith and the outworking of it in love and hope.

Living to please God
Paul reminds his readers that, as God's holy, set-apart people, they are called to live in a particular way.

Hopeful preparation for the day of the Lord
Be prepared in hope for the day when Christ returns in full glory. The Lord's return will come unexpectedly and as a complete surprise.

2 Thessalonians

Author
The apostle Paul.

Audience
The church of Thessalonica.

Date
c. AD 51.

Outline
Opening 1:1-2
Thanksgiving and prayer 1:3-12
The day of the Lord 2:1-17
Idle and disruptive believers 3:1-15
Closing 3:16-18

Purpose
Paul wrote to encourage the Thessalonians in three areas: to hold fast to their faith; to live faithfully as they awaited the coming of Jesus in glory; and to confront troublemakers who were burdening and disrupting the church.

Major themes in 2 Thessalonians

Perseverance of faith through persecution
Persecution of these believers had increased, so Paul wanted to encourage them that it would not be in vain.

The promise of God's justice
God had not forgotten them, and would judge their persecutors in the person of Jesus Christ.

Clarification about Christ's coming
Further truth about what we should expect in these last days, as we await the coming of our Lord in full glory.

The lazy, the unruly, and the undisciplined
"Those unwilling to work will not get to eat." (3:10, NLT).

Ancient Thesssalonica.

1 Timothy

Author
The apostle Paul.

Audience
Timothy, Paul's spiritual son in the faith.

Date
c. AD 62–63.

Outline
Opening 1:1-2
Ordering and organizing the church—administration and public worship, Part 1 1:3–3:16
Ordering and organizing the church—dealing with false teaching, and ministering to different groups in the church, Part 2 4:1–6:19
Closing 6:20-21

About
1 and 2 Timothy and Titus are called Pastoral Epistles—letters written by Paul for pastors and leaders, to help them bring order and to ordain pastors for the churches he planted.

Purpose
To reveal and emphasize the glorious truths of God. Good relationships and spiritual growth can only come when the church grows in maturity, and distinguishes truth from error.

Major themes in 1 Timothy

False teachers and doctrine
Paul tells Timothy to confront false teachers, oppose unorthodox doctrines, and maintain his personal faith—and warns against falling away.

Qualifications for church leaders
A helpful list of qualifications for church officers.

The household of God
What it means to live in the household of God. The proper treatment for widows, and expectations for slaves and workers.

2 Timothy

Author
The apostle Paul.

Audience
Timothy.

Date
c. AD 65–67.

Outline
Opening 1:1-2
Thanksgiving for Timothy's faith 1:3-5
Encouragement to Timothy 1:6–2:13
Instructions for Timothy—warnings about foolish controversies and the last days 2:14–4:8
Closing 4:9-22

About 2 Timothy
This could be called the last will and testament of Paul. Writing from prison and awaiting execution, Paul imparts his final words of wisdom to his spiritual son, Timothy.

Author and audience
Written around AD 65, shortly before Paul was martyred on the orders of the Roman Emperor Nero.

Possibly the most personal and heartfelt of Paul's writings.

Major themes in 2 Timothy

False teachers and doctrine
The unorthodox teaching Paul addressed in his first letter was still a problem. He urges Timothy unapologetically to preach the word of truth.

Suffering and perseverance
From a Roman prison, waiting to be executed, Paul urges his gospel coworker to suffer, as he has, for the gospel.

Faithfulness in life and ministry
Paul instructs Timothy to carry out his ministry with dedication, faithfully preaching the apostolic message. He offers his own life as an example of faithfulness to ministry and godliness.

Timeline of Paul's Christian Ministry

All dates are approximate.

AD 34	Converted on the Damascus road.
37	First visit to Jerusalem (GALATIANS 1:18; ACTS 9:26-30). Returns to Tarsus.
47-48	Ministers in Antioch (ACTS 11:25-26).
48	Second visit to Jerusalem (GALATIANS 2:1-10; ACTS 11:30).
49	First missionary journey, to the Galatian churches (ACTS 13–14). Apostolic Council in Jerusalem (ACTS 15).
50	Writes Galatians. Second missionary journey begins (ACTS 15:36). Ministers in Thessalonica, arrives in Corinth (ACTS 18:1).
50-51	Writes 1 and 2 Thessalonians.
50-52	Ministers in Corinth. Returns to Antioch (ACTS 18:22).
53	Starts third missionary journey. Begins ministry in Ephesus (ACTS 18:23–19:1).
54	Writes 1 Corinthians.
54-55	Painful visit to Corinth (2 CORINTHIANS 2:1).
55	Leaves Ephesus. Severe letter to Corinth (2 CORINTHIANS 2:4). Ministers in Troas and Macedonia. Writes 2 Corinthians. Arrives in Corinth for the winter (ACTS 20:3).
56	Writes to Rome from Corinth. Travels to Jerusalem. Riot, arrest, and hearing before Felix (ACTS 20–24).
56-58	In prison without trial in Caesarea (ACTS 24:27).
58	Hearings before Festus and Agrippa (ACTS 25–26). Sea journey and shipwreck on Malta (ACTS 27:1–28:10).
59	Arrives in Rome.
59-61	Under house arrest in Rome (ACTS 28:30). Writes Philippians, Ephesians, Colossians, and Philemon.
61	Possibly charges dropped and released.
61-64	Ministers again, possibly in Spain (ROMANS 15:24), Asia Minor (PHILEMON 22; 2 TIMOTHY 4:13), Crete (TITUS 1:5), Corinth (2 TIMOTHY 4:20), Ephesus, and Macedonia (1 TIMOTHY 1:3; 2 TIMOTHY 1:18). Writes 1 Timothy and Titus.
64-65	Re-arrested. Writes 2 Timothy. Tried, and executed in Rome (2 TIMOTHY 4:6, 16).

Roman merchant ship.

Paul the tentmaker

Paul was a tentmaker by trade. He worked in Corinth with his friends Priscilla and Aquila.

In Bible times tents were made from cloth or leather. Fabric woven from goat's hair was common in the desert; wool or leather elsewhere.

Leather for tents had to be tanned by soaking the skins, scraping off the animal hairs, soaking a second time to tighten the skins, then dried. The finished pieces of leather were then trimmed, cut into the shape needed, and holes punched so they could be easily sewn together.

Titus

Author
The apostle Paul.

Audience
Titus, Paul's "true son."

Date
c. AD 57, or possibly c. AD 62–63.

Outline
Opening 1:1-4
Instructions to Titus concerning elders and false teachers 1:5-16
Instructions for godly living 2:1–3:11
Closing 3:12-15

About Titus
Titus is one of three letters known as the Pastoral Epistles, which also include 1 and 2 Timothy. Paul wrote as an older apostle to younger colleagues, to encourage their ministries.

Purpose
Paul wrote to Titus to give instructions for building churches and raising up leaders.

Author and audience
Paul's letter to Titus is deeply personal, from an older, wiser, seasoned apostle to a younger, inexperienced minister.

Major themes in Titus

Faith and salvation in Jesus Christ
Paul calls on Titus to appoint godly leaders and offers a summary of Christian beliefs. He reminds them of the grace manifested in Jesus and the salvation he brought for all.

Appointing church leaders
Appoint church leaders who are blameless, setting an example for the rest of the community of believers. They are also to grasp firmly the gospel message, to teach other believers the truths of the faith.

Right living for the sake of the gospel.
Right living and right believing go hand in hand. When we believe the gospel, and experience the joys of salvation, how can we live other than in light of this mercy?

Philemon

Author
The apostle Paul.

Audience
Philemon, a slave owner.

Date
c. AD 60-61.

Outline
Opening 1-3
Paul's appreciation of Philemon 4-7
Paul's appeal on behalf of Onesimus 8-21
Closing 22-25

Author and audience
Paul's letter to Philemon is written to reconcile two brothers in Christ. Philemon, one of Paul's co-workers in ministry, owned a slave named Onesimus, who stole from him and ran away. Paul led him to the Lord. Paul sent the runaway back to Philemon with this letter, asking his former master to restore Onesimus as a fellow believer.

Major themes in Philemon

Christian belonging in a common faith
When people commit themselves to Christ, they also commit themselves to a community.

The love of Christ performed
Paul wanted Philemon to respond to Onesimus in forgiveness and restoration just as Christ has responded to us. Love forgives, restores, covers sin, and heals broken relationships.

Slavery and brotherhood
This letter seems to be less about slavery and more about the relationship between a slave and his master—now brothers in the Lord—both of whom Paul wants to experience forgiving love.

Hebrews

Author
Unknown; possibly Paul, Barnabas, Apollos, or Priscilla.

Audience
Christians converted from Judaism.

Date
c. AD 50–64.

Outline

Prologue 1:1-3

Jesus' superiority over angels and Moses 1:4–4:13

Jesus' superior priesthood 4:14–7:28

Jesus' superior sacrifice and covenant 8:1–10:18

A call to persevere 10:19–12:29

Roll call of the faithful saints 11:1-40

Final instructions and greetings 13:1-25

Purpose
To prevent readers abandoning their Christian faith and returning to Judaism. The author teaches that Christ is superior to the religious institutions of Moses and the Old Testament. The letter is full of references to the sacrificial system and priesthood of ancient Israel, and explains how Jesus' death has replaced this old religious system.

Author and audience
Hebrews seems to be a sermon contained in a letter. Likely the author is addressing Christians converted from Judaism.

Noah.

Major themes in Hebrews

Christology—the study of Christ, the Messiah

Jesus is our High Priest, greater than Moses, greater than any sacrifice ever offered, greater than any prophet of old.

The reality of heaven

To be in heaven means to be in God's very presence, the place where our ultimate redemption and atonement took place. The old religious order of rules and rituals is no longer necessary because of the final sacrifice made for all people.

Definition and practice of faith

Biblical faith claims a confidence beyond our own because it rests in the character of God, the foundation of our faith. Part of practicing faith is persevering in it. Hebrews warns against turning away in rebellion and unbelief; the divine message that saved us will condemn us if we turn away.

Moses with the Ten Commandments.

Faithful Old Testament Saints

Hebrews 11

People who willingly took God at his word, even when there was nothing to cling to apart from his promise.

Abel
GENESIS 4

Enoch
GENESIS 5

Noah
GENESIS 6

Abraham
GENESIS 12

Isaac
GENESIS 27

Jacob
GENESIS 48

Joseph
GENESIS 50

Moses' parents
EXODUS 2

Moses
EXODUS 2

Rahab
JOSHUA 2; 6

Gideon, Barak, Samson, and Jephthah
JUDGES 4; 6; 11; 13; 15

David, Samuel, and the prophets

James

Author
James, brother of Jesus.

Audience
Jewish Christians.

Date
c. AD 45–47 Difficult to date with any precision.

Outline
Greeting 1:1
Introducing the three themes: wealth, wisdom, trials 1:2–27
Theme 1: Riches and poverty 2:1–26
Theme 2: Wisdom and speech 3:1–4:12
Theme 3: Trials and temptation 4:13–5:18
Closing 5:19–20

About James
The book of James and the book of Galatians are considered the first letters penned by the apostles, most likely between AD 45–47. These are the earliest insights of the first generation of followers of Jesus, mostly Jews.

Author and audience
Aimed at Christians who converted from Judaism, scattered throughout the Roman Empire.

Who was James?

He was Jesus' younger brother.
He refused to believe in Jesus during his lifetime (JOHN 7:5).
He believed after the risen Christ appeared to him (1 CORINTHIANS 15:7).
He became leader of the Jerusalem church (ACTS 12:17; 15:13).
He was known as 'James the Just.'
He was executed by the high priest Ananus in AD 62.

Major themes in James

Wisdom from above
James could be considered a wisdom sermon: the style of the letter is similar to Proverbs. Wisdom is necessary for trying circumstances; it involves insight into God's purposes and leads to spiritual maturity. God is the source of all true wisdom.

Testing and trials
A guide for those whose faith in God is being threatened by daily struggles and hardship—ranging from religious persecution to financial difficulties, from health problems to spiritual oppression.

The law of Moses
The law is relevant to Christian living, not as legalistic rules and rituals, but as love of neighbor and God.

Faith and good deeds
Faith that doesn't involve action is phony: faith that saves is a faith that works.

Poverty and wealth
James tells poor believers they have been blessed with every privilege from God, although society may dismiss them; and warns against favoritism in the church, especially based on the size of one's pocketbook or brand of clothes.

1 Peter

Author
The apostle Peter.

Audience
Churches in northwestern Asia Minor, modern-day Turkey.

Date
c. AD 62–64.

Outline
Opening 1:1-2
Identity as God's chosen people and foreigners 1:3–2:10
Living honorably as foreigners 2:11–3:12
Responding to hostility as foreigners 3:13–4:6
Living in Christian solidarity as foreigners 4:7-19
Suffering together as foreigners 5:1-11
Closing 5:12-14

About 1 Peter
Peter was the first preacher to bring the gospel of Christ to the Jews in Jerusalem.
Peter's letters—part of the General Epistles—are written to strengthen us in our faith.

Purpose
The community of Christ is a holy nation, made up of kings and priests and lovers of God. This is a letter about God and living for him—no matter what the cost, which was primarily persecution.

Author and audience
Written c. AD 62 from "Babylon," a cryptic term for Rome. Peter longed to encourage and strengthen the faith of those persecuted for following Christ.

Major themes in 1 Peter

God the Father, God the Son, God the Holy Spirit
Who God is and what God is like. He is called Father God, the mighty and powerful Creator and Judge, and our merciful and gracious Redeemer. Peter describes Jesus as the "Anointed One," a Hebrew concept for the Messiah; and emphasizes the Holy Spirit, who has set us apart to be God's holy ones.

The nature of our salvation
Peter explains that our salvation is to be reborn into a new family.

Holding fast to our faith in God in the midst of suffering
Peter exhorts his readers not to be surprised at being persecuted as Christians, but to follow the example of Christ, who also suffered; and learn to rejoice in that suffering, as followers of Jesus.

Life in God's family as a spiritual nation
The inevitable outgrowth of our salvation and new birth in Christ is a new way of living, in concert with our new family and a spiritual nation. We are to practice hope and holiness, fear of God, and growth in the knowledge of God, because we have been bought by the blood of Jesus.

Names of the devil

Abaddon, "angel of the bottomless pit"
REVELATION 9:11

adversary
1 PETER 5:8

angel of light
2 CORINTHIANS 11:14

Apollyon
REVELATION 9:11

Beelzebub, prince of the devils
MATTHEW 12:24

Belial
2 CORINTHIANS 6:15

dragon—with seven heads, ten horns, and seven crowns
REVELATION 12:3, 7, 9

evil one
JOHN 17:15

father of lies
JOHN 8:44

god of this world
2 CORINTHIANS 4:4

Lucifer
ISAIAH 14:12

old serpent
REVELATION 12:9; 20:2

prince of the power of the air
EPHESIANS 2:2

prince of this world
JOHN 12:31; 14:30

Satan
JOB 1:6

Tempter
1 THESSALONIANS 3:5

2 Peter

Author
The apostle Peter.

Audience
Churches in northwestern Asia Minor, modern-day Turkey.

Date
c. AD 64–66.

Outline
- Opening 1:1-11
- Peter's reason for writing 1:12-15
- Issue 1: The power and appearing of our Lord 1:16-18
- Issue 2: The reliable and valid prophetic message 1:19-21
- Issue 3: False teachers and their sure destruction 2:1-22
- Issue 4: The certainty of Christ's return—be it delayed—and the destruction unleashed on the Lord's Day 3:1-13
- Closing 3:14-18

Purpose
Peter writes as one facing imminent death, motivated by the false teachings beginning to threaten the health of the churches. But truth will triumph every time—especially when we speak the truth in love.

Major themes in 2 Peter

God the Father, God the Son, God the Holy Spirit
Jesus "our God and Savior" (1:1); "our Lord" (1:2); "our Lord and Savior," and "Christ" (1:11). He is also described as our "sovereign Lord" (2:1). He is the God-Savior, anointed by the Father, who reigns as supreme Lord.

Entrapped humanity and divine deliverance
Humanity is entrapped by corrupt desires, and God's goodness has opened a way to escape this corruption, through deliverance.

Living in light of the end
Ethics (how we live) and eschatology (the end of the world) are intimately connected. We are called to live in the last days in light of the end, the coming day of God.

False teachers and false teaching
Guard against false teachers who slip into the churches. Right teachings are vital to the ongoing purity of the church and our individual godly lives.

Some names for the Holy Spirit

Counselor JOHN 14:16	**Spirit of God** GENESIS 1:2
Eternal Spirit HEBREWS 9:14	**Spirit of his [God's] Son** GALATIANS 4:6
Holy Spirit LUKE 11:13	**Spirit of holiness** ROMANS 1:4
Power of the Most High LUKE 1:35	**Spirit of the Lord** JUDGES 3:10
Spirit ROMANS 8:26-27	**Spirit of sonship** ROMANS 8:15
Spirit of Christ ROMANS 8:9	**Spirit of truth** JOHN 14:17

Fire in Scripture

Fire is a sign God is present. God spoke to Moses from the burning bush in the desert (EXODUS 3:2); by night, a column of fire led Israel through the desert (EXODUS 13:21–22); God appeared to Moses and the people in fire on Mount Sinai (EXODUS 19:18; 24:17–18). In the New Testament, the coming of the Holy Spirit on the day of Pentecost (ACTS 2:1–4) is described as "cloven tongues like as of fire." When John has a vision of Jesus in Revelation 1:14–15 his eyes "were as a flame of fire" and his feet glowed "as if they burned in a furnace."

Fire was important in worship in the Temple. The flame on the altar reminded the people that God was always present (LEVITICUS 6:12–13).

God would use fire to punish the wicked. For example, in the destruction of Sodom and Gomorrah (GENESIS 19:24–25). Fire is a sign of God's anger (PSALM 79:5; 89:46), and God will use it to punish sin and evil in the future (DEUTERONOMY 32:22; ISAIAH 50:10–11; AMOS 7:4). Evil powers will be destroyed by fire at the end of the age (DANIEL 7:11, MALACHI 4:1). Jesus said that the fire of judgment will fall on the earth and its wicked people (MATTHEW 3:11–12; 13:37–42; LUKE 17:29–30). God's final judgment of the evil world includes punishment by fire (2 PETER 3:7), as pictured in Revelation 8:7; 9:18; 14:9–10; 20:9–15.

God uses fire to purify his people. Often this testing is experienced in facing the trials of life (PSALM 66:12; 1 PETER 1:7). God's future judgment will purify his people by fire (ZECHARIAH 13:9; 1 CORINTHIANS 3:12–15).

1 John

Author
The apostle John.

Audience
Communities in Asia Minor experiencing schism.

Date
c. AD 85.

Outline
Opening 1:1-4
Walk in God's light, keep God's commands 1:5–2:11
New status, new love 2:12-17
Believing and living as God's children 2:18–3:24
Test the spirits 4:1-6
Love for one another, love for God 4:7–5:12
Closing 5:13-21

Purpose
To bring the churches back into unity and clarity of faith, and encourage them to hold fast to the tradition and values they had committed themselves to in Christ. John's teachings take us deeper into the truth and ways of God, and love for Jesus Christ.

Author and audience
There is little doubt the apostle John wrote this letter, probably while he was in Ephesus.

Roman lamp.

Major themes in 1 John

Preserving and discerning truth

John was writing to a community troubled by false teachers who distorted the truth of the gospel. The good news is about the one who was the Truth. It is the task of the church to test the spirits, to "test them to see if the spirit they have comes from God" (4:1, NLT).

Warning against antichrists

John warns of antichrists—people who oppose the teachings of Christ, lead people astray, and separate from the true community of Christ's followers.

The character of God

God is pure light; faithfully forgives our sins; the essence of love; the reality of all that is true; and the Father who saves, having sent his Son into the world as its Savior.

The centrality of Christ

Only when we properly understand who Jesus Christ is can we experience the heart of God.

Walking as disciples of Christ

We are to walk in the pure light, not the realm of darkness; we are to walk in self-sacrificing love, not hate.

2 John

Author
The apostle John.

Audience
Communities in Asia Minor experiencing schism.

Date
c. AD 85-90.

Outline
Opening 1-3
Call to walk in truth and love 4-6
Warning against false teachers 7-11
Closing 12-13

Purpose
As with his first letter, John wrote to guard and protect believers from the false teachers. 2 John points us to the truth, and encourages us to hold it fast and never let it go.

Major themes in 2 John

Walking and staying in the truth

Actively walk in the truth and stay in the truth.

Loving one another

Loving one another means following the commands of Christ.

Warning about false teachers

Watch out for antichrists—do not even show them hospitality.

3 John

Author
The apostle John.

Audience
Gaius, a friend of John.

Date
c. AD 85–90.

Outline
Opening 1-4
Call to show hospitality 5-8
An example of inhospitality 9-11
Closing 12-15

About 3 John
The smallest of the New Testament letters. John commends hospitality as a way of expressing Christian love.

Purpose
John's third letter was a general letter, sent to churches throughout Asia Minor (modern Turkey). It carries John's trademarks of showing love and grace to all.

Major themes in 3 John

Walking in the truth
Such walking is a joyful experience for those who are spiritually responsible for others, and for believers, whose souls progress in spiritual health as they maintain their commitment to Jesus.

Christian hospitality
Christian commitment to truth means a commitment to love and support.

Divisions in the body
A major toxin to the body of Christ is division, caused by pride, inhospitality, gossip, slander, malice, and obstruction.

Doing and imitating good
Goodness reflects God's good character and good acts, built on his inspiring love.

Jude

Author
The apostle Jude, half-brother of Jesus.

Audience
Eastern Mediterranean Christians—and all God's lovers.

Date
c. AD 58–60. This letter is difficult to date with any precision.

Outline
Opening 1-2
Reason for writing 3
Arguments against the false teachers 4-16
Call to persevere 17-23
Closing 24-25

Purpose
Intruders had sown the seeds of false teaching among the believers, creating chaos and confusion. Jude urged them to persevere, contend for, struggle for, and defend the truth.

Major themes in Jude

Defend and contend for the faith
We need to struggle as in a great contest, exerting great efforts to promote the noble cause of the gospel's advance—while defending our core beliefs from the threat of false teachers.

Live the faith
False teachers had sneaked into the churches. Believers must live their faith through discipleship, prayer, remaining in God's love, accepting Christ's mercy, being compassionate, evangelistic, and discerning.

The character of God
God keeps us from sin, revealing us as faultless; is heralded as Savior; and possesses endless glory and majesty, power and authority.

Coming salvation and judgment
Along with his salvation, the Lord will bring down judgment upon all the ungodly.

The Seven Churches of Revelation

Ephesus

An ancient city with a population of up to 500,000, situated on a major trade route, and the leading port of Asia Minor in New Testament times. The city was renowned for the worship of Diana (Artemis), whose priestesses acted as cult prostitutes. The great theater of Ephesus, the remains of which still stand, held as many as 25,000 people.

REVELATION 2:1-7

Smyrna

Smyrna—modern Izmir—was a harbor city with a population of around 200,000 in New Testament times. It was famed for its "street of gold," with a temple at each end.

REVELATION 2:8-11

Pergamum

Pergamum housed the second largest library in the Roman Empire, and was famous for its parchment. Home to the Asclepion, where a healing cult was practiced, and to a great altar of Zeus.

REVELATION 2:12-17

Thyatira

Located on an imperial post road, the city had many trade guilds.

REVELATION 2:18-29

Sardis

Destroyed by a great earthquake in AD 17, but rebuilt by the Emperor Tiberius.

REVELATION 3:1-6

Philadelphia

Destroyed by the earthquake of AD 17 and rebuilt by Tiberius. A fortress city on an imperial post road, it was a significant educational center.

REVELATION 3:7-13

Laodicea

Suffered two earthquakes during the New Testament period. World-famous for its strong, red dye, its special eye ointment, and as a banking center.

REVELATION 3:14-22

Revelation

Author
The apostle John.

Audience
Most likely, this letter was addressed to the seven churches mentioned in the opening three chapters of the book. But it also certainly has an application and relevance for every church and believer in every age.

Date
c. AD 64-68, or c. AD 92-95.

Outline
Opening 1:1-20
Christ's letters to the churches 2:1–3:22
John's vision of God's throne room 4:1–5:14
The Lamb opens the sealed scrolls 6:1–8:5
Seven angels sound the trumpets 8:6–11:19
God fights the forces of evil 12:1–15:4
Seven angels bring the seven last plagues—the seven bowls 15:5–16:21
Judgment and destruction, rejoicing and reign 17:1–20:15
A new heaven, a new earth, the new Jerusalem 21:1–22:5
Conclusion 22:6-21

Purpose
This is the Book of Revelation, not the book of revelations. There is one revelation: Christ unveiled to his people.

Author and audience
Possibly written between AD 64-68 under the Emperor Nero, and during his persecution; or maybe AD 92-95, under the Emperor Domitian, who also tried to destroy the church.

Ruins of Laodicea.

Major themes in Revelation

Jesus Christ unveiled
In Revelation we view Jesus as the ascended, glorified Son of God, unveiled before our eyes as Prophet, Priest, and King of kings. As the Prophet, Jesus is the Faithful Witness who speaks only the Father's words. As the High Priest, Jesus is the Firstborn from the dead, who intercedes for us and releases mighty power to us. And as King, Jesus is the Ruler of the kings of the earth.

Jesus' church unveiled
Christ's letter to the churches imparts important truths to every believer, showing the church as God's dwelling place. As Jesus' lovely bride, our reign with him has already begun when we are commissioned to do greater works of Jesus, and spread his glory throughout the earth.

Judgment and destruction of the old order
From the opening of the first of the seven seals, many have understood the truth unveiled in this book as the earth's destruction. Yet it must also be taken symbolically. The old order of the natural realm is passing away and a new order established.

The anger and wrath of the Lamb is corrective and redemptive—not beastly rage, but fiery passion to judge whatever gets between the Lamb and his bride. But, in the end, the world will experience a final judgment—where everything and everyone destructive to God's wonderful world will be cast into the lake of fire.

Divine rescue and renewal: The victory of the Lamb
The end of the world is ultimately about rescue and renewal, for the Lamb of God has won. Though we have to pass through tribulation to enter the kingdom of God, we do so through the blood of Christ, knowing our victory is sure.

One of the characteristics of prophetic apocalyptic writing is the call to persevere. Endurance and faithfulness, conquering and obedience are hallmarks of Revelation.

Jesus is the bright Morning Star, who signals the end of night and the beginning of God's perfect day, the beginning of God's brand new order of righteousness, peace, and pure love.

Interpreting Revelation

Revelation is rooted in the symbolism of the Old Testament, and is full of allusions to the prophetic writings of Scripture. Christians have interpreted and understood Revelation in four different ways: preterist, futurist, historicist, and idealist.

1. Preterist re-viewing of history
This view suggests that most of the book was fulfilled early in the church's history, and many of the symbols relate to events of the first century. Those who hold this view believe Revelation is about faithfulness to God in the face of pagan persecution, and offers hope for God's ultimate, eventual victory.

2. Futurist pre-viewing of history
This view interprets the events as largely happening in the future. The symbols are pointers to the end of the world, previewing what will take place leading up to the return of Christ.

3. Historicist identifying of history
This approach sees Revelation as identifying major movements of church history. Some people also think current events fulfil New Testament apocalyptic symbolism, for instance identifying the Beast with dictators through history, such as Napoleon or Hitler. The seals, trumpets, bowls, and plagues are identified as successive events, with the hope of Christ's return being very near.

4. Idealist symbolizing of history
This interpretation finds significance for the church between Christ's first and second coming in the symbols embedded throughout Revelation. These symbols offer believers in every age spiritual truths unrelated to specific historical events. Revelation is concerned with the battle between good and evil, and between the church and the world, at all periods in Christian history, depicting the continuous victory of believers and Christ.

The Four Horsemen of the Apocalypse

REVELATION 6:1–8

First horseman: Pestilence
On a white horse, with a bow, went forth conquering, and to conquer.

Second horseman: War
On a red horse, with a large sword, had power to take peace from the earth.

Third horseman: Famine
On a black horse. He holds a pair of scales, and is traditionally named famine.

Fourth horseman: Death
On a pale horse. Death and hell are given power to kill with sword, with hunger, with death, and with the beasts of the earth.

"The Four Riders of the Apocalypse" by Dürer.

Millennialisms

Christians hold many differing views about the millennium. The word "millennium" derives from the Latin for "one thousand years," a period mentioned in Revelation 20. Millennial views vary according to how Christ's return—second coming, or second advent—is related to this thousand-year period.

Premillennialism

In this interpretation, Christ returns to inaugurate his kingdom before the millennium. Most premillennialists expect a seven-year period of "tribulation"—cataclysmic events—preceding his appearance. There are subcategories of premillennialism, based on the timing of the "rapture," or "catching up," of Christians, suggested in 1 Thessalonians 4:17:

a. Pre-tribulationalism—the church is raptured before the tribulation
b. Post-tribulationalism—the church is raptured after the tribulation
c. Mid-tribulationism—the church is raptured during the tribulation

Postmillennialism

According to this view, the millennium is a period of righteousness, peace, and blessing brought about by the advance of the gospel and the increasing influence of God's kingdom. At the end of the millennium, Christ will return for the general resurrection and judgment.

Amillennialism

In this interpretation, the millennium is a symbolic concept describing the present rule of Christ in the church. The "last days" began with Jesus's resurrection and ascension, and the "tribulation" refers to the events of the first century AD which led to the destruction of Jerusalem and Herod's temple. Christ will return for judgment after his present reign, and believers enter the kingdom through new life in Christ now and at their death.

New Testament Apocrypha

A number of books known as "New Testament apocrypha," dating from the second century AD to the Middle Ages, were not accepted as Scripture. Some are in the form of gospels, some letters, some Acts, and some apocalypses. The apocryphal gospels focus on alternative parts of Jesus' life—for instance his infancy—and show little interest in his adult ministry. Some are bizarre or offensive, some heretical, and some contain "secret knowledge." Although the apocryphal New Testament books may contain some words of Jesus, it is almost impossible to distinguish them from the worthless material.

Examples of New Testament apocrypha include:

Gospel of Hebrews: which records Jesus' resurrection appearance to James.

Gospel of Peter: which adds miracles to the accounts of the death and resurrection of Jesus.

Gospel of Thomas: which has many sayings similar to the Synoptic Gospels, but with a heretical, Gnostic flavor.

Acts of Peter: which tells how Peter defeated Simon Magus (ACTS 8) and how Paul founded the Roman church.

Stained glass depiction of Christ's second coming.

Some important Church Fathers

Polycarp (AD 69-156), Bishop of Smyrna
During persecution by the Roman Emperor, Polycarp was brought before the provincial governor. When offered freedom if he cursed Christ, he replied "Eighty-six years have I served Christ and he has done me nothing but good; how could I curse him, my Lord and Savior?" He was burned alive.

Ignatius (AD 67-110), Bishop of Antioch
The Emperor Trajan sentenced him to be thrown to wild beasts at Rome. On his way to Rome, he wrote to the Roman Christians, begging them not to try to gain a pardon for him because he longed to die for his Lord.

Justin Martyr (AD 100-167)
Justin traveled as a philosopher, seeking to win people to Christ. He wrote a Defense of Christianity addressed to the Emperor, and died a martyr in Rome.

Irenaeus (AD 130-200), Bishop of Lyons
Noted for his books against the Gnostic heretics. He died a martyr.

Origen (AD 185-254)
Possibly the most learned man of the ancient church. Two-thirds of the New Testament is quoted in his writings. He died as a result of imprisonment and torture under the Emperor Decius.

Tertullian of Carthage (AD 160-220), "The father of Latin Christianity"
A Roman lawyer, after conversion he became a distinguished defender of Christianity.

Eusebius (AD 264-340), Bishop of Caesarea
He wrote an Ecclesiastical History, covering the period from Christ to the Council of Nicaea.

John Chrysostom (AD 345-407), "Golden-mouthed"
The greatest preacher of his day, he became Patriarch of Constantinople. He was banished and died in exile.

Jerome (AD 340-420), "Most learned of the Latin Fathers"
He lived many years in Bethlehem and translated the Bible into the Latin language, becoming known as the Vulgate.

Augustine (AD 354-430), Bishop of Hippo, North Africa
The great theologian of the early church. More than any other, he molded the doctrines of the church of the Middle Ages.

Jerome.

The Church Fathers

What is a "Church Father"?
To be considered a Father of the Church, a candidate had to meet four requirements:

1. Lived before the eighth century AD
2. Be orthodox in doctrine
3. Lived a holy life
4. Be approved by the church

Ecumenical Councils of the church

Nicaea (AD 325)
Condemned Arianism.

Constantinople (AD 381)
Called to settle Apollinarianism.

Ephesus (AD 431)
Called to settle the Nestorian Controversy.

Chalcedon (451)
Called to settle the Eutychian Controversy.

Constantinople II (553)
Called to settle the Monophysite Controversy.

Constantinople III (680)
Defined the doctrine of Two Wills in Christ.

Nicaea II (787)
Sanctioned the use of ikons.

Constantinople (869)
Final schism between East and West.

Rome (1123)
Decided bishops should be appointed by the pope.

Rome (1139)
An effort to heal schism between East and West.

Rome (1179)
Called to enforce ecclesiastical discipline.

Rome (1215)
Called to carry out the will of Pope Innocent III.

Lyons (1245)
Called to settle quarrel between pope and Emperor.

Lyons (1274)
An effort to unite the church in the East and West.

Vienne (1311)
Suppressed the Knights Templar.

Constance (1414-18)
Called to heal papal schism.

Basel (1431-49)
Called to reform the church.

Rome (1512-18)
Another effort to reform the church.

Trent (1545-63)
Called to respond to the Reformation.

Vatican (1869-70)
Declared the infallibility of the pope.

Vatican II (1962-65)
Attempt to reform the church.

Essential Bible Manuscripts

There are more copies of the New Testament than of any other document in ancient history.

We possess more than 6,000 manuscript copies of either the entire Greek New Testament or parts of it. By contrast, we have only about 650 manuscript copies of Homer's *Iliad*, and these date from AD 200 to 300, more than a thousand years after it was composed. There are just nine good extant copies of Caesar's *Gallic Wars* and 8 manuscripts of Herodotus' *History*.

The three oldest and most important extant Greek manuscripts of the Bible are:

Codex Vaticanus
Dating to c. AD 350, this manuscript contains the entire Bible and Septuagint, except Genesis 1—46, Psalms 105—137, and the New Testament after Hebrews 9:14.
HOUSED IN THE VATICAN LIBRARY, ROME.

Codex Sinaiticus
Dating to early in the fourth century, this manuscript—discovered in the nineteenth century at St. Catherine's Monastery, Sinai—contains the entire New Testament except 24 verses and 145 leaves of the Septuagint—roughly half the Old Testament.
HOUSED IN THE BRITISH LIBRARY, LONDON.

Codex Alexandrinus
Dating to the early fifth century, this contains the entire New Testament, except 34 chapters (mainly Matthew), and the entire Septuagint, except 10 leaves.
HOUSED IN THE BRITISH LIBRARY, LONDON.

Popular English translations of the Bible

Amplified Bible
Includes alternate (amplified) readings in brackets to help the reader understand the text. First published in 1965.

Authorized Version (AV)
See King James Version.

Christian Standard Bible (CSB)
Balances accuracy and readability. Popular for its contemporary language and theological faithfulness. First published in 2017 as revision of Holman Christian Standard Bible.

Douai-Rheims Bible
Roman Catholic translation produced in the early seventeenth century. Mostly translated from the Latin Vulgate. Until the 1970s, the standard English translation of the Bible for the Roman Catholic Church.

English Standard Version (ESV)
A modern English translation, first published in 2001 by Crossway.

Good News Bible (GNB)
See Today's English Version.

Jerusalem Bible (JB)
Roman Catholic translation, first published in 1966.

King James Version (KJV)
Until recently, the King James Version was the most widely used English translation of the Bible. First published in 1611, and authorized by King James I, its language greatly influenced spoken English and English literature.

The Living Bible (TLB)
A thought-for-thought translation of the Bible, widely used since its first publication in 1971.

New American Bible (NAB)
Sometimes called the Confraternity Bible, first published in 1970, it is the translation mostly used by Catholics.

New American Standard Bible (NASB)
First published in 1971, popular as an accurate word-for-word translation.

New English Bible (NEB)
A thought-for-thought translation published in 1970. More popular in the United Kingdom than the United States.

New International Version (NIV)
Popular since first publication in 1978. It has surpassed the King James Version as the most widely-used English translation of the Bible.

New Jerusalem Bible (NJB)
Revision of the Jerusalem Bible, first published in 1985.

New King James Version (NKJV)
A popular revision of the King James Version, first published in 1982. Many difficult and archaic words have been updated; "thee" and "thou" replaced with "you" etc.

New Living Translation (NLT)
Complete revision of the Living Bible, first published in 1996.

New Revised Standard Version (NRSV)
See: Revised Standard Version.

Revised English Bible (REB)
Revision of the New English Bible, first published in 1989.

Revised Standard Version (RSV)
Used by many mainstream denominations. First published in 1952. In 1990 a revised edition, the New Revised Standard Version (NRSV) was published.

The Passion Translation
Reintroduces the passion of the Bible to the English reader. First published in 2017.

Today's English Version (TEV)
Published by the American Bible Society, popular since first publication in 1976. It uses simple English and is a thought-for-thought translation. Also called the "Good News Bible."

Some key Bible passages

The creation story
GENESIS 1:1–2:7

The fall
GENESIS 3:1-24

The flood and the covenant with Noah
GENESIS 6:1–9:17

The call of Abraham and the divine covenant made with him
GENESIS 12:1-9

The Mosaic Law Covenant revealed at Sinai, including the Ten Commandments
EXODUS 19–24

The Ten Commandments
EXODUS 20:1-17

The Davidic Covenant, the promise of a new temple and an eternal kingdom
2 SAMUEL 7

The shepherd's psalm
PSALM 23

God is my refuge
PSALM 91

The birth of Jesus
MATTHEW 1:18–2:23; LUKE 1:26–2:40

The golden rule
LUKE 6:31

The Sermon on the Mount
MATTHEW 5–7

The Beatitudes
MATTHEW 5:3-11

The Lord's Prayer
LUKE 11:2-4

The Prodigal Son
LUKE 15:11-32

The Good Samaritan
LUKE 10:29-37

The Last Supper
MATTHEW 26:17-30; MARK 14:12-26

The death of Christ
LUKE 23:26-56; JOHN 19:16-42

Christ, the Eternal Word
JOHN 1:1-8

God so loved the world
JOHN 3:1-21

Jesus, the Way to the Father
JOHN 14:1-14

Jesus, the True Vine
JOHN 15:1-17

The resurrection of Christ
MATTHEW 28; LUKE 24; JOHN 20

The ascension of Christ
ACTS 1:1-12

The coming of the Holy Spirit
ACTS 2:1-21

The conversion of Paul
ACTS 9:1-31

Life in the Spirit
ROMANS 8:1-17

The love chapter
1 CORINTHIANS 13

Children of Light
EPHESIANS 4:17-24

Faith and endurance
JAMES 1:2-18

The faith chapter
HEBREWS 11

Some model prayers in the Bible

A blessing
NUMBERS 6:24-26

A doxology praising God
JUDE 24-25

Confession
PSALM 32; PSALM 51; EZRA 9:5-15

Dedication
2 CHRONICLES 6:14-42

Dependence
2 CHRONICLES 20:6-12

Despair
PSALM 73

For believers
EPHESIANS 1:16-23; EPHESIANS 3:14-21

For blessing
PSALM 90

For deliverance
ISAIAH 37:14-20

For guidance
PSALM 25:4-5

For healing
ISAIAH 38:3, 9-20

For hope
PSALM 42:5-6

For love and discernment
PHILIPPIANS 1:9-11

For restoration
DANIEL 9:4-19

For salvation
JONAH 2:2-9

For spiritual wisdom
COLOSSIANS 1:9-12

For strength and fullness
EPHESIANS 3:14-21

For unity
JOHN 17

For wisdom
1 KINGS 3:3-9

Intercession
GENESIS 18:16-33; EXODUS 32:11-13

National crisis
2 KINGS 19:14-19

Petition
ACTS 4:24-30

Praise
LUKE 1:46-55

Praising God
1 SAMUEL 2:1-10

Recommitment
JONAH 2:2-9

Thanksgiving
1 SAMUEL 2:1-10; PSALMS 16; 65

The Lord's Prayer
MATTHEW 6:9-13; LUKE 11:2-4

Trust
PSALM 23

When wickedness prospers
PSALM 37:1-4

Bible reading plan

This plan will take you through the entire Bible in one year, reading part of the Old and New Testament daily.

January

1.	Luke 5:27-39; Genesis 1–2; Psalm 1
2.	Luke 6:1-26; Genesis 3–5; Psalm 2
3.	Luke 6:27-49; Genesis 6–7; Psalm 3
4.	Luke 7:1-17; Genesis 8–10; Psalm 4
5.	Luke 7:18-50; Genesis 11; Psalm 5
6.	Luke 8:1-25; Genesis 12; Psalm 6
7.	Luke 8:26-56; Genesis 13–14; Psalm 7
8.	Luke 9:1-27; Genesis 15; Psalm 8
9.	Luke 9:28-62; Genesis 16; Psalm 9
10.	Luke 10:1-20; Genesis 17; Psalm 10
11.	Luke 10:21-42; Genesis 18; Psalm 11
12.	Luke 11:1-28; Genesis 19; Psalm 12
13.	Luke 11:29-54; Genesis 20; Psalm 13
14.	Luke 12:1-31; Genesis 21; Psalm 14
15.	Luke 12:32-59; Genesis 22; Psalm 15
16.	Luke 13:1-17; Genesis 23; Psalm 16
17.	Luke 13:18-35; Genesis 24; Psalm 17
18.	Luke 14:1-24; Genesis 25; Psalm 18
19.	Luke 14:25-35; Genesis 26; Psalm 19
20.	Luke 15; Genesis 27:1-45; Psalm 20
21.	Luke 16; Genesis 27:46–28:22; Psalm 21
22.	Luke 17; Genesis 29:1-30; Psalm 22
23.	Luke 18:1-17; Genesis 29:31–30:43; Psalm 23
24.	Luke 18:18-43; Genesis 31; Psalm 24
25.	Luke 19:1-27; Genesis 32–33; Psalm 25
26.	Luke 19:28-48; Genesis 34; Psalm 26
27.	Luke 20:1-26; Genesis 35–36; Psalm 27
28.	Luke 20:27-47; Genesis 37; Psalm 28
29.	Luke 21; Genesis 38; Psalm 29
30.	Luke 22:1-38; Genesis 39; Psalm 30
31.	Luke 22:39-71; Genesis 40; Psalm 31

February

1.	Luke 23:1-25; Genesis 41; Psalm 32
2.	Luke 23:26-56; Genesis 42; Psalm 33
3.	Luke 24:1-12; Genesis 43; Psalm 34
4.	Luke 24:13-53; Genesis 44; Psalm 35
5.	Hebrews 1; Genesis 45:1–46:27; Psalm 36
6.	Hebrews 2; Genesis 46:28–47:31; Psalm 37
7.	Hebrews 3:1–4:13; Genesis 48; Psalm 38
8.	Hebrews 4:14–6:12; Genesis 49–50; Psalm 39
9.	Hebrews 6:13-20; Exodus 1–2; Psalm 40
10.	Hebrews 7; Exodus 3–4; Psalm 41
11.	Hebrews 8; Exodus 5:1–6:27; Proverbs 1
12.	Hebrews 9:1-22; Exodus 6:28–8:32; Proverbs 2
13.	Hebrews 9:23–10:18; Exodus 9–10; Proverbs 3
14.	Hebrews 10:19-39; Exodus 11–12; Proverbs 4
15.	Hebrews 11:1-22; Exodus 13–14; Proverbs 5
16.	Hebrews 11:23-40; Exodus 15; Proverbs 6:1–7:5
17.	Hebrews 12; Exodus 16–17; Proverbs 7:6-27
18.	Hebrews 13; Exodus 18–19; Proverbs 8
19.	Matthew 1; Exodus 20–21; Proverbs 9
20.	Matthew 2; Exodus 22–23; Proverbs 10
21.	Matthew 3; Exodus 24; Proverbs 11
22.	Matthew 4; Exodus 25–27; Proverbs 12
23.	Matthew 5:1-20; Exodus 28–29; Proverbs 13
24.	Matthew 5:21-48; Exodus 30–32; Proverbs 14
25.	Matthew 6:1-18; Exodus 33–34; Proverbs 15
26.	Matthew 6:19-34; Exodus 35–36; Proverbs 16
27.	Matthew 7; Exodus 37–38; Proverbs 17
28.	Matthew 8:1-13; Exodus 39–40; Proverbs 18

Bible reading plan continued

March

1.	Matthew 8:14-34; Leviticus 1–2; Proverbs 19
2.	Matthew 9:1-17; Leviticus 3–4; Proverbs 20
3.	Matthew 9:18-38; Leviticus 5–6; Proverbs 21
4.	Matthew 10:1-25; Leviticus 7–8; Proverbs 22
5.	Matthew 10:26-42; Leviticus 9–10; Proverbs 23
6.	Matthew 11:1-19; Leviticus 11–12; Proverbs 24
7.	Matthew 11:20-30; Leviticus 13; Proverbs 25
8.	Matthew 12:1-21; Leviticus 14; Proverbs 26
9.	Matthew 12:22-50; Leviticus 15–16; Proverbs 27
10.	Matthew 13:1-23; Leviticus 17–18; Proverbs 28
11.	Matthew 13:24-58; Leviticus 19; Proverbs 29
12.	Matthew 14:1-21; Leviticus 20–21; Proverbs 30
13.	Matthew 14:22-36; Leviticus 22–23; Proverbs 31
14.	Matthew 15:1-20; Leviticus 24–25; Ecclesiastes 1:1-11
15.	Matthew 15:21-39; Leviticus 26–27; Ecclesiastes 1:12–2:26
16.	Matthew 16; Numbers 1–2; Ecclesiastes 3:1-15
17.	Matthew 17; Numbers 3–4; Ecclesiastes 3:16–4:16
18.	Matthew 18:1-20; Numbers 5–6; Ecclesiastes 5
19.	Matthew 18:21-35; Numbers 7–8; Ecclesiastes 6
20.	Matthew 19:1-15; Numbers 9–10; Ecclesiastes 7
21.	Matthew 19:16-30; Numbers 11–12; Ecclesiastes 8
22.	Matthew 20:1-16; Numbers 13–14; Ecclesiastes 9:1-12
23.	Matthew 20:17-34; Numbers 15–16; Ecclesiastes 9:13–10:20
24.	Matthew 21:1-27; Numbers 17–18 Ecclesiastes 11:1-8
25.	Matthew 21:28-46; Numbers 19–20; Ecclesiastes 11:9–12:14
26.	Matthew 22:1-22; Numbers 21; Song of Songs 1:1–2:7
27.	Matthew 22:23-46; Numbers 22:1-40; Song of Songs 2:8–3:5
28.	Matthew 23:1-12; Numbers 22:41–23:26; Song of Songs 3:6–5:1
29.	Matthew 23:13-39; Numbers 23:27–24:25; Song of Songs 5:2–6:3
30.	Matthew 24:1-31; Numbers 25–27; Song of Songs 6:4–8:4
31.	Matthew 24:32-51; Numbers 28–29; Song of Songs 8:5-14

April

1.	Matthew 25:1-30; Numbers 30–31; Job 1
2.	Matthew 25:31-46; Numbers 32–34; Job 2
3.	Matthew 26:1-25; Numbers 35–36; Job 3
4.	Matthew 26:26-46; Deuteronomy 1–2; Job 4
5.	Matthew 26:47-75; Deuteronomy 3–4; Job 5
6.	Matthew 27:1-31; Deuteronomy 5–6; Job 6
7.	Matthew 27:32-66; Deuteronomy 7–8; Job 7
8.	Matthew 28; Deuteronomy 9–10; Job 8
9.	Acts 1; Deuteronomy 11–12; Job 9
10.	Acts 2:1-13; Deuteronomy 13–14; Job 10
11.	Acts 2:14-47; Deuteronomy 15–16; Job 11
12.	Acts 3; Deuteronomy 17–18; Job 12
13.	Acts 4:1-22; Deuteronomy 19–20; Job 13
14.	Acts 4:23-37; Deuteronomy 21–22; Job 14
15.	Acts 5:1-16; Deuteronomy 23–24; Job 15
16.	Acts 5:17-42; Deuteronomy 25–27; Job 16
17.	Acts 6; Deuteronomy 28; Job 17
18.	Acts 7:1-22; Deuteronomy 29–30; Job 18
19.	Acts 7:23–8:1a; Deuteronomy 31–32; Job 19
20.	Acts 8:1b-25; Deuteronomy 33–34; Job 20
21.	Acts 8:26-40; Joshua 1–2; Job 21
22.	Acts 9:1-25; Joshua 3:1–5:1; Job 22
23.	Acts 9:26-43; Joshua 5:2–6:27; Job 23
24.	Acts 10:1-33; Joshua 7–8; Job 24
25.	Acts 10:34-48; Joshua 9–10; Job 25
26.	Acts 11:1-18; Joshua 11–12; Job 26
27.	Acts 11:19-30 Joshua 13–14; Job 27
28.	Acts 12; Joshua 15–17; Job 28
29.	Acts 13:1-25; Joshua 18–19; Job 29
30.	Acts 13:26-52; Joshua 20–21; Job 30

Bible reading plan continued

May

1.	Acts 14; Joshua 22; Job 31
2.	Acts 15:1-21; Joshua 23–24; Job 32
3.	Acts 15:22-41; Judges 1; Job 33
4.	Acts 16:1-15; Judges 2–3; Job 34
5.	Acts 16:16-40 Judges 4–5; Job 35
6.	Acts 17:1-15; Judges 6; Job 36
7.	Acts 17:16-34; Judges 7–8; Job 37
8.	Acts 18; Judges 9; Job 38
9.	Acts 19:1-20; Judges 10:1–11:33; Job 39
10.	Acts 19:21-41; Judges 11:34–12:15; Job 40
11.	Acts 20:1-16; Judges 13; Job 41
12.	Acts 20:17-38; Judges 14–15; Job 42
13.	Acts 21:1-36; Judges 16; Psalm 42
14.	Acts 21:37–22:29; Judges 17–18; Psalm 43
15.	Acts 22:30–23:22; Judges 19; Psalm 44
16.	Acts 23:23–24:9; Judges 20; Psalm 45
17.	Acts 24:10-27; Judges 21; Psalm 46
18.	Acts 25; Ruth 1–2; Psalm 47
19.	Acts 26:1-18; Ruth 3–4; Psalm 48
20.	Acts 26:19-32; 1 Samuel 1:1–2:10; Psalm 49
21.	Acts 27:1-12; 1 Samuel 2:11-36; Psalm 50
22.	Acts 27:13-44; 1 Samuel 3; Psalm 51
23.	Acts 28:1-16; 1 Samuel 4–5; Psalm 52
24.	Acts 28:17-31; 1 Samuel 6–7; Psalm 53
25.	Romans 1:1-15; 1 Samuel 8; Psalm 54
26.	Romans 1:16-32; 1 Samuel 9:1–10:16; Psalm 55
27.	Romans 2:1–3:8; 1 Samuel 10:17–11:15; Psalm 56
28.	Romans 3:9-31; 1 Samuel 12; Psalm 57
29.	Romans 4; 1 Samuel 13; Psalm 58
30.	Romans 5; 1 Samuel 14; Psalm 59
31.	Romans 6; 1 Samuel 15; Psalm 60

June

1.	Romans 7; 1 Samuel 16; Psalm 61
2.	Romans 8; 1 Samuel 17:1-54; Psalm 62
3.	Romans 9:1-29; 1 Samuel 17:55–18:30; Psalm 63
4.	Romans 9:30–10:21; 1 Samuel 19; Psalm 64
5.	Romans 11:1-24; 1 Samuel 20; Psalm 65
6.	Romans 11:25-36; 1 Samuel 21–22; Psalm 66
7.	Romans 12; 1 Samuel 23–24; Psalm 67
8.	Romans 13; 1 Samuel 25; Psalm 68
9.	Romans 14; 1 Samuel 26; Psalm 69
10.	Romans 15:1-13; 1 Samuel 27–28; Psalm 70
11.	Romans 15:14-33; 1 Samuel 29–31; Psalm 71
12.	Romans 16; 2 Samuel 1; Psalm 72
13.	Mark 1:1-20; 2 Samuel 2:1–3:1; Daniel 1
14.	Mark 1:21-45; 2 Samuel 3:2-39; Daniel 2:1-23
15.	Mark 2; 2 Samuel 4–5; Daniel 2:24-49
16.	Mark 3:1-19; 2 Samuel 6; Daniel 3
17.	Mark 3:20-35; 2 Samuel 7–8; Daniel 4
18.	Mark 4:1-20; 2 Samuel 9–10; Daniel 5
19.	Mark 4:21-41; 2 Samuel 11–12; Daniel 6
20.	Mark 5:1-20; 2 Samuel 13; Daniel 7
21.	Mark 5:21-43; 2 Samuel 14; Daniel 8
22.	Mark 6:1-29; 2 Samuel 15; Daniel 9
23.	Mark 6:30-56; 2 Samuel 16; Daniel 10:1-21
24.	Mark 7:1-13; 2 Samuel 17; Daniel 11:1-19
25.	Mark 7:14-37; 2 Samuel 18; Daniel 11:20-45
26.	Mark 8:1-21; 2 Samuel 19; Daniel 12
27.	Mark 8:22–9:1; 2 Samuel 20–21; Hosea 1:1–2:1
28.	Mark 9:2-50; 2 Samuel 22; Hosea 2:2-23
29.	Mark 10:1-31; 2 Samuel 23; Hosea 3
30.	Mark 10:32-52; 2 Samuel 24; Hosea 4:1-11a

Bible reading plan continued

July

1. Mark 11:1-14; 1 Kings 1; Hosea 4:11b–5:4
2. Mark 11:15-33; 1 Kings 2; Hosea 5:5-15
3. Mark 12:1-27; Kings 3; Hosea 6:1–7:2
4. Mark 12:28-44; 1 Kings 4–5; Hosea 7:3-16
5. Mark 13:1-13; 1 Kings 6; Hosea 8
6. Mark 13:14-37; Kings 7; Hosea 9:1-16
7. Mark 14:1-31; 1 Kings 8; Hosea 9:17–10:15
8. Mark 14:32-72; 1 Kings 9; Hosea 11:1-11
9. Mark 15:1-20; Kings 10; Hosea 11:12–12:14
10. Mark 15:21-47; 1 Kings 11; Hosea 13
11. Mark 16; 1 Kings 12:1-31; Hosea 14
12. 1 Corinthians 1:1-17; 1 Kings 12:32–13:34; Joel 1
13. 1 Corinthians 1:18-31; 1 Kings 14; Joel 2:1-11
14. 1 Corinthians 2; 1 Kings 15:1-32; Joel 2:12-32
15. 1 Corinthians 3; 1 Kings 15:33–16:34; Joel 3
16. 1 Corinthians 4; 1 Kings 17; Amos 1
17. 1 Corinthians 5; 1 Kings 18; Amos 2:1–3:2
18. 1 Corinthians 6; 1 Kings 19; Amos 3:3–4:3
19. 1 Corinthians 7:1-24; 1 Kings 20; Amos 4:4-13
20. 1 Corinthians 7:25-40; 1 Kings 21; Amos 5
21. 1 Corinthians 8; 1 Kings 22; Amos 6
22. 1 Corinthians 9; 2 Kings 1–2; Amos 7
23. 1 Corinthians 10; 2 Kings 3; Amos 8
24. 1 Corinthians 11:1-16; 2 Kings 4; Amos 9
25. 1 Corinthians 11:17-34; 2 Kings 5; Obadiah
26. 1 Corinthians 12; 2 Kings 6:1–7:2; Jonah 1
27. 1 Corinthians 13; 2 Kings 7:3-20; Jonah 2
28. 1 Corinthians 14:1-25; 2 Kings 8; Jonah 3
29. 1 Corinthians 14:26-40; 2 Kings 9; Jonah 4
30. 1 Corinthians 15:1-34; 2 Kings 10; Micah 1
31. 1 Corinthians 15:35-58; 2 Kings 11; Micah 2

August

1. 1 Corinthians 16; 2 Kings 12–13; Micah 3
2. 2 Corinthians 1:1– 2:4; 2 Kings 14; Micah 4:1–5:1
3. 2 Corinthians 2:5–3:18; 2 Kings 15–16; Micah 5:2-15
4. 2 Corinthians 4:1–5:10; 2 Kings 17; Micah 6
5. 2 Corinthians 5:11–6:13; 2 Kings 18; Micah 7
6. 2 Corinthians 6:14–7:16; 2 Kings 19; Nahum 1
7. 2 Corinthians 8; 2 Kings 20–21; Nahum 2
8. 2 Corinthians 9; 2 Kings 22:1–23:35; Nahum 3
9. 2 Corinthians 10; 2 Kings 23:36–24:20; Habakkuk 1
10. 2 Corinthians 11; 2 Kings 25; Habakkuk 2
11. 2 Corinthians 12; 1 Chronicles 1–2; Habakkuk 3
12. 2 Corinthians 13; 1 Chronicles 3–4; Zephaniah 1
13. John 1:1-18; 1 Chronicles 5–6; Zephaniah 2
14. John 1:19-34; 1 Chronicles 7–8; Zephaniah 3
15. John 1:35-51; 1 Chronicles 9; Haggai 1–2
16. John 2; 1 Chronicles 10–11; Zechariah 1
17. John 3:1-21; 1 Chronicles 12; Zechariah 2
18. John 3:22-36; 1 Chronicles 13–14; Zechariah 3
19. John 4:1-26; Chronicles 15:1–16:6; Zechariah 4
20. John 4:27-42; 1 Chronicles 16:7-43; Zechariah 5
21. John 4:43-54; 1 Chronicles 17; Zechariah 6
22. John 5:1-18; 1 Chronicles 18–19; Zechariah 7
23. John 5:19-47; Chronicles 20:1–22:1; Zechariah 8
24. John 6:1-21; Chronicles 22:2–23:32; Zechariah 9
25. John 6:22-59; 1 Chronicles 24; Zechariah 10
26. John 6:60-71; 1 Chronicles 25–26; Zechariah 11
27. John 7:1-24; 1 Chronicles 27–28; Zechariah 12
28. John 7:25-52; 1 Chronicles 29; Zechariah 13
29. John 8:1-20; 2 Chronicles 1:1–2:16; Zechariah 14
30. John 8:21-47; 2 Chronicles 2:17–5:1; Malachi 1:1–2:9
31. John 8:48-59; 2 Chronicles 5:2-14; Malachi 2:10-16

Bible reading plan continued

September

1.	John 9:1-23; 2 Chronicles 6; Malachi 2:17–3:18
2.	John 9:24-41; 2 Chronicles 7; Malachi 4
3.	John 10:1-21; 2 Chronicles 8; Psalm 73
4.	John 10:22-42; 2 Chronicles 9; Psalm 74
5.	John 11:1-27; 2 Chronicles 10–11; Psalm 75
6.	John 11:28-57; 2 Chronicles 12–13; Psalm 76
7.	John 12:1-26; 2 Chronicles 14–15; Psalm 77
8.	John 12:27-50; 2 Chronicles 16–17; Psalm 78:1-20
9.	John 13:1-20; 2 Chronicles 18; Psalm 78:21-37
10.	John 13:21-38; 2 Chronicles 19; Psalm 78:38-55
11.	John 14:1-14; 2 Chronicles 20:1–21:1; Psalm 78:56-72
12.	John 14:15-31; 2 Chronicles 21:2–22:12; Psalm 79
13.	John 15:1–16:4a; 2 Chronicles 23; Psalm 80
14.	John 16:4b-33; 2 Chronicles 24; Psalm 81
15.	John 17; 2 Chronicles 25; Psalm 82
16.	John 18:1-18; 2 Chronicles 26; Psalm 83
17.	John 18:19-38a; 2 Chronicles 27–28; Psalm 84
18.	John 18:38b–19:16a; 2 Chronicles 29; Psalm 85
19.	John 19:16b-42; 2 Chronicles 30; Psalm 86
20.	John 20:1-18; 2 Chronicles 31; Psalm 87
21.	John 20:19-31; 2 Chronicles 32; Psalm 88
22.	John 21; 2 Chronicles 33; Psalm 89:1-18
23.	1 John 1; 2 Chronicles 34; Psalm 89:19-37
24.	1 John 2; 2 Chronicles 35; Psalm 89:38-52
25.	1 John 3; 2 Chronicles 36; Psalm 90
26.	1 John 4; Ezra 1–2; Psalm 91
27.	1 John 5; Ezra 3–4; Psalm 92
28.	2 John; Ezra 5–6; Psalm 93
29.	3 John; Ezra 7–8; Psalm 94
30.	Jude; Ezra 9–10; Psalm 95

October

1.	Revelation 1; Nehemiah 1–2; Psalm 96
2.	Revelation 2; Nehemiah 3; Psalm 97
3.	Revelation 3; Nehemiah 4; Psalm 98
4.	Revelation 4; Nehemiah 5:1–7:4; Psalm 99
5.	Revelation 5; Nehemiah 7:5–8:12; Psalm 100
6.	Revelation 6; Nehemiah 8:13–9:37; Psalm 101
7.	Revelation 7; Nehemiah 9:38–10:39; Psalm 102
8.	Revelation 8; Nehemiah 11; Psalm 103
9.	Revelation 9; Nehemiah 12; Psalm 104:1-23
10.	Revelation 10; Nehemiah 13; Psalm 104:24-35
11.	Revelation 11; Esther 1; Psalm 105:1-25
12.	Revelation 12; Esther 2; Psalm 105:26-45
13.	Revelation 13; Esther 3–4; Psalm 106:1-23
14.	Revelation 14; Esther 5:1–6:13; Psalm 106:24-48
15.	Revelation 15; Esther 6:14–8:17; Psalm 107:1-22
16.	Revelation 16; Esther 9–10; Psalm 107:23-43
17.	Revelation 17; Isaiah 1–2; Psalm 108
18.	Revelation 18; Isaiah 3–4; Psalm 109:1-19
19.	Revelation 19; Isaiah 5–6; Psalm 109:20-31
20.	Revelation 20; Isaiah 7–8; Psalm 110
21.	Revelation 21–22; Isaiah 9–10; Psalm 111
22.	1 Thessalonians 1; Isaiah 11–13; Psalm 112
23.	1 Thessalonians 2:1-16; Isaiah 14–16; Psalm 113
24.	1 Thessalonians 2:17–3:13; Isaiah 17–19; Psalm 114
25.	1 Thessalonians 4; Isaiah 20–22; Psalm 115
26.	1 Thessalonians 5; Isaiah 23–24; Psalm 116
27.	2 Thessalonians 1; Isaiah 25–26; Psalm 117
28.	2 Thessalonians 2; Isaiah 27–28; Psalm 118
29.	2 Thessalonians 3; Isaiah 29–30; Psalm 119:1-32
30.	1 Timothy 1; Isaiah 31–33; Psalm 119:33-64
31.	1 Timothy 2; Isaiah 34–35; Psalm 119:65-96

Bible reading plan continued

November

1.	1 Timothy 3; Isaiah 36–37; Psalm 119:97-120
2.	1 Timothy 4; Isaiah 38–39; Psalm 119:121-144
3.	1 Timothy 5:1-22; Jeremiah 1–2; Psalm 119:145-176
4.	1 Timothy 5:23–6:21; Jeremiah 3–4; Psalm 120
5.	2 Timothy 1; Jeremiah 5–6; Psalm 121
6.	2 Timothy 2; Jeremiah 7–8; Psalm 122
7.	2 Timothy 3; Jeremiah 9–10; Psalm 123
8.	2 Timothy 4; Jeremiah 11–12; Psalm 124
9.	Titus 1; Jeremiah 13–14; Psalm 125
10.	Titus 2; Jeremiah 15–16; Psalm 126
11.	Titus 3; Jeremiah 17–18; Psalm 127
12.	Philemon; Jeremiah 19–20; Psalm 128
13.	James 1; Jeremiah 21–22; Psalm 129
14.	James 2; Jeremiah 23–24; Psalm 130
15.	James 3; Jeremiah 25–26; Psalm 131
16.	James 4; Jeremiah 27–28; Psalm 132
17.	James 5; Jeremiah 29–30; Psalm 133
18.	1 Peter 1; Jeremiah 31–32; Psalm 134
19.	1 Peter 2; Jeremiah 33–34; Psalm 135
20.	1 Peter 3; Jeremiah 35–36; Psalm 136
21.	1 Peter 4; Jeremiah 37–38; Psalm 137
22.	1 Peter 5; Jeremiah 39–40; Psalm 138
23.	2 Peter 1; Jeremiah 41–42; Psalm 139
24.	2 Peter 2; Jeremiah 43–44; Psalm 140
25.	2 Peter 3; Jeremiah 45–46; Psalm 141
26.	Galatians 1; Jeremiah 47–48; Psalm 142
27.	Galatians 2; Jeremiah 49–50; Psalm 143
28.	Galatians 3:1-18; Jeremiah 51–52; Psalm 144
29.	Galatians 3:19–4:20; Lamentations 1–2; Psalm 145
30.	Galatians 4:21-31; Lamentations 3–4; Psalm 146

December

1.	Galatians 5:1-15; Lamentations 5; Psalm 147
2.	Galatians 5:16-26; Ezekiel 1; Psalm 148
3.	Galatians 6; Ezekiel 2–3; Psalm 149
4.	Ephesians 1; Ezekiel 4–5; Psalm 150
5.	Ephesians 2; Ezekiel 6–7; Isaiah 40
6.	Ephesians 3; Ezekiel 8–9; Isaiah 41
7.	Ephesians 4:1-16; Ezekiel 10–11; Isaiah 42
8.	Ephesians 4:17-32; Ezekiel 12–13; Isaiah 43
9.	Ephesians 5:1-20; Ezekiel 14–15; Isaiah 44
10.	Ephesians 5:21-33; Ezekiel 16; Isaiah 45
11.	Ephesians 6; Ezekiel 17; Isaiah 46
12.	Philippians 1:1-11; Ezekiel 18; Isaiah 47
13.	Philippians 1:12-30; Ezekiel 19; Isaiah 48
14.	Philippians 2:1-11; Ezekiel 20; Isaiah 49
15.	Philippians 2:12-30; Ezekiel 21–22; Isaiah 50
16.	Philippians 3; Ezekiel 23; Isaiah 51
17.	Philippians 4; Ezekiel 24; Isaiah 52
18.	Colossians 1:1-23; Ezekiel 25–26; Isaiah 53
19.	Colossians 1:24–2:19; Ezekiel 27-28; Isaiah 54
20.	Colossians 2:20–3:17; Ezekiel 29-30; Isaiah 55
21.	Colossians 3:18–4:18; Ezekiel 31-32; Isaiah 56
22.	Luke 1:1-25; Ezekiel 33; Isaiah 57
23.	Luke 1:26-56; Ezekiel 34; Isaiah 58
24.	Luke 1:57-80; Ezekiel 35–36; Isaiah 59
25.	Luke 2:1-20; Ezekiel 37; Isaiah 60
26.	Luke 2:21-52; Ezekiel 38–39; Isaiah 61
27.	Luke 3:1-20; Ezekiel 40–41; Isaiah 62
28.	Luke 3:21-38; Ezekiel 42–43; Isaiah 63
29.	Luke 4:1-30; Ezekiel 44–45; Isaiah 64
30.	Luke 4:31-44; Ezekiel 46–47; Isaiah 65
31.	Luke 5:1-26; Ezekiel 48; Isaiah 66

Biblical Records

The Bible's longest and shortest, according to the King James Version.

Shortest reign:
Zimri ruled Israel for seven days, then committed suicide by burning his palace around him. (1 KINGS 16:15)

Longest reign:
Manasseh started to reign when he was twelve and ruled Judah for fifty-five years. (2 KINGS 21:1)

Youngest king:
Joash (Jehoash) was seven when he became king of Judah, and reigned for forty years. (2 CHRONICLES 24:1)

Longest Old Testament book:
Psalms—150 chapters and 2,461 verses.

Shortest book in the Old Testament:
Obadiah—21 verses and just 670 words.

Shortest book in the New Testament:
2 John—13 verses and just 298 words.

Longest chapter in the Bible:
Psalm 119—176 verses.

Shortest chapter in the Bible:
Psalm 117—2 verses and just 33 words.

The two shortest Bible verses:
"Eber, Peleg, Reu" (1 CHRONICLES 1:25) and "Jesus wept" (JOHN 11:35).

Longest verse in the Bible:
Esther 8:9—90 words.

Total number of verses in the Bible:
30,442; Old Testament: 22,485; New Testament: 7,957.

Longest name in the Bible:
Maher-shalal-hash-baz (ISAIAH 8:1, 3)—the prophet Isaiah's son.

Shortest prayer in the Bible:
"Lord, save me" (MATTHEW 14:30), cried by Peter, terrified while walking on Lake Galilee.

Does the Bible Really Say That?

It is often said, "Money is the root of all evil"; but the Bible actually says, "the love of money is the root of all evil" (1 TIMOTHY 6:10).

It is often said that Esau sold his birthright to his brother for a "mess of pottage"; however, the words "mess of" do not appear in the King James Bible (GENESIS 25:30–34): only "red pottage" and "pottage of lentils."

It is commonly said that, after Elijah prayed for fire from heaven, he saw "a cloud no bigger than a man's hand." The King James Version actually reads: "Behold, there ariseth a little cloud out of the sea, like a man's hand" (1 KINGS 18:44).

The phrase "The lion shall lie down with the lamb" is frequently quoted as if from Scripture. But the King James Version reads: "The wolf also shall dwell with the lamb, and the leopard shall lie down with the kid; and the calf and the young lion and the fatling together; and a little child shall lead them" (ISAIAH 11:6).

According to the book of Genesis, Adam and Eve did not eat an apple. The fruit they tasted is simply referred to as the fruit of the "tree of the knowledge of good and evil" (GENESIS 2:17).

The book of Jonah says God sent "a great fish"—not a whale—to swallow the prophet Jonah, when he was thrown overboard in a storm.

The Bible never describes Mary Magdalene (MARY OF MAGDALA) as a prostitute. Apart from her presence at the resurrection (LUKE 24:10), the only other reference to her is when Jesus cured her of seven demons (LUKE 8:2).

According to Genesis, Adam did not eat an apple.

The word "prodigal" doesn't occur in the Bible story about the runaway son. It was added as a subheading and means "wasteful" or "lavish," referring to his life in exile. It has nothing to do with leaving home—or returning (LUKE 15:11–32).

What some famous people said about the Bible

The holy scriptures are our letters from home.
AUGUSTINE OF HIPPO (AD 354–430)

I have found in the Bible words for my inmost thoughts, songs for my joy, utterances for my hidden griefs, and pleadings for my shame and my feebleness.
SAMUEL TAYLOR COLERIDGE (1772–1834), ENGLISH POET

The first and almost the only book deserving of universal attention is the Bible.
JOHN QUINCY ADAMS (1767–1848), US PRESIDENT

This Bible is for the Government of the People, by the People, and for the People.
JOHN WYCLIFFE (c. 1320–1384), ENGLISH REFORMER

The Bible, the whole Bible, and nothing but the Bible is the religion of Christ's church.
CHARLES HADDON SPURGEON (1834–1892), ENGLISH BAPTIST PREACHER

Most people are bothered by those passages in Scripture which they cannot understand; but as for me, I always noticed that the passages in Scripture which trouble me most are those that I do understand.
MARK TWAIN (1835–1910), AMERICAN AUTHOR

Abraham Lincoln.

To the Bible men will return; and why? Because they cannot do without it.
MATTHEW ARNOLD (1822–1888), ENGLISH POET

Unless God's word illumine the way, the whole life of men is wrapped in darkness and mist, so that they cannot but miserably stray.
JOHN CALVIN (1509–1564), FRENCH REFORMER

It is the best book that ever was, or will be, known in the world…
CHARLES DICKENS (1812–1870), ENGLISH NOVELIST

The Word of God is greater than heaven and earth, yea, is greater than death and hell, for it forms part of the power of God, and endures everlastingly...
MARTIN LUTHER (1483–1546), GERMAN REFORMER

We account the Scriptures of God to be the most sublime philosophy.
SIR ISAAC NEWTON (1643–1727), ENGLISH POLYMATH

The Bible makes the best people in the world.
THOMAS JEFFERSON (1743–1826), AMERICAN PRESIDENT

I believe the Bible is the best gift God has ever given to man.
ABRAHAM LINCOLN (1809–1865), AMERICAN PRESIDENT

The Bible has been the Book that held together the fabric of Western civilization....
H. G. WELLS (1866–1946), ENGLISH NOVELIST

This is a Book worth more than all the others that were ever printed.
PATRICK HENRY (1736–1799), AMERICAN FOUNDING FATHER

The existence of the Bible as a book for the people is the greatest benefit which the human race has ever experienced.
IMMANUEL KANT (1724–1804), GERMAN PHILOSOPHER

Living in Bible Times

Daily life

Tent living

In Bible times, some people moved from place to place as nomads, searching for good pasture for their flocks and herds. Abraham and Sarah lived like this after they came to the Promised Land (GENESIS 18:1–15). When the annual rainy season arrived, grass sprang up in the valleys and plains. The nomads, who lived in moveable tents, would drive their sheep to feed on the fresh grass, and continue to wander looking for good pasture until the dry season. They would then return to a populated place, where they prepared the sheep and goats' wool to sell at a nearby town or city market. People ate and slept in their tents, but mainly worked outdoors, looking after their animals. Their sheep, goats, and cattle were the only way to make a living.

The nomads' tents were quite simple, normally rectangular, and roughly 9 by 15 feet (3 by 5 meters). Originally, the covering would have been made of animal skins; later, tents were made from pieces of woven black goat's hair, sewn together by the women. Tents gave protection from rain and sun. The covering became waterproof after the rain soaked and shrank it. If the covering became torn, it could be repaired by darning. The goat's-hair cover was quite thick, giving warmth and protection from wind and rain in winter. On hot days, the sides of the tent were lifted to allow in light and fresh air.

Inside the women's section of a tent.

Tents normally had at least two sections, separated by a sheet or curtain hanging from the roof. Women and children lived in the smaller section, and the men occupied the larger area. Abraham's wife, Sarah, was in the women's section when she heard visitors tell her husband that she was going to have a son (GENESIS 18:10–12). The tent door was just a flap that could be raised and lowered (GENESIS 18:1). Apart from the father of the family, no males were allowed inside the tent. Any other men had to stay outside at the "porch," which had a special covering. The father would eat there with male visitors, and sleep with them there too. It was seen as bad manners to leave a visitor to sleep alone.

Inside the tent the ground was covered with mats, skins, and carpets. The family stored cooking pots, food, and other belongings inside the tent. They dug a hole in the ground in the middle of the tent and lit a fire there to cook food. Families living in tents had little furniture because they were constantly moving on. They might have had straw mats to sit on and an animal skin as a table. They stored water, milk, and butter in bottles made out of goatskins. There would be a little clay lamp filled with olive oil to light the tent.

Houses

In Bible times, a house was mainly a place of shelter, where people slept at night. The family spent little time inside the house during the day; they would be working in the fields or doing jobs in the yard. However, the wealthy owned larger houses where they entertained guests. Houses were often built in clusters, in little villages or small towns, preferably near a well or spring. Usually people built houses near one another, to help them feel safe.

The poorest lived in simple houses with just one room, sometimes measuring only 10 feet (3 meters) square. If the family owned an ox or donkey, this space was also a stable. The family lived on a raised platform that separated them from the animals. The animals were fed with hay in a manger, or feeding box. A mother would sometimes lay her baby in the manger to keep it safe while she was working around the house and the animals were out in the fields (LUKE 2:7).

Houses were usually built from mud or clay bricks that had been dried in the sun, or from rough stones and rubble. If wood was available, the walls were strengthened with timber beams. The houses were quite roughly built; in a storm or flood, a house might collapse (MATTHEW 7:24–27). Walls were quite thick, to keep the house cool on hot, summer days and warm during the cold, winter nights. Often insects and snakes lived in the uneven walls (AMOS 5:19).

The house would have a flat roof made of wooden branches laid across wooden beams. The gaps were filled with smaller branches before the roof was coated with clay. Such a roof was not very watertight; after rain, it had to be smoothed down with a stone roller. It was through such a roof that the sick man was lowered to Jesus' feet to be healed (LUKE 5:19). The family reached the roof via stairs outside the house. Often they dried grain and fruit, such as olives and figs, on the roof. On summer nights, the family would sleep on the roof, and the men would go up to the roof to pray. A Jewish law said there had to be a low wall around the roof to prevent people falling (DEUTERONOMY 22:8).

Most houses had just one little unglazed window, high in the wall. The house would also have a single small door, often made of sycamore wood. The door was opened at sunrise, to show that the family welcomed visitors; but it was closed again at sundown, to keep the family safe. It would be blocked with a wooden bar.

On the right-hand doorpost, Jewish families fixed a little box; inside it was a parchment with words from Jewish scripture (DEUTERONOMY 6:4–9, 11:13–21). As the men went in and out, they touched this *mezuzah*, praying, "May God keep my going in and coming out."

Sometimes the family lit a fire in the lower area, to warm the room and to cook. Most houses had no chimney, so smoke went everywhere, making people cough and splutter. On the raised platform, the family would eat their meals, sit talking, and sleep at night. They stored their food and pots on shelves and niches in the walls. Families had little furniture; they were generally poor, and anyway spent little time indoors during the daytime. They stored clothes and other belongings in a wooden chest that could be turned upside down for use as a dinner table. Some families also owned wooden stools or chairs to sit on, but most people usually sat on the floor.

The poor slept on animal-skins; richer people had rough mattresses—some even owned wooden beds. As pillows, people often used goatskins stuffed with wool or feathers. The family would sleep in a row; father at one end, mother at the other, and the children in between. They bundled up their bedding each morning.

Cutaway of house in Bible times.

Every family had an oil lamp in the house, on a shelf or upturned pot. Cheaper lamps were made of clay; expensive ones of bronze or other metal. Such lamps burned olive oil, pitch (tar), or wax, and had a wick made from flax. A lamp was left burning all night; the light showed that there were people indoors sleeping.

Larger houses were often built in a U-shape, opening on to an inner courtyard where animals were kept. Sometimes wealthy people built a room on the roof, reached by outside stairs (2 KINGS 4:10; MARK 14:15). Such an upper room could be big enough to hold a gathering of people (ACTS 12:12–17). Families living in a large home would have servants, and sometimes a doorkeeper.

Inside a house of Bible times.

Housework

Mostly people got up before daybreak, to start work before the sun grew too strong. After breakfast, the men and older boys went to the fields to work; younger boys often looked after the family's animals, such as the goats or chickens.

The women now began their daily tasks. One important job was grinding the grain into flour, ready to bake bread. Women crushed the grain in a hand-mill, its two flat stones grinding against each other. Two women would sometimes mill together (MATTHEW 24:41). Wheat or barley bread had to be baked every day except the Sabbath, when work was forbidden. Poor people usually ate bread made from barley. Wheat bread was of better quality and more expensive. To make bread, the women mixed the flour they had milled with salt and water. If they wanted the bread to rise, they added some dough from the previous day's bread to act as yeast (MATTHEW 13:33). The dough was left to warm by the fire so that the yeast could work through it. The bread was then ready to bake.

People sometimes baked "unleavened" bread, with no added yeast, or "leaven." This bread didn't rise and was eaten at some religious feasts (EXODUS 12:15; MATTHEW 26:17).

There were several methods of baking. In early times, the dough was placed on heated, flat stones (1 KINGS 19:6). Sometimes bread was baked on a big, shallow bowl turned upside down over a fire. The dough was rolled thin before being laid on top of the dish to bake. There were also large upside-down earthenware conical ovens: a fire was lit at the bottom, and the dough put inside to bake.

Another important daily chore was fetching water (GENESIS 24:11–13). This was often done by the older girls, who took goatskin bottles or clay pitchers to a spring or well to fill with water (see GENESIS 24:1–27). They then carried the water back, balancing the container on their hips, shoulders, or head. Because of the summer heat, water was often fetched from the well early morning or in the cool of the evening. The well became a popular place to gather.

The house also had to be swept and tidied every day, while the animals' area also needed cleaning out. The oil lamps were refilled with oil and their wicks trimmed.

In addition, the clothes had to be washed in a fast-flowing stream or by bashing the dirt out of the damp clothing between flat stones. The women used soap made from olive oil or a vegetable.

At midday, when the sun was at its hottest, the family would find a shady place and rest. It was too uncomfortable to work.

Food

Families ate bread at every meal. Jesus taught his followers to pray: "Give us each day our daily bread" (LUKE 11:3). Bread had to be baked almost every day because in a hot country, such as Palestine, it dried and crumbled quickly. People didn't use knives to cut bread; they tore off pieces with their bare hands. Sometimes, when men were in the fields reaping wheat, they would roast a few ears of grain on a fire and eat them warm.

Women grind grain.

The Jews drank the milk of sheep, goats, and camels. They also used their milk to produce cheese, butter, and a kind of yogurt (GENESIS 18:8; 2 SAMUEL 17:29). People grew and ate various vegetables, and cooked stews made from beans, lentils, gherkins, and cucumbers (GENESIS 25:27–34; EZEKIEL 4:9), adding root vegetables and herbs as flavoring.

The Jews also ate plenty of fruit. In addition to grapes, the land was rich in pomegranates, figs, dates, olives, almonds, and pistachio nuts (JEREMIAH 24:2; GENESIS 43:11; DEUTERONOMY 8:8). People ate grapes fresh and also dried, as raisins (1 SAMUEL 25:18). Similarly, they ate figs fresh and baked in cakes (MATTHEW 21:19). People ate olives as a staple food, as well as preserving them in brine. Olive oil was used for cooking, rather than butter or animal fat (1 KINGS 17:12).

Honey from wild bees was important as a sweetener (JUDGES 14:8–9). People ate the honey from the comb, but also used it to make sweet-cakes. John the Baptist ate wild honey (MATTHEW 3:4). A different kind of sweetener was made by boiling grape juice down into a syrup.

Most families couldn't afford to eat meat. The commonest meat was young goat, or kid, but people also ate lamb. Cows provided milk, and were also used for plowing. Sheep gave both milk and wool. If a cow or sheep was killed, its value for other uses was lost, so beef and lamb were eaten only on special occasions (1 KINGS 4:23). People sometimes also roasted birds, such as pigeons, geese, quails, and partridge.

Baking bread.

Loaves and fish mosaic, Galilee.

Fish were common and plentiful. In Jesus' time, there were many fishermen working on the Sea of Galilee (LUKE 11:11). Fish were boiled or roasted over coals (JOHN 21:9–13). Salt was important for adding flavor (JOB 6:6) and for preserving food. People discovered how to salt fish so that they could be dried and preserved for eating.

People enjoyed spicy food. Black cumin and coriander were used instead of pepper. Mint and anise were also utilized, particularly in stews.

The juice of grapes was used to make wine. Available water was often dirty and full of germs, so it was safer to drink wine. Diluted wine was also drunk regularly in Bible times (MATTHEW 9:17; 21:33; JOHN 2:1–11).

In wealthy homes, a servant poured washing water for guests (2 KINGS 3:11, NRSV). A prayer of thanks was said before eating.

Jewish people held feasts when people got married, on birthdays, at burials, and at sheep-shearing. They also ate well if there were guests to entertain. For festivals such as Passover and harvest, people would add meat to the stew – and they might also have sweet pastries. Feasts were celebrated with much singing and dancing.

In New Testament times, guests at a banquet sometimes lay on couches arranged on three sides, with their head facing the table and their legs away from it. They used their right hand to eat. A servant washed guests' feet, served food, and waited on the guests (LUKE 7:36–38). The host was in the center, with the place of honor to his left. Food at banquets was lavish: wine was served, the best lamb roasted, and cheeses, vegetables, dates, honey, and figs all served.

People took off their sandals when they entered a house; otherwise they would dirty their clothes and the rug. When a visitor entered a wealthy home, a servant would wash his feet (JOHN 13:4–5). In large houses, a room was sometimes set apart for a guest (2 KINGS 4:10). If a family was away from home, they would wait at a well or at the city gate until someone invited them to stay in their home (GENESIS 24:13–14; JUDGES 19:15).

Meals

Breakfast was not a big meal: it usually consisted of bread and cheese, perhaps with some fruit or olives. The main meal was in the evening, after work was finished. It was often a vegetable stew or lentils (GENESIS 25:29, 34). Everyone would scoop food from the shared pot, using a piece of bread called a "sop." There were no knives or forks to eat with. The family might finish the meal with fruit.

Since people ate with their hands, cleanliness was important. Before eating, everyone washed their hands.

A family meal.

What people wore

Men's clothing

Most Jewish men wore an inner garment, an outer garment, and sandals. The inner garment, or tunic, was made of wool, linen, or cotton and worn next to the skin. It would be held in at the waist by a belt made of leather or cloth. Sometimes the belt had a pouch to hold money or other valuables (MARK 6:8). When a man needed to free himself for work, he tucked his tunic into his belt, or "girded" himself, to allow freedom of movement. Some men also wore a loincloth beneath the tunic.

In addition, men wore an outer cloak or robe made of woolen cloth, which could be wrapped around the body to keep warm. It was looser and longer than the tunic, with slits rather than sleeves for the arms. The apostle Paul asked some friends to send his warm cloak when he was a prisoner in a Roman jail (2 TIMOTHY 4:13). John the Baptist wore a cloak of camel's hair that protected him from the cruel weather of the wilderness. Rich men wore cloaks of expensive silk or linen, with wide sleeves and blue fringes (MATTHEW 23:5). Men tied a sash or belt of leather around their waist; expensive ones were made of cotton or even silk.

Men's clothing.

In Bible times, people didn't wear nightclothes. At night, they loosened their belts and lay down in their tunics, often using their cloak as a bedcover. When sleeping outdoors, the shepherd used his cloak as both bedding and blanket.

Jewish men had jewels and adornments. They often wore a ring on a finger or a cord around their neck. These rings were sometimes used to press into wax on important letters, to make a unique seal that showed who the letter came from. Some people wore magic charms or "amulets," believing they would ward off evil spirits.

Men often wore a skull-cap, with a band of cloth around the edge. Many men also wore a headdress made from a square of cloth folded in half, kept in place with a twisted band of wool or cotton.

Jewish Scripture said men should bind God's laws on their hand and between their eyes. To do this literally, they would tie on the forehead and arm little square boxes ("phylacteries" or *tefillin*) containing tiny parchment rolls, on which were written words of Scripture.

The very poor often went barefoot—as did people who were in mourning. Most men wore leather sandals, sometimes with wooden soles, tied to the feet with thongs. Jesus' disciples wore sandals like this (see MARK 6:9).

Women's clothing

Like the men, women wore a tunic of wool, cotton, or linen; however, women's tunics were worn down to the ankles, and were often blue. They usually had a V-neck, with embroidery around the edges. Like the men, women lifted the hem of their tunic when doing heavy work, such as carrying water. The women's outer garment was also longer than men's, usually covering the feet, and was fastened with a belt at the waist.

Jewish women wore their hair long, and often in plaits. Like the men, women usually wore squares of material on their heads, fastened with plaited cords to protect them from the sun. If unmarried, women wore a veil over their faces in public (GENESIS 24:65). Married women did not always go veiled; but if a man approached a woman in public, she covered her face with her veil.

Jewish women wore many jewels and ornaments, such as bracelets on the wrist and above the elbow. They often also wore ankle bangles that jangled as they walked.

Women usually wore earrings, often in the form of gold rings or hoops (EZEKIEL 16:12). They also used make-up, painting their eyelashes and sometimes staining their fingers and toes with henna (ISAIAH 3:18–21). Women liked to use perfumes and scents, such as frankincense and myrrh from Africa, aloes and nard from India, and saffron from Palestine.

Family life

The father was the head of the home, ruling the family clan. He was in complete control. Normally, the eldest son became head of the family when his father died. In Bible times, women came second to men and were much of the time separated from the men. On a journey, the man might ride a donkey, while the woman was on foot. In public, women walked behind the men. Women worked hard physically, grinding the grain (MATTHEW 24:41), and putting up the tents.

When a wife became pregnant, people believed it was a sign that God was blessing the home (LUKE 1:25). Jewish parents thought that having many children was a sign that God approved (DEUTERONOMY 28:4). The more children, the better—especially if they were boys. If a woman was childless, people sometimes made fun of her, or pitied her.

When a pregnant woman was ready to give birth, the family would call a midwife (EXODUS 1:15–19). The newborn baby was washed, and then rubbed down with salt, water, and oil. After this, the baby was wrapped up tightly with strips of bandage. People believed that this would help the baby's legs and arms to grow straight. Mary wrapped baby Jesus in such "swaddling clothes" (LUKE 2:7).

When a boy child was eight days old, he was circumcised, as a sign that he was being given back to God (GENESIS 17:10). From about the age of three, the father began to teach his son stories from the Hebrew Law, or "Torah," and to train him in his craft or trade. Joseph taught his son Jesus his craft as a carpenter.

When a boy reached the age of thirteen, he was regarded as a man, with a special ceremony to mark this stage in his life: he was said to have become a "son of the Law." The father fastened phylacteries on his son's arm and forehead to show his devotion to the Law in his mind and heart. When he was twelve, Jesus went to the Temple with his parents for his last Passover as a child (LUKE 2:41–49).

In Jesus' day, boys of six and over went to school at the "house of the book." The schoolteacher was paid by the members of the synagogue, the Jewish meeting-place. The teacher sat cross-legged on a little platform in front of the

Boys learn to read and write.

boys, who squatted on the floor. The boys were taught to read and write, and learned long passages of Scripture by heart.

Marriage

Marriage happened at quite a young age. Jewish rabbis set twelve as the minimum age for marriage for girls, and thirteen for boys. The marriage was arranged by parents. After a wife had been selected, the bride's father had to be paid for the loss of his daughter, and he had also to give his daughter a dowry (GENESIS 24:59–61).

For a year the couple were "betrothed" to be married (MATTHEW 1:18–20), during which time the man prepared a home for his bride and the bride's family made her wedding clothes and arranged the marriage feast. At the wedding, the bride and groom made a legal agreement and a blessing was said. Then followed the wedding banquet, usually given by the bride's family. The bride and groom would sit under a special canopy. Feasting could continue for as long as seven days (JUDGES 14:12), with much drinking, eating, dancing, and singing.

Health and medicine

The Jews had many special rules to help them lead healthy lives. They were commanded to keep one day in seven as a day of rest. They were instructed not to eat specific unhealthy foods, and to make sure that their food and their homes were clean.

People suffered from many different illnesses and diseases, including leprosy, blindness, deafness, epilepsy, and as cripples (MARK 1:32–34). Many Jews believed illness came as a result of their sins. If someone was ill, they would ask: "Was this person a sinner—or his mother or father?" (JOHN 9:2–4).

People believed they ought to pray to God when they were ill—but sometimes they copied surrounding nations by wearing lucky charms to keep away evil spirits. They started using simple natural drugs and knew how to clean wounds and bandage them, using natural ointments. A herb called myrrh mixed with wine was used as a pain-killer.

In Jesus' time, some doctors were trained by the Greeks to undertake surgery. They took vows promising to put the life of their patient first and not to share personal details about their patients.

Death and burial

In Bible times, many people died before old age, through illness, poverty, or famine. As soon as someone died, their friends and relatives started to wail and lament. This let their neighbors know that someone had passed away. Some rich families paid for mourners to come and lament for them (JEREMIAH 9:17–18). While they were mourning, people often wore rough goat's-hair clothes, or tore their clothes, to show how sad they felt.

It was important to bury the dead quickly, before the body started to rot, as the weather was often very hot. Normally the body was washed and wrapped in linen before it was carried to the place of burial on a stretcher.

People were often buried in caves or tombs dug out of the rock (JUDGES 8:32; MATTHEW 27:59–60). There were not enough caves, so, when bodies had rotted away, the bones were collected and saved in bone-boxes called "ossuaries" to make space for new bodies. Burial caves were closed up with huge rocks. Sometimes the cave door was a circular stone, rolled in a slot across the opening (see LUKE 24:1–2). Poorer people were sometimes buried more simply (LUKE 7:14). The stretcher carrying their body was laid on the ground, covered with earth, and surrounded by rocks.

A bone-box, or "ossuary."

Occupations of Bible times

Farming

Farmers of Bible times grew mainly wheat and barley, and sometimes also millet. Barley was a poor person's crop, grown on less fertile soil; wheat was regarded as more valuable and grown on fertile land.

In the dry climate of Palestine, the soil became hard during the long, hot summer. The farmer waited for the "early" rains of October and November to soften the soil before plowing. He often plowed the ground and sowed seed at the same time. The plow was a T-shaped wooden tool with a sharp spike that cut through the soil, drawn by two donkeys or two oxen, attached by a yoke fastened around their necks.

The farmer walked across his field, scattering handfuls of seed, while another man followed with the plow, burying the seeds to prevent birds from snatching them. Barley was ready to harvest in April or May. The farmer cut it with a sickle (JEREMIAH 50:16). The grain was then tied in sheaves ready for threshing, when oxen pulled a threshing board across the grain. After this, the farmer separated the grain from the chaff by tossing it in the air. The chaff was blown away on the wind, but the heavier grain fell to the ground. After it had been sifted, the farmer would store his precious grain. Harvest was an important time, providing grain for the next year's bread; it was celebrated with much feasting.

Plowing.

Olive trees grow well in dry lands such as Palestine. They have deep roots and can find water far down in the earth. In Bible times, most families had olive trees, often growing in small groves. The olives were ready to pick in September and October. Some olives were eaten raw, others were preserved in salt water, but most were crushed to make olive oil.

Olive oil was eaten with barley bread for breakfast, used for frying, and poured over salads. It was also used instead of butter, and regarded as an essential cooking ingredient. Olives could also be used to make soap, as medicine and as an ointment for wounds, or fuel for lamps (MATTHEW 25:3–4)—and even as a laxative. Bodies were usually anointed with olive oil before burial, and Jewish prophets, priests, and kings were all anointed with it. Olive oil could also be included as a part of the wage allotment for workers (2 KINGS 4:5; 2 CHRONICLES 2:10).

Vines and grapes

In Bible times, the grape harvest was almost as important as the grain harvest. Grape vines were best planted on a hillside (ISAIAH 5:1), where the grapes caught the sun and the rain ran off the slope. A hillside could be stepped in terraces along the slope. Often the farmer built a stone wall around his vineyard to protect it, sometimes with a tower from which a watchman could guard it (SONG OF SONGS 2:15; JEREMIAH 49:9).

Grape harvest was a festival time, with singing and dancing as well as plenty of hard work. Some of the grapes were eaten fresh, some dried in the sun to produce raisins, and others crushed into juice. Most were pressed to make wine. Wine was also used to clean flesh wounds (LUKE 10:34). It could be mixed with a substance called "gall," made from animal bile, to relieve pain. Jesus was offered this painkiller when he was dying on the cross (MATTHEW 27:34).

Fig trees were common in Israel. Figs were commonly eaten fresh, but were also dried on roofs for consuming throughout the year. Figs were used to make cakes and also medicinally (2 KINGS 20:7).

The shepherd

Sheep were valued highly by the Jews as they provided wool, meat, and milk, while sheepskins and goatskins could be used to make tents. Wool was also bartered for essential goods, and even the sheep's horns were used, to make trumpets (LEVITICUS 25:9) and to contain oil.

In Bible times, the shepherd kept goats and sheep in the same flock. Goats gave milk, which could be used to make a kind of yogurt. Goat's hair made coarse cloth for covering tents and clothes, while goatskin leather was used to make water bottles.

A shepherd sometimes looked after the sheep and goats belonging to everyone in his village. In winter after rain, there was plenty of grazing near the village. After the grain harvest, the sheep and goats grazed on the stubble that had been left behind. When the summer sun dried the grass, the shepherd had to lead the flocks further away to find pasture (1 CHRONICLES 4:39–40).

The shepherd also searched for a stream to water the sheep. If there was no flowing water, he had to find a well to draw water for the sheep and goats to drink. The shepherd normally walked ahead of his sheep, leading them to pasture; his sheep followed because they recognized his voice. The shepherd also had to guard his flock from the wild animals that roamed the country (1 SAMUEL 17:34–36). Lions, bears, jackals, and hyenas all sought animals such as sheep to eat. At night the shepherd would find a safe place to shelter his sheep (LUKE 2:8). He would often take them to a cave, and sleep across the entrance, to prevent wild animals from getting in (JOHN 10:7).

Shepherd.

In the village, there would sometimes be a stone sheepfold. The shepherd watched out for straying sheep, to restore them quickly to the fold (LUKE 15:3–7). At the end of summer, the sheep would be sheared. When sheep-shearing was finished, the shepherds celebrated with feasting (1 SAMUEL 25).

Shepherds' tools included a club or "rod," a heavy weapon, used to protect their sheep from predators. The shepherd's staff was a 6-foot (1.8 meter) stick used to snare sheep that strayed. It also helped the shepherd as he was walking over rugged land. The shepherd could also use the staff to count the sheep and guide them into the sheepfold at night. The shepherd would have a leather sling for throwing stones at wild animals and a "scrip," or leather bag, to carry food. Some shepherds also had a pipe to play while watching their sheep and goats.

The fisherman

In Jesus' time, many fishermen worked on the Sea of Galilee. Numerous fishing villages surrounded the lake. Some fishermen used a cast net (MARK 1:16–17), a circular net measuring about 17 feet (5 meters) across, with weights around the edge. When a fisherman saw fish in shallow water, he would wade into the water and "cast" the net over them. Peter and Andrew were casting nets when Jesus called them to follow him (MATTHEW 4:18). Some fishermen also used a rod and line.

Fishermen in Jesus' time used small sail boats, with a single sail and a long steering oar, capable of holding about four men. After a day's fishing, they would leave their nets to dry, and mend any tears in them. If they were fishing from a boat, fishermen would often use a seine net (LUKE 5:4), a long net about 10 feet (3 meters) wide that was let out behind the boat. Fish were then caught in the net as the boat sailed along. In contrast, the dragnet was about 8 feet (2.4 meters) wide, but perhaps 300 feet (100 meters) long. Launched from two boats, the nets formed a circle in which all kinds of fish could be caught.

Fishermen combine for a big catch.

The potter

In Bible times, clay was used to make jars for water, pots for meat, bowls and jars for oil and flour, and cups and pitchers for drinking. The earliest potters made bowls and jugs by rolling out long snakes of clay and coiling them up. They then smoothed down the surface, before leaving the pot to dry and harden. Later, potters discovered they could make smooth, round pots on a flat, turning wheel.

Oil lamps, which had a lip on one side, were made by pressing clay into a wooden mold to shape them. The potter also made things by hand, such as toys, ornaments, and little figurines. Once the clay object had dried, the potter put it in a kiln to "fire" it. The clay pots would come out hard; however they broke easily if knocked or dropped.

The carpenter

The carpenter built houses and made furniture, used tools such as a handsaw and axe. Isaiah mentions four other carpenter's tools: the measuring line, marking tool, plane, and a tool for making circles (ISAIAH 44:13). The carpenter did smaller jobs too, making doors and door frames, wooden locks, tables, stools, and chests for the home, and plows, yokes, and shovels for the farmer.

The leatherworker

Leather was used in Bible times to make bottles, belts, soldiers' helmets, shields, and slings. The leatherworker prepared his leather by skinning a goat or ox, scraping the skin to remove the hair, and soaking the skin in lime to remove any remaining hair. Next, he softened the leather, rubbed it with dog droppings and hammered it. Sometimes he would dye it before making sandals, belts, or other saleable items.

Leather was used to make awnings, walkway coverings, sunshields for houses and public buildings, and for coats, drinking flasks, and tents. Goatskins were also used as liquid containers: the leg and tail openings were sewn up and the neck opening became the mouth of the bottle.

Tentmaking.

Music of Bible times

Music was very important to the Israelites. Musicians sang or played their instruments during temple services, special feasts, weddings, and funerals.

Lyre player.

Instruments of Bible times included:
The lyre had strings made of twisted grass or dried animal gut. Young David played a lyre to soothe King Saul, and it was also the chief instrument of the Temple orchestra.
The harp, which had twelve strings, was louder and lower in pitch than the lyre. It was also important in the Temple orchestra.
Brass cymbals were large and loud and played in pairs, one in each hand. Smaller, one-handed cymbals dangled on strings, and had a higher, tinkling sound.
The tambourine was made of two skins stretched over a wooden hoop and beaten like a drum. Moses' sister Miriam played the tambourine in rejoicing when the Egyptians were defeated (EXODUS 15:20).
The curved trumpet, made from a hollow ram's horn, could sound only two or three notes. It was used to call people to worship and to battle.
The trumpet of Bible times was made of metal, and was straight, long, and ended in a bell-shape. It had no valves.
The pipe consisted of two reeds—and probably two pipes—made of wood, ivory, or bone. It made a wailing sound and was played at joyful occasions and funerals.
The flute, a long, straight instrument made of hollowed-out wood or bone, was often played by shepherds, but also at celebrations and funerals.

Towns and cities

Towns and cities of Bible times were small by modern standards. They were usually walled (LEVITICUS 25:29, 31), and villages were often sited nearby so city-dwellers could protect the villagers from their enemies. The walls were vital for protection. The walls of ancient Jericho, built around 5,000 BC, were roughly 6.5 feet (2 meters) thick with towers 30 feet (9 meters) high. The ancient city of Babylon had an outer wall 11 feet (3.4 meters) thick, an inner wall 21 feet (6.4 meters) thick, and a tower spaced every 60 feet (18 meters).

Towns and cities were often built on a hill to make attack difficult, since any approaching enemy had to climb a steep slope. When a city was destroyed, the rubble was flattened and the victors built a new city on top. After a number of such destructions, the city level would rise to create a mound.

The gate was a city's weakest point and needed careful defense. If an enemy took the gate, he could capture the entire city. City gates were shut at night, to avoid strangers or enemies entering in darkness. For added protection, two sets of gates separated by a yard were built in later years. If the enemy broke through the outer gate, he still had to break down the inner gate. Meanwhile the defenders could drop rocks and weapons on to attackers in the yard below. Often towers were constructed next to the gate, to serve as a lookout for the city's defenders. There were also towers at corners of the wall, so that the defenders could shoot arrows and hurl stones at invading forces.

The marketplace, normally sited near the city gate or on a busy street, was a very important center in towns and cities of Bible times. The court of elders of the city would convene at the city gate, where important news was also announced. Also, the Jewish prophets frequently spoke God's message to their people at the gate.

Marketplace.

Bartering and bargaining were both common in the market. But the marketplace was not solely for doing business, it was also a gathering place. Children played (MATTHEW 11:16) and workers looked for jobs there (MATTHEW 20:3–4). Because it was a meeting-place, Paul went to the marketplace (or "agora") in Athens to preach the good news (ACTS 17:17).

Streets of Bible times were often merely narrow alleyways, with houses and other buildings right up to the street. Household waste and debris were thrown into the unpaved street, which rapidly became filthy. The narrow, dark streets could also become dangerous, with wild dogs roaming. By contrast, Roman streets were wide, straight, and paved— and the Romans built drains to carry away any sewage.

There was little rain during the long summer, so water was vital for towns in Bible times. A reliable water supply was important for the inhabitants and also to raise herds and flocks successfully. Settlements were normally built near to a water supply. There were cisterns to store water throughout Israel; some formed in the natural limestone rock. Man-made pools were also used to store water, for instance two pools excavated at Gibeon. There was also a pool at Samaria (1 KINGS 22:38) and several in Jerusalem. The Romans built aqueducts to carry water into Jerusalem.

Travel

Land travel

Palestine is a bare, hilly country. In Bible times it was difficult for travel and there were few good roads. Travel was also dangerous, so people left home only if they had to. Most travelers journeyed on foot; those who could afford to went on horseback or by horse-drawn carriage. The roads were often dangerous, with thieves lying in wait. Jesus told a story about a man who was set upon by thieves on the road to Jericho (LUKE 10:30–35).

The best roads were built by the Romans. They were straight and level, enabling the Roman army to march rapidly when necessary. There was a popular saying: "All roads lead to Rome." In Roman times, a mounted courier could cover 75 miles (120 kilometers) in a day, changing horses on the way. Nevertheless, distances were so great that it still took more than 50 days to travel from Rome to Caesarea in Palestine.

The donkey was used to carry both people and goods. People also used donkeys to turn heavy mill-wheels and water-wheels. The camel was an adaptable beast of burden; it could store enough water to last several days, making it ideal for crossing the desert. Abraham used camels for long journeys (GENESIS 24:10–11, 64), as did his grandson Jacob (GENESIS 31:17). In Bible times camels were used by merchants journeying across the desert (JUDGES 6:5). Mules were little used until the time of David but had become common by the time of the prophet Isaiah (ISAIAH 66:20).

Travel

Horses were used by the Egyptians and Assyrians to pull war chariots (EXODUS 14:9). Later, David and his son Solomon used horses and chariots (2 SAMUEL 8:4; 2 CHRONICLES 1:14; 9:25). Ox-wagons could be used to haul heavy goods.

Sea travel

Palestine had no natural harbors on the Mediterranean coast, apart from north of Mount Carmel. The Israelites were not great sailors, and were quite scared of the sea. In Bible times, the Philistines, Phoenicians, Greeks, and Romans built most of the ships on the Mediterranean.

Solomon had a fleet of Phoenician ships that traded with Spain, Ophir, and southern India (1 KINGS 9:26–28; 10:22). In Jesus' time, the Romans sailed large ships that traded with the ports of Palestine. These merchant ships had two massive oars used as rudders, a tiller, a square mainsail, and sometimes extra sails. Some of them carried grain from Egypt to Rome, while smaller vessels traded up and down the Mediterranean coast of Palestine.

For part of the year no ships sailed because the weather was too dangerous. Roman law forbade sailing between 10 November and 10 March. As a prisoner, Paul had to sail to Rome aboard a big grain ship. Such ships were difficult to handle in stormy weather, and his vessel met with turbulent seas and hurricane-force winds. Finally, it was wrecked off the coast of the island of Malta (ACTS CHAPTER 27), though without any fatalities.

Cutaway of small Roman merchant ship.

The religion of Israel

Religious life

For the Israelites, worshiping God was not a matter of going to services. Although services and other religious practices were important, being God's people involved the whole of life. For the Jews, there was no difference between religious and non-religious activities. If they treated people unfairly or disobeyed the commandments, religious observance counted for nothing.

Worshiping God involved living one's life the way God had laid down. Family life, working life, social and political life all had to be carried out in a way that honored God and reflected his Law. Regulations about worship are found along with laws about farming, fighting, clothing, commerce, loving, and learning. All of them were important in people's relationship with God; all could be seen as part of worship.

Nevertheless, the occasions when people took part in specific religious activities were important.

Levites

Israel was divided into twelve tribes, among which the tribe of Levi acted as assistants to the priests, looking after the religious aspects of life.

In the early days, when Israel was travelling in the desert, the Levites were responsible for the Tabernacle, and for carrying the tent and the Ark of the Covenant from place to place. Later they were responsible for cleaning the Temple and looking after its furniture and implements. They also supervised the collection and distribution of gifts for the Temple and the poor.

The Levites were not assigned an area of the country, like the other tribes. Instead, they were allocated small sections throughout the country, so they could help with local religious activities. They received payment from funds raised by gifts and taxes on the people.

From the time of Solomon, some Levites were trained as singers and musicians for worship in the Temple.

Priests

The spiritual leaders of Israel were the priests, who came from one clan of the Levi tribe. The priests were all descended from Moses' brother, Aaron. Every boy born into a priestly family was prepared for priest's work from childhood, but served as a priest only between the age of thirty and fifty.

The priests led worship within the Temple and also made the sacrifices. When the people brought sacrifices to offer to God, the priests had to ensure they were properly prepared before offering them. People who had recovered from an infectious illness or a skin disease like leprosy had to have their health checked by a priest.

The priests of Israel wore special clothing to show that they had been set apart for their sacred duties. Their costume, called an ephod, was made of white linen or Egyptian cotton (1 SAMUEL 2:18–19).

Priests sacrifice in front of the Tabernacle.

The high priest

One priest was appointed high priest. Once a year, on the Day of Atonement, he alone entered the Most Holy Place in the innermost part of the Temple, where the Ark of the Covenant was kept. The high priest also worked alongside the king and the prophets in leading the nation.

The high priest wore elaborate clothes. His top garment was an ephod embroidered in sacred colors—scarlet, blue, and purple—and interwoven with gold. On each shoulder he wore a semi-precious stone inscribed with the names of the twelve tribes of Israel, to symbolize the unity of the twelve tribes of the nation gathered to worship God.

Over his ephod he wore a jeweled breastplate, with a pouch holding two stones, Urim and Thummim (EXODUS 28:15–30), that were used for casting lots. Beneath the ephod the high priest wore a blue tunic with 72 miniature golden bells hanging from its hem. He could not move without setting the little bells tinkling. The high priest also wore a linen turban on his head (EXODUS 28:37).

The Tabernacle

The Tabernacle was a portable sanctuary—a holy place for worshiping God—created in the desert. It symbolized God's presence with his people and was where his will was communicated. When the people of Israel were journeying from Egypt through the wilderness towards the Promised Land, they lived in tents, so the Tabernacle was also a tent. It was designed so it could easily be dismantled when the Israelites moved their camp and then reassembled at the next halting place.

The Israelites anticipated that once peace and security had been secured, a permanent national shrine would be set up (DEUTERONOMY 12:10–11). However, this did not happen until the time of King Solomon, when the first Temple was erected (2 SAMUEL 7:10–13; 1 KINGS 5:15–19). The Tabernacle was a forerunner of the Temple. They are both closely linked historically, by their similar construction, and by their theology.

The best source of information about the Tabernacle is the book of Exodus. Exodus chapters 25–28 describe the construction and furniture of the Tabernacle, while chapters 35–40 recount how it was made. We are also given the specifications for Solomon's Temple (1 KINGS 6; 2 CHRONICLES 3–4) and the Temple seen in the prophet Ezekiel's vision (EZEKIEL 40–43)—both of which followed the basic plan of the Tabernacle.

The outer courtyard of the Tabernacle was rectangular, 100 cubits (about 150 feet or 45 meters) long on its north and south sides and 50 cubits (about 75 feet or 23 meters) wide on its east and west sides (EXODUS 27:9–18; 38:9–20). Enclosing this space was a fence, its framework consisting

The Tabernacle in the Israelite camp.

of 60 acacia wood pillars, 5 cubits (about 7.5 feet or 2.3 meters) high (EXODUS 27:18). The base of each pillar stood in a brass socket, and each pillar was held upright by cords (EXODUS 27:9–18; 35:17–18) fastened to brass tent pegs (EXODUS 27:19) that were driven into the ground inside and outside the court. Curtains of fine-twined linen, probably white or natural in color, were sewn together end to end to form a continuous screen right round the Tabernacle area. Each curtain was 22.5 feet (6.8 meters) long, and 7.5 feet (2.3 meters) high, so no one could peer over the fence.

A central entrance, about 30 feet (9 meters) wide and 5 cubits (about 7.5 feet or 2.3 meters) high, was at the eastern end of the Tabernacle court. This entrance was screened by an embroidered curtain woven from blue, purple, and scarlet material, and finely twisted linen (EXODUS 38:18). The entrance curtain was probably set back from the fence, to allow entry at both ends. This was the only entrance into the Tabernacle courtyard (EXODUS 27:16–18; 38:18).

Anyone entering the Tabernacle court was confronted immediately by the bronze altar of burnt offering, where sacrifices were offered to God. By Mosaic Law, this was the only place where sacrifices could be made. The altar stood at the east end of the court, probably about halfway between the entrance and the Tabernacle itself (EXODUS 40:29), reminding the people that they could not approach God except by the place of sacrifice. The altar consisted of a hollow box of acacia wood, 5 cubits (about 7.5 feet or 2.3 meters) square by 3 cubits (about 4.5 feet or 1.4 meters) high. It was lined with bronze inside and out to protect it from the heat, and was light enough to be carried on the bronze-covered poles that passed through bronze rings fixed at each corner (EXODUS 27:1–8; 38:1–7).

The Ark of the Covenant

The ark was a portable holy chest, built to hold the most sacred relics of Israel's history. It was constructed according to instructions given by God to Moses, and is sometimes also called "the ark of the Testimony" or "the ark of God." It was made of acacia wood overlaid with gold, with two cherubim standing on top, their outstretched wings touching.

The ark served as a container for the two tablets of the Law that Moses brought down from Mount Sinai, a sample jar of manna—the miraculous food thar God provided in the wilderness—and Aaron's rod that budded. The ark's cover, also known as the "mercy-seat," was the place where the high priest came once a year—on the Day of Atonement—to spill blood to atone for the people's sins. The Israelites believed God's presence was manifest between the two cherubim on the top of the ark, which made the ark the holiest item in the worship of ancient Israel.

The Ark of the Covenant.

The history of the Tabernacle

It was at Mount Sinai—identified with today's Jebel Musa in the Sinai Peninsula, at the base of which stands St Catherine's Monastery—that Moses received the Law. When the Jews turned away from God and started to worship the golden calf in the wilderness, Moses angrily shattered the tablets of stone inscribed with the Ten Commandments. After the people repented, Moses climbed Mount Sinai once again to intercede with God.

God renewed his covenant with Israel, gave them a second copy of the Law, and invited them to offer the materials needed to construct the Tabernacle. The people responded generously, giving much more than was required (EXODUS 36:5–6). The Tabernacle was completed on the first day of the first Jewish month (Abib, March–April) in the second year after the Exodus from Egypt. The cycle of sacrifices and worship that God had laid down for the new sanctuary now commenced (EXODUS 40:2).

Unlike the provisional tabernacle (EXODUS 33:7–14), this permanent, but mobile, Tabernacle was sited at the very center of the Jewish encampment. It must have appeared very impressive, with Mount Sinai as its backdrop. Moses and Aaron set up their tents on the east side of the Tabernacle, with the remaining three families of priests on the other three sides—the family of Kohath to the south; the family of Gershon on the west; and the family of Merari on the north—serving as the "bodyguard" of Israel's ruler, God, and preventing any unauthorized intrusion into the sacred area. Outside the inner square, in a wider square, the tribes of Judah, Zebulun, and Issachar camped on the eastern side, under the standard of Judah; Ephraim, Manasseh, and Benjamin to the west, under the standard of Ephraim; the less conspicuous tribes of Dan, Asher, and Naphtali, to the north, under the standard of Dan; and Reuben, Simeon, and Gad on the south side, under the standard of Reuben.

Into the wilderness

The Israelites remained at the foot of Mount Sinai for a year, until the Tabernacle and its furnishings were completed. They then set off again, heading for the Promised Land (NUMBERS 10:11). When the Israelite army organized the people for the march, the Tabernacle—carried on the shoulders of Levites—remained in the center, with the tribes from the east and south of the camp marching in front, those from the north and west to the rear (NUMBERS 2).

Although the Bible records the route taken by the Israelites in the wilderness, most of the places named in the itinerary in Numbers 33 are today unknown. Two sites can probably be identified: Hazeroth and Kadesh. Hazeroth has usually been identified as Ein Hudra, an oasis in the Gulf of Aqaba. Kadesh–barnea is today usually identified as the valley of Ein el-Qudeirat, a lush oasis based around the largest spring locally.

The Israelites arrived at Kadesh-barnea almost a year after leaving Sinai. From here, Moses sent out twelve spies to reconnoiter the Promised Land (NUMBERS 13). When all the spies except Joshua and Caleb returned with

St. Catherine's Monastery, Sinai.

discouraging reports, the Israelites panicked. Their fear turned to fury, in a mass uprising, and Moses' and Aaron's lives were saved only by God's direct intervention at the Tabernacle (NUMBERS 14:1–10). Because they failed to trust God, the Israelites were condemned to remain in the wilderness until every adult who had departed from Egypt perished (NUMBERS 14:20–25).

It was 38 years before the Israelites, the Tabernacle in their midst, set out again for the Promised Land. After leaving Kadesh-barnea, circling around Edom, and defeating the Amorites and Og, king of Bashan, they encamped on the Plains of Moab (NUMBERS 33:48–49), at the oasis formed by springs in the foothills of Moab. From here, Moses climbed Mount Pisgah (also known as NEBO, DEUTERONOMY 34:1) to survey the Promised Land, which he was not to be permitted to enter (DEUTERONOMY 3:27).

Mount Sinai.

Crossing Jordan

When Moses died, Joshua took over leadership of his people. After having dispatched two spies across the Jordan river to the ancient city of Jericho, he prepared the Israelites to enter the promised land of Canaan. The Ark of the Covenant was positioned at the head of the Israelite marching column and the people were ordered to follow it over the Jordan (JOSHUA 3:3–4), which dried up for their crossing. Gilgal, the site of the Israelites' first camp on the west side of the Jordan, became their first permanent settlement, and during the early stages of the Israelite conquest of Canaan, the Tabernacle was located here (JOSHUA 4:19; 5:10; 9:6; 10:6, 43).

The Ark figured prominently in the destruction of the stronghold of Jericho, carried around the city every day for seven days, before the "great shout" on the seventh day, after which the city walls fell. However, the Israelites failed to take the city of Ai, because of the sin of one man, Achan. Joshua and the elders of the nation fell before the Ark and implored God's help, before achieving success at the second attempt.

After the Israelites had captured the central highlands of Palestine, the Tabernacle was transferred there. Although the exact location is not clear, it was probably sited in turn at Shiloh, near Bethel, in the mountains of Ephraim (JOSHUA 18:1, 9–10; 22:9, 12); at Shechem, a city lying between Mount Gebel and Mount Gerizim, where the desert covenant was renewed (JOSHUA 8:30–35; 24); at Mizpah (JUDGES 20:1); and Bethel (JUDGES 20:18, 26). Finally, the Ark was taken back to Shiloh, perhaps because of that town's central position, and because it belonged to the powerful tribe of Ephraim.

The Tabernacle remained in Shiloh for the entire period of the Judges of Israel, although the Ark of the Covenant was removed from it during the time of Eli (1 SAMUEL 4:4), and never returned. By the time of the prophet Samuel, the sanctuary at Shiloh—now called the "house of the Lord"—appears to have become a more permanent structure, with doors (1 SAMUEL 1:7; 3:3, 15). This building likely replaced the earlier Tabernacle, which—with the passing of years and the wear and tear of moving—had deteriorated. It seems unlikely that Moses' Tabernacle survived beyond the period of the Judges.

The history of the Tabernacle

The capture of the Ark

During the time of Samuel, the warlike "Sea-Peoples," or Philistines, who had settled along the Mediterranean coast, threatened the existence of the Israelites. In about 1050 BC, after a major defeat at Aphek, the leaders of Israel carried the Ark into battle, in an effort to compel God to fight for his people (1 SAMUEL 4:1–11). But the Philistines once more emerged victorious, capturing the Ark and destroying the sanctuary at Shiloh.

After this battle, the Philistines took the Ark to Ashdod, where its presence caused the Philistine deity Dagon to collapse and plague to break out. It was therefore moved on to Gath, and then to Ekron, but the plague followed. At last, seven months after the capture of the Ark, the terrified people of plague-ridden Ekron returned it to Beth-shemesh in Israel (1 SAMUEL 6:1–14). From Beth-shemesh, the Ark was sent to Kiriath-jearim, above the modern village of Abu Ghosh, Israel—only 8 miles (13 kilometers) from Jerusalem—where for 20 years it was kept in the house of Abinadab, guarded by his son, Eleazar (1 SAMUEL 7:1–2).

When David became king over all Israel, he made Jerusalem his capital city. On Mount Zion, next to his palace, he set up a new Tabernacle for the Ark. In the first attempt to bring the Ark to its new home, David ignored the instruction that it be carried on priests' shoulders, and had it transported in a cart. When the oxen stumbled, Uzzah held the Ark to steady it, and was killed for his lack of reverence (1 SAMUEL 6:1–7). David then stored the Ark for a further twenty years, in the house of a foreigner, Obed-Edom (2 SAMUEL 6:10). Finally, the Ark was carried into Jerusalem on the shoulders of Levites (1 CHRONICLES 15–16), with David dancing before it.

Solomon's Temple

Because he was a "man of war," King David was not permitted to build a Temple, although he collected the money and materials for its construction. His son Solomon built the first temple in Jerusalem; it was twice the size of the Tabernacle which it replaced and on which it was modelled.

David purchased the site for the temple from Araunah the Jebusite. Its location is identified with Mount Moriah—modern Jerusalem's Temple Mount—where, years before, Abraham had been told to sacrifice his son Isaac. The Temple took seven years to build.

In front of the splendid Temple stood the bronze altar of sacrifice and the "molten sea," a huge tank supported on the backs of twelve bronze oxen and holding gallons of water, used by the priests for ritual washing. The Temple entrance was flanked by two great pillars, called Jachin and Boaz.

The Ark of the Covenant was situated in the innermost room of the Temple, the Most Holy Place or "Holy of Holies." The only major item surviving from Moses' Tabernacle, the Ark still contained the tablets of the Law, although the pot of manna and Aaron's rod had disappeared.

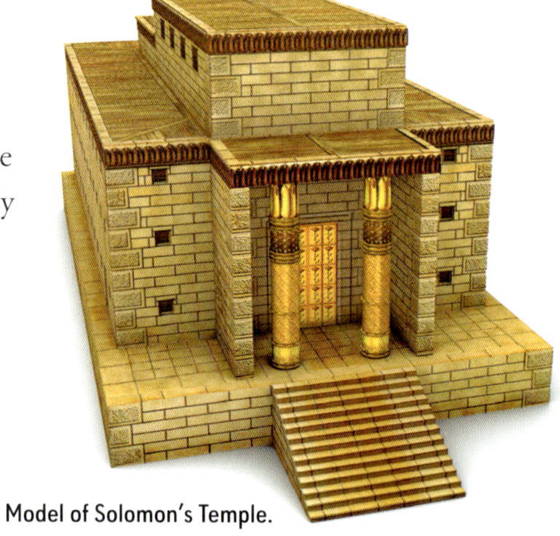

Model of Solomon's Temple.

The synagogue

Synagogues probably did not appear until the Jews were exiled in Babylonia (597–536 BC). After Solomon's Temple had been destroyed in 586 BC, the Jewish people needed an alternative place of worship: the synagogue filled this need. When they returned from exile to Palestine, the Jews built synagogues as places of worship in towns throughout the land, often situated at the highest point in the town or at crossroads. Its entrance often faced Jerusalem.

The Greek word "synagogue" means "bring together": the synagogue became the local religious meeting place for Jews. Men entered through the main door and sat together; the women had a separate door, usually leading to stairs to the gallery, where they sat with the children.

Jerusalem

Jerusalem is first named in the Bible when Abraham met Melchizedek, a mysterious king from Salem, or Jerusalem, who blessed the patriarch (GENESIS 14:18–20). Egyptian records from as far back as the nineteenth century BC refer to Jerusalem, as do fourteenth century BC clay tablets known as the Amarna Letters, found in Egypt. When the Israelites entered the Promised Land, they failed to drive the Jebusites out of their fortified town of Jebus (Jerusalem). After David became ruler of the united kingdom of Judah and Israel, he needed a new capital city. Jerusalem was ideally positioned for this purpose, belonging to neither of the two jealous kingdoms. David's commander, Joab, led a successful assault on Jerusalem, which now became known as "the City of David" (2 SAMUEL 5:6–10).

The Jebusites boasted that Jerusalem—perched on a hill with three steep sides—could never be captured. But David took Jerusalem by surprise when Joab's men climbed a water-shaft that tunneled beneath the city walls (2 SAMUEL 5:8). Having captured the city, King David strengthened Jerusalem's fortifications and brought the Ark of the Covenant within its walls, making this the political and religious center for God's people. David bought a threshing floor from the Jebusite Araunah, and on this site built an altar of sacrifice (2 SAMUEL 24:13–25). By tradition, this is Mount Moriah, where Abraham so nearly sacrificed his son Isaac (GENESIS 22:2). Jerusalem's most important building, the Temple, was to be built on the same site (2 CHRONICLES 3:1–2).

Besieged, destroyed, rebuilt

Jerusalem reached its greatest glory under Solomon, with the building of his palace and Temple there. Then followed a pattern of decline, siege, surrender, deportation, repatriation, and rebuilding.

In 925 BC King Shishak of Egypt came to Jerusalem and plundered the treasures of the Temple (2 CHRONICLES 12:9). Later, Jerusalem suffered famine when the Assyrian Sennacherib laid siege to it and shut up King Hezekiah "like a bird in a cage." The Bible records an amazing escape: "the angel of the LORD set out and struck down one hundred and eighty-five thousand in the camp of the Assyrians; when morning dawned, they were all dead bodies. Then King Sennacherib of Assyria left, went home, and lived in Nineveh" (2 KINGS 19:35–36).

Between the reign of Solomon and Jerusalem's destruction by King Nebuchadnezzar in 587 BC, Jerusalem was plundered eight times. The last king of Judah in Jerusalem, Zedekiah, was put in chains and taken to Babylon (2 KINGS 25:1–21), along with the precious Temple treasures.

Exile and return

King Jehoiachin and the leading citizens of Jerusalem were exiled by Nebuchadnezzar in 597 BC, followed by the rest of the able-bodied people, with King Zedekiah, in 587 BC. For 70 years the Israelites languished in Babylon, with their beloved city and Temple in ruins. Then King Cyrus of Persia issued an edict permitting the rebuilding of the Temple.

Gradually, Jerusalem was repopulated. Sheshbazzar was made governor of Judah in 538 BC; then Zerubbabel and Joshua led more exiles back to Jerusalem in 525 BC; as did Ezra in 458 BC. Nehemiah came to Jerusalem in 445 BC, with an armed escort. Nehemiah inspected the broken-down walls of Jerusalem and rebuilt them. "After fifty-two days of work the entire wall was finished" (NEHEMIAH 2:1–20; 6:15).

Jerusalem in the time of Solomon.

How the Bible came down to us

Books and scrolls

How the Bible was written down

The earliest permanent surface for writing was stone. The first reference to writing in the Bible regards the Ten Commandments, which were written on stone. The first pen was a chisel. For writing, the Assyrians, Greeks, and Romans used boards made from wood—sometimes ivory—covered with wax, and used a pointed stick as a stylus or pen.

In ancient Babylonia, clay was shaped into thin, flat, rectangular bricks for writing on. Words were pressed into the soft clay with a wedge-shaped stylus, then the clay was baked in the sun to harden. "Libraries" of such clay tablets have been discovered by archaeologists. People even used broken bits of pottery called "sherds" or "potsherds" to write notes, bills, and even shopping lists.

Papyrus plant.

The ancient Egyptians learned to make papyrus paper many years before the pyramids were built. They used the pith, or inner stalk, of Nile River papyrus reeds that grew in the marsh areas of the country. The thick, wet stems were laid criss-cross on top of each other and then beaten till they melded together to make a smooth, flat surface. This sheet could be written on once it had been dried in the sun. Papyrus was quite expensive, but it could be re-used by washing or scraping. The word "paper" is derived from "papyrus." The Egyptians wrote using brushes made out of reeds, and ink derived from plants and insects.

To make a smooth writing material called "parchment," the skins of sheep, goats, calves, and antelopes were dried, scraped, and cleansed. After this, the skins were stretched and beaten flat, ready to write on. Pens were made from reeds, with one end cut to a sloping edge and then split. Ink was created by mixing soot with oil or gum.

Books with pages had not yet been invented when the Bible was written down: people wrote on scrolls made out of sheets of papyrus, parchment, or even thin copper. These sheets were sewn or glued together to form a long strip, up to 30 feet long and 12 inches wide. Each end was fastened around a wooden rod; the reader unrolled the scroll with one hand and rolled it up with the other. When they were not in use, scrolls were wrapped in cloths and stored in tall jars for protection. There were drawbacks however: scrolls were awkward to carry, and it could take time to locate a short passage of Scripture on a long scroll. The apostle Paul wrote from prison in Rome asking his helper Timothy to bring him his "scrolls, especially the parchments" (2 TIMOTHY 4:13).

Copper scrolls.

Christians first collected together the books of the New Testament in the second century. They were probably among the earliest people to replace the scroll. In its place they started to combine a number of sheets of papyrus or parchment, fold them in half, sew them along the fold, and then add more folded sheets. This forerunner of our "book" was sometimes bound in a harder, more durable, cover. This early form of book was called a codex. The book had arrived!

Languages of the Bible

The earliest form of writing appeared nearly 5,500 years ago in Mesopotamia (modern day Iraq). The original simple pictures or images were gradually replaced by a series of characters that represented the sound of the local language, Sumerian. From around 2800 BC these characters were impressed into damp clay using a reed stylus, creating the wedge-shaped marks that we know as "cuneiform." From around 3200 BC the Egyptians created their own images or symbols to represent words, or parts of words. These are known as "hieroglyphs," from Greek words for "sacred carving." The Egyptians painted these symbols on papyrus—and even on walls.

The Babylonians did not have access to papyrus, and it was not easy to draw on clay. For this reason, their pictures became increasingly simplified, until words became standard shapes, pressed into the clay tablets with wedge-shaped sticks. This form of writing is known as "cuneiform," meaning "wedge-shaped."

In Canaan, around 1500 BC, a specific symbol—or letter—was for the first time linked to each sound in the language. About 25 letters were required for this purpose. There was now no need to learn hundreds of different shapes for the hundreds of different words. Any word could be written down by listening to its sounds and choosing the letters that matched. This simple concept spread quickly to other languages.

Most of the Old Testament is written in Hebrew, the language of the Israelite people. The Hebrew alphabet has 22 consonants but no vowels; vowel sounds have to be added by the reader. Hebrew is read from right to left, and therefore from back to front, so the first page of a Hebrew Bible is our last page.

Aramaic was the language of the Persians, the major power in the Middle East for two hundred years from around 550 BC, so it became the language used by traders

Cuneiform clay tablet.

Hebrew writing.

in that region. Some parts of the books of the Old Testament prophets such as Daniel, and Jeremiah, and the writings of Ezra, were written in Aramaic. By New Testament times, Aramaic had also become the everyday language of the Jews: Jesus would have spoken Aramaic. However, Hebrew remained the language of Jewish prayer and worship. The educated spiritual leaders of the Jewish people understood Hebrew, but when the Hebrew Bible was read out loud in a synagogue service, a translator interpreted it in Aramaic for the rest of the congregation. Some parts of the Old Testament have survived in Aramaic manuscripts called "Targums" (Hebrew for "translations"). These documents help us to discover the meaning of the original Hebrew.

In 331 BC, the Macedonian King, Alexander the Great conquered and occupied Persia. He ruled the entire known ancient world, and the language of his people—"common" (*koiné*) Greek—became the language understood by most people of that time. When followers of Jesus were writing what became the New Testament, they wrote in *koiné* Greek. In a few places they retained the original Aramaic words. For example, *"abba"* (MARK 14:36) is an Aramaic word meaning "dad." When Jesus said to Jairus's daughter, "*Talitha, koum!*" those were his actual Aramaic words—meaning, "Get up, my child!" (MARK 5:41).

The Greek alphabet was the first to include letters for vowels, and, unlike Hebrew, Greek is written from left to right. In Revelation 1:8, God says: "I am the *Alpha* and the *Omega*..."—the first and last letters of the Greek alphabet—"who is, and who was, and who is to come." In other words, God is eternal, without beginning or end.

Who Wrote the Bible?

Different parts of the Bible were written by different people over a long period of time. Only later were the many different parts collected together into a single book. Scholars are not sure when the books of the Old Testament were first written down; the period of their writing covered many centuries. Although there can be no certainty on this issue, there is a valid body of evidence that suggests that much—if not all—of the Old Testament was probably formally written down and collected together over a period of more than a thousand years, beginning most likely around the mid-Second Millennium (c.1500 BC) at the time of Moses, and concluding around 200 BC during the Second Temple period. At the same time, it is recognized that oral tradition almost certainly preceded the transcribing of the sacred Hebrew Scriptures—traditions that date back to the earliest times of Israel's patriarchs and ancestors. And there is a significant scholarly consensus that Moses, the leading prophetic figure of the Old Testament period—under the inspiration of the Spirit of God—gathered together some of these earliest oral traditions, edited them, and

Scribes copying.

produced the first five books of the Old Testament, now known as the Pentateuch.

By around the third century BC, the Jews recognized a number of their books as "holy," directly inspired by God. These books were also unambiguously affirmed by Jesus in Luke 24:44, after his resurrection, as having divine canonical authority. Our Lord categorized them as the three sections of the Jewish canon of Scripture—namely, the Law (of Moses), the Prophets, and the Psalms (the Writings). He affirmed that everything must be fulfilled that is written about him in these books. This is clear evidence that by the beginning of the third decade of the 1st century AD, the format and content of the Jewish Scriptures—what we now call the Old Testament—was recognized throughout Judea as Holy Scripture. Some 60 years later, at the Council of Jamnia (or Yavneh) in AD 90, this list of canonical books was re-affirmed for the expanding New Testament church. The theory that Jamnia formally canonized the Old Testament for the first time, has now been largely discredited. This council merely reinforced what was already widely known and accepted.

In early times, Jewish scribes were often the only people who could read and write. They drew up wills and other legal documents, and kept written records. When new copies of Old Testament scrolls were needed, these scribes had the sacred task of preserving, copying out, and explaining the teachings of the Old Testament.

Matthew, Mark, Luke, and John wrote the four Gospels based on eye-witness accounts of Jesus' life. The stories about Jesus' birth at Bethlehem, his life and miracles, and his death and resurrection—which we know from the Gospels of Matthew, Mark, Luke, and John—were all written down before about AD 100. The apostle Paul and other apostles wrote a number of letters to explain to believers about their faith, and to instruct them as to how Christians should behave. Some of these letters were written earlier than the Gospels, from around AD 50. The full canonicity of all 27 books of the New Testament, however, would not be recognized by all of Christendom for several centuries. It was not until around the mid-4th century AD, that the New Testament as we know it today was recognized.

Scrolls from the Dead Sea

In 1947 a Bedouin shepherd-boy noticed a hole in the cliffs of the barren hills west of the Dead Sea. When he tossed a stone down the hole, he heard the sound of breaking pots. He ventured inside and found a large number of earthenware jars—and inside them leather parchments covered in Hebrew writing. Eventually, roughly 400 scrolls were found in a series of caves near a place called Qumran. They were discovered to be

Dead Sea Scrolls were found in these caves.

the library of the Essenes, a Jewish religious sect, and included parts of almost every book in the Hebrew Old Testament. A Jewish community called the Essenes lived nearby around the time of Jesus, following a basic, monastic lifestyle. Carbon 14 dating and other research has shown that these "Dead Sea Scrolls" were written between 200 BC and AD 70. The Isaiah Scroll is almost complete, and is more than one thousand years older than our next oldest surviving copy of the book of Isaiah. The almost perfect correlation between the text of these two scrolls of the Book of Isaiah, separated by more than a millennium, is irrefutable evidence that testifies to the accuracy of the transmission of the text of the Hebrew Scriptures down through the ages. It gives us great confidence, that under the guidance of the Holy Spirit, the people of God—in both the Old and New Covenant ages—can be assured that our sacred Scriptures have been accurately preserved and transmitted throughout history.

What is the Septuagint?

In what is known as the dispersion, or "diaspora," Jewish people spread all over the Mediterranean world in early Christian times. At this time, the Jews often spoke Greek rather than Hebrew. The Old Testament was first translated from Hebrew into Greek in the second and third centuries BC, in a version known as the "Septuagint," a translation made in Alexandria, Egypt. The word "Septuagint" comes from the Latin for 70; by tradition 70 (or perhaps 72) scholars made this translation, which is sometimes written as LXX (70 in Roman numerals).

What is the oldest Bible?

Our earliest surviving complete text of the New Testament was originally copied out not long after AD 300. It was discovered at St Catherine's Monastery, at the foot of Mount Sinai, Egypt, and is known as *Codex Sinaiticus*. A German scholar named Constantine von Tischendorf (1815–1874) was visiting this remote monastery in 1844 when he encountered some ancient parchments with early Greek writing. They turned out to be part of the Old Testament dating from the fourth century AD. Eventually, Tischendorf found enough parchment pages to make almost a complete Bible. The *Codex Sinaiticus* is now preserved in the British Library, London. Other important early manuscripts of the Bible in Greek include the *Codex Vaticanus*, now in the Vatican Library, Rome, and the *Codex Alexandrinus*, also in the British Library.

Page of the Codex Sinaiticus.

Scribes and translators

Copying the Bible

After the Roman Empire collapsed in AD 476, Christian monks protected, preserved, and passed on the texts of the Bible. When a Bible wore out, monks spent years making a fresh copy. Every codex had to be copied out by hand, a long and laborious process. Sometimes mistakes were made, when a monk or scribe became tired, or because he was working in poor light. Sometimes a scribe deliberately changed things because he wanted to put the Scriptures into his own words or fit them to his point of view. The monks often worked in a scriptorium, or writing room, each man silent at his desk. Because of the danger of fire destroying priceless manuscripts, the room had no heat and no candlelight.

The first translations of the Bible

By AD 300, the New Testament had been translated into several languages, including Latin and Syriac, which was spoken in what is today part of Turkey. Syriac missionaries took the Christian gospel—and the Bible—eastward as far as China, India, Armenia, and Georgia.

The Armenian and Georgian alphabets were likely specially created so that the Bible could be written down in these languages. The Bible was also translated into Coptic, a form of ancient Egyptian—the language of the North African Christians—and Sahidic, a dialect of Coptic. In the fourth century, the language of the Germanic Ostrogoths had still not been written down, but around AD 350 Bishop Ulfilas, a Christian missionary to the Goths, translated the Bible into their language, which he committed to writing.

A Latin scholar called Jerome, born in northern Italy in about AD 345, became concerned about the impact of copyists' mistakes on the Bible text. He traveled widely, learning many languages, and transcribing many parts of the Scriptures. Around AD 382, Pope Damasus asked Jerome to make a completely new translation of the Gospels, Psalms, and other Old Testament books, partly to eliminate mistakes which had crept into various Bible versions. By this time, most Christians in the West spoke Latin and could not understand the Greek New Testament. So, in AD 386 Jerome moved to a monastery in Bethlehem, where he set about translating the Hebrew and Greek texts of the entire Bible into Latin. A Jewish rabbi helped him learn Hebrew so that he could translate directly from the Old Testament text. Jerome's Latin translation of the Bible, known as the Vulgate, or "Common Version," was the main Bible used by the Roman Catholics for centuries.

Monks copying.

Precious Bibles

In the Middle Ages, books were made of parchment—the skin of a sheep, goat, or calf. The latter animal's skin was known as vellum (from the French word *veau*, for "calf") a particularly fine parchment. In time, the monks began to illustrate the pages, resulting in the decorated books we know as "illuminated" manuscripts. Sometimes the copyists would add a painted border to the page, and often the first letter of a paragraph or chapter would be enlarged almost to fill the page, and then be decorated with patterns, flowers, or little figures. Quill pens, made from sharpened feathers, and basic brushes were the only tools available, but the results were exquisite.

In the fifth and sixth centuries AD, Irish monks traveled to Scotland and northern England, explaining the Christian faith and setting up monasteries, bringing with them the skill to create beautiful Celtic designs. The Book of Kells,

Part of an illuminated Bible.

a magnificent, illuminated book of the Gospels, originating from the island of Iona, western Scotland, is now preserved at Trinity College, Dublin. Most were less ornate than The Book of Kells, but even plain books took years to copy. They were also much valued, so when a Bible was placed in a monastery chapel, or a cathedral, it would often be chained to the reading-desk to stop anyone from stealing it.

The Bible for the people

In the Middle Ages most Bibles, however beautiful, were still written in Latin—a language the majority of people did not understand. Some men determined to change this by translating the Bible into their own vernacular language. In around 1175, Peter Waldo, a wealthy merchant from Lyons, France, took Jesus' words literally and gave away all his possessions. His followers, the Waldensians, translated the Bible into the Provençal language—and probably also into Italian, German, Piedmontese, and Catalan.

The first translation of any part of the Bible into the Anglo-Saxon language was a version of the Psalms, made about AD 700 by Bishop Aldhelm of Sherborne, in southern England. Before his death in AD 735, the Venerable Bede, Abbot of Jarrow, north-east England, translated part of John's Gospel.

John Wycliffe (c. 1330–1384) longed for the Bible to be translated into English so that ordinary people could understand it. By 1384 some of his followers, such as Nicholas of Hereford and John Purvey, had translated the

Burning Bibles.

entire Bible. This "Wycliffe Bible" was banned in 1408; nevertheless, hundreds of copies were made and sold secretly. Ordinary people could rarely read, so Wycliffe's followers—poor priests or "Lollards"—traveled from town to town, reading and explaining the Bible. Some of them were burned at the stake as heretics, with the Bibles tied around their necks. Despite this, around 170 copies of this version survive.

In fifteenth-century Prague, capital of Bohemia (now the Czech Republic) John Huss (1374–1415), the Rector of Charles University, started denouncing the greed, immorality, and ambition of priests. Influenced by Wycliffe's teachings, he was accused of heresy, imprisoned, and eventually burned at the stake. However, his followers began translating the Bible into Czech and a Czech New Testament appeared in 1475.

Printed Bibles

In fifteenth-century Mainz, Germany, the age of printed books began. The first complete book, printed by the pioneer Johann Gutenberg, was the Latin Bible, in 1454 or 1455. A complete copy is now worth around $35 million. Before long, presses sprang up across Europe—from Rome and Paris, to Cracow and London. Soon there were printed Bibles everywhere. William Caxton set up the first printing press in London by 1476, and the first printed Hebrew Old Testament appeared at Soncino, Italy, in 1488, produced by a group of Italian Jews.

The Dutch scholar Erasmus of Rotterdam (1466–1536), prepared the first printed edition of the Greek New Testament in 1516; it formed the basis for many modern European translations of the New Testament.

The German Reformer, Martin Luther (1483–1546), believed a good translation could be made only directly from the original language, and that it needed to be in everyday speech. While in hiding from persecution, he started to translate the Bible into vernacular German. The complete Luther Bible was published in 1534, one of the earliest in the language of the people. Even today, Luther's translation which helped shape the modern German language—remains the best-loved German Bible.

John Wycliffe

John Wycliffe (c. 1330–1384) is sometimes known as the "Morning Star of the Reformation." He lived in England during the fourteenth century, when the Roman Catholic church was suffering increasingly from corruption. Wycliffe was one of the great thinkers of his age, and wrote many important works of philosophy and theology. But he did not confine himself to the academic life.

In his forties, Wycliffe became involved in politics, siding with the government in its disputes with the papacy. During that time, his views became increasingly radical, as he questioned a number of accepted Catholic beliefs. Just when his ideas became most radical, the political situation changed, and his government no longer required his services. Wycliffe's ideas were condemned, and he had to retire. There he continued to write and encourage those seeking reform. His followers, the "Lollards," translated the Bible into English and journeyed widely preaching, but were fiercely persecuted and driven underground. However, Wycliffe's ideas paved the way for the Protestant Reformation, some 150 years after his death.

John Wycliffe.

Wycliffe's Bible contained many mistakes of translation and copying. Even after the invention of printing, there was no printed Bible which the English could read in their own language. It was pronounced illegal to translate or print any part of the Bible. However, William Tyndale (c. 1490–1536), the celebrated English biblical scholar and linguist, declared to a bishop, "If God spare my life … I will cause the boy that drives the plough to know more of the Bible than you do." Exiled in Germany, Tyndale translated the New Testament into everyday English from the original Greek. Printed copies were smuggled into England in 1526, but before he could finish translating the Old Testament, Tyndale was betrayed and burnt at the stake. For 300 years, English-speaking Protestants largely read the King James Version of the Bible, translated in 1611—closely based on Tyndale's version.

William Tyndale

William Tyndale (c. 1490-1536) could be called the father of the English Bible. Tyndale was determined to produce an accurate English version, translated from the original Hebrew and Greek, and make it available to all of God's people. The church authorities opposed this plan. Tyndale was therefore forced to go underground, to become "God's outlaw." He succeeded in translating all of the New Testament and some of the Old, but was betrayed by an enemy agent, and paid for his work with his life. In the end he triumphed, because his translation became the basis for almost all English translations of the Bible until recent times.

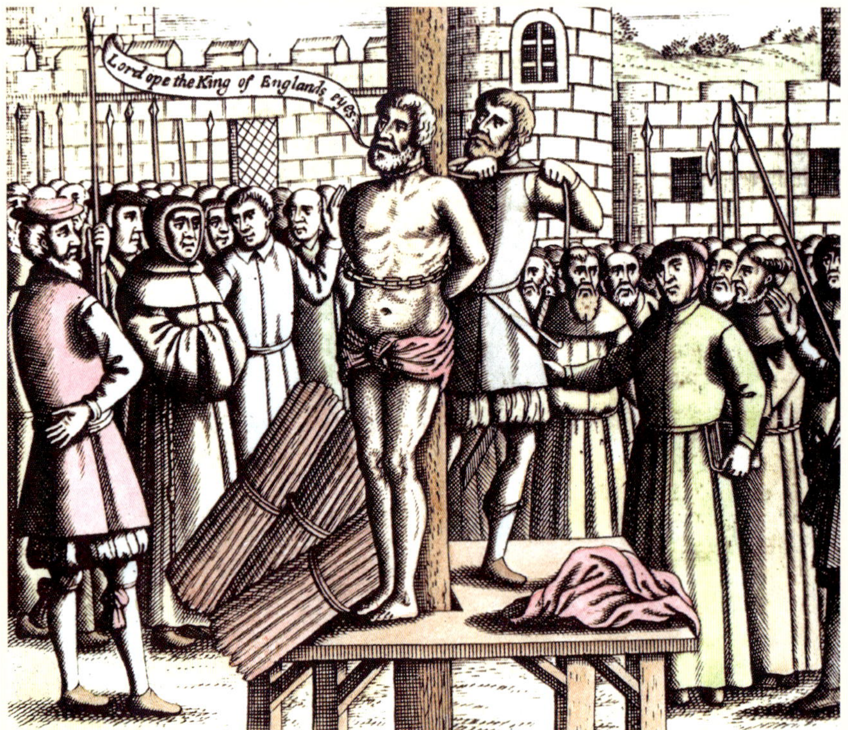

William Tyndale.

The expanding church

Timeline of Christianity

AD 62	James stoned to death
64–68	Great Fire of Rome; Nero blames and persecutes Christians
66–73	First Jewish-Roman War: Herod's Temple destroyed
72	Thomas martyred in India
c. 117	Ignatius, Bishop of Antioch, fed to lions in Rome
112	Pliny reports Christianity in Bithynia
c. 125	Rylands Library Papyrus P52, oldest known New Testament fragment
132–135	Bar Kokhba revolt. Jerusalem renamed Aelia Capitolina
150	Gospel reaches Portugal and Morocco
c. 160	Polycarp martyred
167	Pope sends Fuganus and Duvianus to convert Britons
174	First Christians reported in Austria
177	Persecution in Lyon, France
190	Tertullian says Christianity ranks throughout society, North Africa
200	First Christians reported in Switzerland and Belgium
202	Emperor Severus forbids conversion to Christianity
206	Abgar, King of Edessa, takes up Christian faith
250	Denis establishes church in Paris
c. 270	Anthony begins monastic movement
280	First rural churches in northern Italy
300	Probably 10 percent of the world population Christian Part of the Bible available in 10 different languages
301	Armenia first kingdom to adopt Christianity
303–312	Emperor Diocletian persecutes Christians
313	Edict of Milan: Constantine ends persecution, tolerates Christianity
325	First Council of Nicaea
325	Aksum (Modern Ethiopia) makes Christianity state religion
325	Church of the Nativity, Bethlehem
328–373	27 books of New Testament canon recognized
330	Constantine moves capital of Roman Empire to Byzantium, renames it Constantinople
c. 350	Codex Sinaiticus and Codex Vaticanus: earliest surviving Christian Bibles
360	Julian the Apostate, last non-Christian Emperor
363–364	Council of Laodicea
370–379	Basil the Great, Bishop of Caesarea
396–430	Augustine, Bishop of Hippo
c. 390	Ninian evangelizes Picts in Scotland
400	Jerome's Vulgate published
c. 400	Ethiopic Bible Peshitta Bible in Syriac (Aramaic)
406	Armenian Bible
410	Rome sacked by Alaric and Visigoths
432	Patrick begins mission in Ireland.
440–461	Pope Leo the Great stops Attila the Hun at Rome
451	Council of Chalcedon
455	Vandals sack Rome
476	Emperor Romulus Augustus deposed: often seen as fall of Western Roman Empire
496	Clovis I, King of the Franks, baptized
529	Benedict of Nursia establishes first monastery, Monte Cassino, Italy
563	Columba goes to Scotland, evangelizes Picts, sets up monastery at Iona
590–604	Gregory the Great, often seen as greatest pope, reforms church
596	Augustine of Canterbury evangelizes Jutes
622	Muhammad founds Islam, after fleeing to Mecca
664	Synod of Whitby unites Celtic Christianity with Roman Catholicism in Britain

Timeline of Christianity

718	Pope sends Boniface to evangelize Germans
730-787	Byzantine Emperor Leo III bans Christian icons
731	Bede writes English Church History
732	Battle of Tours stops Islam expanding westward
781	Nestorian Stele, Daqin Pagoda, and Jesus Sutras: evidence of Christianity in China
800	Charlemagne crowned first Holy Roman Emperor of the West
849-865	Ansgar, "Apostle of the North," evangelizes North Germany, Denmark, Sweden
863	Cyril and Methodius evangelize Slavs, translate Bible into Slavonic
909	Benedictine Abbey of Cluny founded, France
966	Duke Mieszko I of Poland baptized; Poland becomes Christian
c. 988	Kievan Rus' adopts Christianity
c. 1000	Stephen of Hungary crowned; Hungary becomes Christian
1054	East-West Schism between Eastern (Orthodox Christianity) and Western (Roman Catholic) churches
1065	Westminster Abbey consecrated
1095-1291	10 Crusades, first called by Pope Urban II at Clermont
1098	Monastery of Cîteaux founded; growth of Cistercian order
1118	Knights Templar founded, to defend Holy Land
1154-1159	Pope Adrian IV, first and only English pope
1163	Notre Dame de Paris
1205	Francis of Assisi founds Franciscan order
1274	*Summa Theologiae*, by Thomas Aquinas
1291	Acre, last Crusader city, falls
1305-1378	Avignon Papacy: Popes move to Avignon, France
1326	Metropolitan Peter moves from Kiev to Moscow
1380-1382	Wycliffe Bible
1414-1418	Council of Constance; Jan Hus burned at stake
1453	Fall of Constantinople, overrun by Ottoman Empire
1454-1455	Gutenberg Bible, first printed Bible
1473-1481	Sistine Chapel built
1478	Spanish Inquisition established
1483	Martin Luther born
1492	Columbus opens New World to Christianity
1517	Luther's Ninety-five Theses; Reformation begins
1519	Huldrych Zwingli begins Reformed tradition
1521	Luther at Diet of Worms
1522	Luther Bible
1525	Anabaptist movement begins
1526	Tyndale New Testament
1530	Augsburg Confession, first doctrinal statement of Lutheran Church
1534	Henry VIII establishes independent Church of England
1536	Calvin's *Institutes of the Christian Religion*
1536-1540	Monasteries in England, Wales, and Ireland dissolved
1537	Lutheranism made state religion of Norway and Denmark

Notre Dame, Paris.

1540	Jesuits founded by Ignatius of Loyola; help reconvert Poland, Hungary, and south Germany; send missionaries to New World, India, and China
1542	Roman Inquisition established
1545-1563	Catholic Council of Trent: Counter-Reformation begins
1549	Episcopalian Book of Common Prayer written by Thomas Cranmer
1553-1558	Mary I of England persecutes reformers
1560-1598	French Wars of Religion
1566	Index of Prohibited Books published
1571	Dutch Reformed Church established
1572	John Knox founds Scottish Presbyterian Church
1572	St. Bartholomew's Day Massacre: Many French Protestants murdered
1596	Ukrainian Catholic Church formed
1598	Edict of Nantes grants toleration to French Protestants (Huguenots)
1609	Baptists founded by John Smyth
1609-1610	Douay-Rheims Bible, first Catholic English translation
1611	King James Version published
1620	Plymouth Colony founded by Puritans
1648	George Fox founds Quakers
1678	John Bunyan publishes *Pilgrim's Progress*
1730-1749	First Great Awakening in North America
1735	Welsh Methodist revival
1738	Led by John Wesley, Methodist movement begins
1741	Handel performs *Messiah* for first time
1767-1815	Suppression of Jesuits
1780	Robert Raikes begins Sunday schools
1784	Roman Catholicism introduced in Korea
1789-1815	John Carroll, first American Catholic bishop
1789-1801	France dechristianized in French Revolution
1791	First Amendment to US Constitution
1801	Cane Ridge Revival, Kentucky
1816	Bishop Richard Allen founds African Methodist Episcopal Church, first African-American denomination
1828	Plymouth Brethren founded
1830	Charles Finney's revivals lead to Second Great Awakening in America
1845	Southern Baptist Convention formed
1847	Lutheran Church-Missouri Synod founded
1854	Immaculate Conception becomes Catholic dogma
1865	William Booth founds Salvation Army
1869-1870	First Vatican Council asserts Papal Infallibility
1886	Moody Bible Institute founded
1899	Gideons International founded
1904	Welsh Revival
1905	French law separates Church and State
1906-1909	Azusa Street Revival, Los Angeles, starts modern Pentecostal movement
1907	Church of God in Christ formed as Pentecostal body
1908	Church of the Nazarene founded

Salvation Army founder, William Booth.

1909	Scofield Reference Bible published
1910	Edinburgh Missionary Conference launches modern missions movement
1924	KFUO (AM)—first religious radio station in USA—founded
1925	Scopes Trial
1925	United Church of Canada formed
1945	Dietrich Bonhoeffer executed by Nazis
1947	Dead Sea Scrolls discovered
1948	World Council of Churches founded
1948	State of Israel established
1949	Billy Graham preaches first Los Angeles crusade
1950	Mother Teresa founds Missionaries of Charity
1951	Campus Crusade for Christ founded
1952	C. S. Lewis' *Mere Christianity* published
1957	United Church of Christ founded
1962–1965	Second Vatican Council
1970s	Jesus movement begins in USA
1973	New International Version of Bible
2013	Francis, an Argentinian, first non-European pope of modern times

Symbols of Christianity

In the first centuries of thc church, a number of different icons or signs were used by Christians

Symbol	Meaning
Alpha-Omega	The first and last letter of the Greek alphabet—showing God is all that can be, without beginning or end
Anchor	Faith
Bread and wine	The death of Christ; the Lord's Supper
Chi-Rho	The first two letters of "Christ" in Greek—so, Jesus Christ
Cross	The death of Christ
Dove	The Holy Spirit—at Jesus' baptism
Fire	The Holy Spirit—at Pentecost
Fish	"Jesus Christ"—the initial letters in Greek of "Jesus Christ, God's Son, Savior"—spelling ICHTHUS—Greek for "fish"
Lamb	The sacrifice of Jesus on the cross
Shepherd	Jesus—his loving care for his people
Ship	The Christian church—derived from Noah's ark
Vine	Jesus' union with his people; the wine of the Lord's Supper

Chi-Rho symbol.

Palm crosses.

How Christianity first spread

The Christian faith began in Palestine, the Jewish Promised Land, which had been ruled by foreign nations for much of its history because of its favorable strategic location. Egypt and Assyria had fought over it for centuries, until Babylon conquered Assyria, and with it, Palestine. The Persians allowed some Jews to return from exile to Palestine, before the Greeks under Alexander the Great conquered the land around 300 BC. There then followed rule by the Seleucid and Hasmonean dynasties until Rome captured Jerusalem in 63 BC. Palestine remained under Roman rule at the time of the birth of Jesus.

Christianity came into a world of great religious diversity. Even in first-century Roman Palestine there was not only Judaism, but also worship of the Roman emperor, mystery cults, and various kinds of Greek philosophy.

After Jesus' death, his followers in Jerusalem formed a community of believers that spread rapidly, first to Samaria, then to Phoenicia, Gaza, and Egypt, and later to the cities of Antioch and Damascus in Syria, and to the island of Cyprus. The message was carried by journeying preachers and missionaries. The first believers were all Jews, but they were soon joined by gentiles. These first believers were variously known as followers of "the Way," "Christians," and "Nazarenes."

In AD 62 James, leader of the Jerusalem believers, was executed, leading to some believers leaving the city, thus weakening its Jewish Christian community. During the First Jewish-Roman War (AD 66–73), the Romans utterly destroyed Herod's Temple and sacked Jerusalem. Most of the inhabitants were killed, committed suicide, or fled. The destruction of the Temple ended the Jewish priesthood and system of sacrifices, and was an enduring catastrophe for Judaism.

The Christian community probably left Jerusalem just before the siege, taking refuge at Pella, beyond the Jordan river, although some believers later returned. Christian communities near the Mediterranean coast, founded by the apostles, survived, as did Christian groups at Capernaum and Rimmon, in Galilee, and Cochaba, in Gaulanitis (modern Golan, Israel).

After the failure of the Jewish Bar Kokhba Revolt (AD 132–135), their Sanhedrin court moved away from Jerusalem to Jamnia, in Galilee. Following these two rebellions against Rome, many Jews were killed, expelled, or sold into slavery while pagans, Samaritans, and Jews were converting to Christianity. Together, these changes resulted in Christians becoming a majority in Palestine by the second century AD.

Over several generations, Christianity gradually separated from Judaism, with the destruction of the Temple and disaster of the two Jewish Wars accelerating this division. Increasingly, Christian missionaries directed themselves at gentiles in the Holy Land and elsewhere around the Mediterranean.

The Romans assault Jerusalem.

What happened to the twelve apostles?

There are many stories, traditions, and legends about the mission of the twelve apostles. They are believed to have traveled widely, carrying the message of the risen Christ. Many suffered persecution for their faith, frequently meeting violent deaths.

The apostle Peter is said to have preached in Antioch, Pontus, Galatia, Cappadocia, and in Rome itself. Peter's brother, Andrew, is believed to have preached to the Scythians (in modern Georgia) and Thracians (in modern Bulgaria), to have evangelized Byzantium (modern Istanbul), and to have been crucified at Patras, in Achaia (modern Greece). "Doubting" Thomas supposedly preached to the Parthians, the Medes, the Persians, the Hyrcanians, the Bactrians, and the Margians, and even reached India. The Mar Thoma Christians of India regard Thomas as their founder. Philip possibly preached in Carthage, North Africa, and in Phrygia (modern Turkey).

The apostle Matthew is held to have written his Gospel in Antioch, and to have preached in Persia, Parthia, and Ethiopia. Bartholomew—also known as Nathanael—is said to have journeyed to India with Thomas, taking Matthew's Gospel, as well as visiting Armenia, Ethiopia, and Southern Arabia. James, the son of Alphaeus, may have evangelized in Syria, while Simon the Zealot is said to have preached in Persia. James, one of the sons of Zebedee, preached in Judea—and, according to legend, as far away as Spain. His brother John was banished to the Aegean island of Patmos, and is the only one of the Twelve believed to have died a natural death, in the city of Ephesus. An early tradition claims that he escaped unharmed after being thrown into boiling oil in Rome. Judas—also known as Lebbaeus or Thaddaeus—preached in Edessa, Armenia, and in Mesopotamia, and died at Berytus, modern Lebanon. Matthias—chosen by lot to replace the traitor, Judas Iscariot—according to tradition traveled with Andrew to Syria.

Ancient theater, Ephesus.

The first-century church

Paul and the other Jewish apostles carried the Christian message to areas far beyond Palestine. With the specific aim of evangelizing gentiles, they traveled widely in Asia Minor (modern Turkey) and Greece, visiting Jewish synagogues—where their message often met opposition—but also speaking with gentiles in the marketplace. Following their visits, they left behind them small, uncertain groups of Jewish and gentile Christians, whose faith was strengthened by further visits and by letters such as those included in the New Testament.

By the end of the first century, Christianity was still found mainly in the eastern part of the Roman Empire, concentrated in Asia Minor—where Jewish communities had long been present, attracting to their synagogues God-fearing gentiles. There were also Christian communities in Italy—in Rome itself, in Puteoli, on the Bay of Naples—and possibly also in Spain. The only church we know of that was outside the Roman Empire was at Edessa, beyond the Euphrates River.

We know the names of towns and cities with Christians from the New Testament—for instance the seven churches of Revelation chapters 1–3—and from contemporary letters. The Early Church Father, Ignatius of Antioch, mentions churches he knew at Magnesia and Tralles, and later writers mention a Christian community at Alexandria, Egypt, the home of Apollos, one of Paul's helpers.

Coin of Emperor Nero.

During the reign of the notorious Emperor Nero (AD 54–68), the first major state persecution of Christians took place, but it was short-lived and concentrated in Rome, so it did not hinder the overall spread of the church. A letter of Pliny the Younger, governor of the Roman province of Bithynia (on the northern coast of modern Turkey), shows that—only eighty years after Jesus' crucifixion—Christianity had grown to a strength where it was impacting the Roman Empire. Around AD 110, Pliny wrote to the Emperor Trajan describing the trials he was organizing to discover and execute Christians:

Forum, Rome.

> "... many of every age, of every social class, even of both sexes, are being called for trial and will be called. Not only cities, but villages, and even rural areas have been invaded by the infection of this superstition."

Pliny was writing from a remote Roman province, yet—within a few generations of its beginning—Christianity had clearly entered every level of society.

Ninety years later, around AD 200, Tertullian, a Roman lawyer who had converted to Christianity, wrote a letter to Roman magistrates defending Christianity against persecution, boasting proudly (though exaggerating) that "nearly all citizens of all cities are Christians."

A Christian Empire?

During the second century AD, Christian communities spread widely westward and northward, as far as Gaul (modern France) and Germany. Many groups of believers were established in North Africa, laying the foundations for the strong church that existed there in the third century. In Egypt, Christianity started to extend beyond the great city of Alexandria into surrounding rural areas. Further Christian communities were founded in Mesopotamia, while in the Christian stronghold of Asia Minor the church spread both northward and eastward.

During the period of the Roman emperors Nerva, Trajan, Hadrian, Antoninus Pius, Marcus Aurelius, Lucius Verus, and Commodus (AD 96–192), Christians were largely left in

Persecution of the first Christians

Date	Emperor	Persecution	Well-known martyrs
64	Nero	Emperor blamed Christians for fire in Rome.	Paul, Peter
c. 90-96	Domitian	Sporadic persecution, mainly in Rome and Asia Minor. Christians punished for refusing to worship the emperor.	Clement of Rome, John (exile to Patmos)
98-117	Trajan	Sporadic. Christians executed when found, but not hunted down.	Ignatius, Symeon, Zozimus, Rufus
117-138	Hadrian	Sporadic. Similar to Trajan's policy.	Telesphorus
161-180	Marcus Aurelius	Emperor was Stoic, so opposed to Christianity. Christians blamed for natural disasters.	Justin Martyr, Pothinus, Blandina
202-211	Septimus Severus	Forbade conversion to Christianity.	Irenaeus, Perpetua
235-238	Maximus	Christian clergy executed.	Ursula, Hippolytus
249-251	Decius	First empire-wide persecution. Return to paganism—so extermination of Christianity.	Fabianus
257-260	Valerian	Christians forbidden to assemble, their property confiscated.	Origen, Cyprian
303-311	Diocletian	Worst persecution of all. Churches were destroyed, Bibles burned, Christians' civil rights suspended, sacrifice required to Roman gods.	Alban

peace, unharmed by the authorities, which helped greatly the growth of Christianity throughout the empire. By the end of the third century the shape of the Christian world looked quite different. As the church expanded westward—as far as Roman Britain—the city of Rome, along with Alexandria and Antioch—became a very important center.

In AD 312, the Emperor Constantine the Great (AD 274–337) won a decisive battle at the Milvian Bridge, outside Rome, after having called upon the "God of the Christians" and putting a Christian symbol on his shield. Although he continued to tolerate other faiths, his granting of toleration for Christianity in 313 opened up a new era for the long-oppressed Christians. They were now free for the first time both to worship in public and to build churches. Constantine moved his capital to Byzantium—renaming it Constantinople—where he even erected new churches at public expense.

By the time Constantine died, in 337, the Christian Church was firmly established in the Roman Empire. In 380, the Christian Emperor Theodosius recognized the majority position of Christianity in the Roman state by making the faith the only official state religion. Christianity had conquered a mighty empire.

Earlier in the fourth century, Armenia had become the first ever country to adopt Christianity as its official religion. In other parts of the world, particularly in Africa and western Asia, the Church had also made significant progress. Only a little more than three hundred years after the death of Christ, the new religion appeared to be on the brink of even greater victories.

However, Christianity had lost some of its original zeal, together with much of its earlier simplicity. Christian leaders became confidants of emperors, and Christianity popular with the masses.

Constantine the Great.

Augustine of Hippo

Augustine of Hippo (AD 354–430) stands at a turning-point, living at the end of the period of the church's initial growth, when the Roman Empire was crumbling into decay. However, he also looked forward to the church of the Middle Ages, which he strongly influenced. Brought up in Roman North Africa, by his pious mother, Augustine led a dissolute adult life until "the light of faith flooded into [his] heart." Augustine then turned to a life of preaching and teaching, becoming a fearless defender of Christianity.

Augustine left his mark in a tightly-argued system of theology based on the letters of the apostle Paul. He developed a doctrine of predestination: No reason can be given why some are saved and the rest damned—it is due solely to God's inscrutable choice. Similar ideas were later taken up by Bernard of Clairvaux, Martin Luther, and particularly John Calvin. Augustine's classic books, his *Confessions*—often called the first Western autobiography—and the *City of God*, have influenced generations of Christians.

Augustine of Hippo.

What did monks do for the church?

Most religions include people who take their beliefs more seriously and exactingly than the rest. Sometimes they reject things other people consider normal and good—for example marriage and sex. Sometimes, searching for greater piety, they pray more, at more inconvenient times. And sometimes they withdraw to a solitary life, devoted to cultivating the soul, or to a community life, apart from the world, but with others of similar persuasion.

In Jesus' time, John the Baptist was a solitary ascetic, living simply in the Judean wilderness and preaching a stern message of repentance. Some early Christian groups in the centuries immediately afterwards followed a similar path. James, first leader of the Jerusalem church, was noted for his frequent fasting and prayer.

After Constantine officially tolerated and recognized Christianity, the church began to attract many new members—but ethical and spiritual standards fell because it seemed less was now demanded of believers. Those seeking a purer form of Christianity started to withdraw from the churches—and from society itself. Monastic life came to be seen as the ideal for the most devout.

Some started to follow the life of the hermit, a person dedicated to God. Anthony the Great (c. 256–356), a young Egyptian, is the earliest well-known Christian hermit. He is said to have spent fifteen years living among tombs in the desert, before moving to the middle of the desert in order completely to escape human society and cultivate a closer relationship with God. Ultimately, he set up a community of monks at Mount Colzim, near the Red Sea.

Many other hermits withdrew, to the deserts of Syria and Egypt, temporarily or permanently retreating from society in the search for a more spiritual way of life. Living alone or in small groups, they dedicated themselves to prayer and meditation, often also attempting feats of exceptional spiritual endurance, such as fasting and sleep deprivation.

The first Christian monastery we know of was set up around 320 by Pachomius, who founded an ascetic community at Tabennisi, by the Nile River. Rejecting the most extreme rigor, Pachomius set out regular routines for meals and worship. Further communities followed, at first only for men. Pachomius created a lasting template for a community of monks, sometimes living in a single building, following a set rule.

By the end of the fourth century, monastic living had spread from Egypt throughout the Christian world, in both town and country. By this time, there were at least 300 monastic houses in the city of Constantinople alone. Others were located in remote spots such as St Catherine's, Mount Sinai; rock-cut caves in Cappadocia; and the Holy Mountain of Athos, Greece.

Basil the Great (330–379), Bishop of Caesarea, Cappadocia, founded a community that emphasized significant new features. He decided that monks and hermits should be better integrated into the local church, and that communal rather than solitary prayer should take priority in the monastery. Basil also wanted monasteries to serve society: his own community offered medical help, relief for the poor, and education to those living nearby. Basil's model is still observed by Orthodox Christians today.

Monastery of St Anthony, Egypt.

What did monks do for the church?

Martin of Tours (d. 397) pioneered monasticism in Western Europe. He set up a monastery at Marmoutier, France, noted for its austerity and holiness, which helped hasten the spread of Christianity into France.

The Roman statesman Cassiodorus (c. 485–c. 585), founded a monastery at Vivarium, in Calabria, southern Italy, which introduced the study and copying of ancient manuscripts, an activity that became associated with Christian monasteries and helped save many important texts.

Benedict of Nursia (c. 480–c. 547)—the so-called "Father of Western Monasticism"—created the standard "rule" for monasteries in Western Europe. He is said to have set up the influential monastery of Monte Cassino, southern Italy, in 528. His hugely significant rule divided a monk's life into two essential activities—prayer and work—and demanded vows of poverty, chastity, and obedience. Benedict also insisted that the monastery should provide care for the weak and the sick, and hospitality to strangers. Daily life in a Benedictine monastery was built around a set pattern of seven prayer services: Matins (or Lauds), Prime, Terce, Sect, Nones, Vespers, and Compline. Gradually the Rule of Benedict replaced all other rules in the monasteries of Western Europe, and Benedictine monks set up monastic houses throughout the West. Even today, most monasteries observe the Rule of Benedict.

Beyond the reach of Rome, a different form of monastery sprang up in Ireland. Irish monks became noted for their devotion to Christ, their mystical spirituality, their scholarship, their asceticism, their restlessness, and their evangelistic zeal. Irish monasteries became known for their libraries and richly illustrated manuscripts, with their intricate Celtic designs. While

Medieval monastery.

What did monks do for the church?

monks elsewhere were required to remain in one location, Irish monks had a tradition of wandering. The monks often traveled in groups of twelve, imitating the twelve apostles, and establishing churches and holy days.

The monasteries played a vital role in the conversion of Europe. In the fifth century, the Briton Ninian founded a monastery and preached in southern Scotland. Columba (c. 521–597) founded several monasteries in Ireland before sailing to the island of Iona, off the west coast of Scotland. With his followers he then evangelized in Scotland, and his disciple, Aidan (d. 651), journeyed to Northumbria, north-east England, founding the monastery of Lindisfarne. Another disciple of Columba, Columban (c. 543–615), founded monasteries in France and northern Italy. Willibrord (658–739), "Apostle to the Frisians," founded the monastery of Echternach, which grew into a major missionary center. Possibly the most remarkable missionary of this period was Boniface (c. 675–754), the "Apostle of Germany," who founded several monasteries, including Fulda (c. 743), where he was buried after he was martyred.

In 596 Pope Gregory the Great sent Augustine (d. c. 604), to Canterbury with a group of around forty monks to preach to the Anglo-Saxons. Arriving in 597, he converted King Aethelbert and became the first Bishop of Canterbury. Paulinus (d. 644) followed with a second mission, arriving in England in 604, and converted King Edwin of Northumbria.

Monasteries soon succumbed to worldly temptations. Rich benefactors made lavish donations to them in return for prayers, so that successful monasteries acquired vast estates. The monastic life began as a calling but was often corrupted into a profession; monastic scholarship frequently dwindled into dry traditionalism.

What were the Crusades?

During the eleventh century the Muslim Seljuk Turks conquered Asia Minor (modern Turkey), parts of which had been Christian ever since the mission of the apostle Paul. In 1095, the Eastern Emperor asked for help from Christians in the West, as the Turks were threatening Constantinople, the home of Eastern Christianity. The Crusades were a response to more than four centuries of Islamic conquest, during which Muslims had captured two-thirds of the Christian world.

At the Council of Clermont in 1095, Pope Urban II called upon Christian nations to push back Islam in a Crusade. He presented the Crusaders with several goals: rescue the Eastern Christians, recover the Holy Land—and particularly the holy city of Jerusalem—from Muslim occupation, and open up access to the Holy Land for Christian pilgrims. This triggered not just the First Crusade, but also the entire crusading movement, which lasted for centuries.

Thousands of knights took a vow of the cross and prepared for war, partly as an act of penitence. Crusaders believed they were simultaneously on a military

Crusaders attack Jerusalem.

expedition blessed by the pope, and on a pilgrimage to the Holy Land, for which they expected the guarantee of entry to heaven.

From the very outset the First Crusade (1096–1099) seemed to be on the edge of disaster. It had no single leader, poor supply lines, and no detailed strategy and huge numbers died in battle, or from disease and starvation. Despite this, the Crusaders restored Christian rule to the major center of Antioch, and in July 1099 they captured Jerusalem itself. The Crusade had occurred at a particularly opportune moment when Islam was temporarily split internally. However, the First Crusade was alone in significantly resisting the military progress of Islam.

There was widespread support for a second crusade. Preached by Bernard of Clairvaux, and led by Louis VII of France and Conrad III of Germany, it failed miserably. Most of its warriors were killed en route, while those who actually reached Palestine worsened things by attacking Damascus, a strong ally of the Christians. The Muslims grew in strength. Their legendary leader, Saladin, united the Islamic Near East, preaching *jihad* against the Christians. At the Battle of Hattin (1187) he wiped out the Christian armies. Christian cities surrendered to him, culminating in the disastrous capitulation of Jerusalem.

The Third Crusade (1189–1192), led by Frederick Barbarossa of Germany, Philip II Augustus of France, and Richard the Lionheart of England appeared to be very grand. But the aged Frederick drowned while crossing a river, and his army returned home having never reached the Holy Land. After two attempts, Richard abandoned the struggle to reconquer Jerusalem, and agreed terms with Saladin that ensured peace in the region and free access to Jerusalem for unarmed pilgrims.

Numerous squalid military expeditions followed, and warriors, pilgrims, and traders traveled continually between Europe and the Holy Land. A few Crusaders sustained a toehold in the Holy Land, but far from converting locals to Christianity, they often took up Eastern customs themselves. The Crusades finally ended in 1270, leaving a poisonous heritage of ill-feeling between Christians and Muslims.

Why did people go on pilgrimage?

Pilgrimage to Christian holy sites had been undertaken ever since the fourth century. Such journeys became more frequent in medieval times, as they claimed to offer the prize of God's grace—and even eternal life. From the eleventh century onward, journeys to holy sites became a major enterprise.

The pilgrims mainly visited three places: Rome, and the traditional tombs of Peter and Paul; Jerusalem, and other sites associated with Jesus in the Holy Land; and Santiago de Compostela, in Northern Spain, where the alleged tomb of the apostle James was discovered around 830. After the 1099 recapture of Jerusalem, the Holy Land became particularly popular with pilgrims; the Christian orders of knights were founded to make travel there safer. Following the murder and canonization of Archbishop Thomas Becket (c. 1118–1170), Canterbury became a favorite destination for English pilgrims, famously described by Geoffrey Chaucer in his *Canterbury Tales.*

Santiago de Compostela Cathedral.

Francis of Assisi

The Italian Francis of Assisi (1181/2-1226) rejected his family fortune in obedience to Jesus' words in the Gospels, and took up a wandering life, followed by a few friends. They begged from the rich, gave to the poor, tended the sick, and preached to anyone they met.

In time, Francis' followers became recognized as a new Christian order, the Franciscans—nicknamed "Grey Friars" for their grey costume. They took similar vows to other monks, but were constantly on the road, not based in a single location or building. They broke away from the monastic ideal of living apart from the world, desiring to bring the faith to ordinary people by living among them.

Although Francis is often associated with the birds and wild animals, his mission was largely to the cities of medieval Italy. His friend Clare (c.1193-1253) established an order for women similar to the Franciscans, known as the Poor Clares.

Mission was a key concern of the Franciscans. Francis travelled to Egypt in 1219; in later years Franciscans journeyed to Hungary, Spain, and the East—even as far as Central Asia and India.

Francis of Assisi.

Why did the Reformation happen?

Martin Luther (1483–1546) was born into a world ripe for reform. As a young monk, he struggled with the age-old Christian question: 'What must I do to be saved?' After much anguish, he finally found his answer in the New Testament writings of Paul. Luther recovered Paul's teachings about justification by grace through faith in Jesus Christ. In contrast with the teaching of the medieval church that we are saved by faith and works, he discovered that the New Testament emphasis was on 'faith alone.' Gradually, Luther worked out the basic Protestant doctrines: the authority of the Bible, and salvation by personal faith in Christ.

Initially, Luther called for reformation of the church along biblical lines. On October 31, 1517, he nailed his Ninety-Five Theses to the door of the Castle Church in Wittenberg, questioning the medieval system of repentance and forgiveness—and even the authority of the pope. Luther became the voice of the Protestant Reformation but was soon joined by many others.

The pope did not respond to Luther's plea for reform and his cause soon expanded into the Protestant Reformation. The concept of a reformation based on the Bible spread quickly across Europe. Ulrich Zwingli introduced the Reformation in Zurich, Switzerland, in 1518, and Martin Bucer preached similar doctrines in Strasbourg, Germany, beginning in 1523. Eventually their followers became a part of the Reformed tradition in the church.

The other leading Reformer was John Calvin (1509–1564), whose work resulted not only in the Presbyterian and Reformed churches, but also the Puritan movement in England and America.

But not everyone was satisfied with the reforms of Luther and Calvin. Many wanted to forget about reforming the old church and instead return directly to the New Testament. During the sixteenth century, the most important expression of this Radical Reformation was Anabaptism. Unlike Luther and Calvin, the Anabaptists rejected the possibility of a state church, and emphasized what they claimed was the Bible's example of a 'gathered fellowship' made up solely of baptized believers. For them, the true church included solely believers who had openly and deliberately confessed Christ and followed him in baptism. One important branch of the Anabaptists was led by the former Dutch priest, Menno Simons (1496–1561), who believed Christians should not use violence: “Since we are to be conformed to the image of Christ, how can we fight our enemies with the sword?” To this day the Mennonites, who have preserved many of the best traditions of the Radical Reformation, are committed to pacifism.

Eventually the various strands of Protestantism resulted in four distinct movements: Lutheran, Calvinist (Reformed and Presbyterian), Episcopalian and Anabaptist.

Martin Luther

Martin Luther (1483-1546) was the father of the Protestant Reformation. He was educated within the medieval Roman Catholic church and became a monk and a priest. But his study of the Scriptures, and his personal spiritual struggle, led him to an evangelical breakthrough. He came to teach the basic principles of Protestant Christianity: justification by grace alone through faith alone, and the Bible as the only ultimate authority for Christian belief and practice.

He led a movement in sixteenth-century Europe to reform theology, purify the church and help Christians understand biblical Christianity.

Luther’s achievements as pastor, scholar, theologian and Christian were monumental, and have influenced the church profoundly to this day. He was far from perfect, but his fellow reformer, Philip Melanchthon, provided a fitting epitaph for Luther, saying that God had given a violent age a violent physician.

Martin Luther.

John Calvin

John Calvin (1509-1564), the exiled Frenchman who became chief pastor of Geneva, was the supreme Bible teacher of the Reformation. His massive book of doctrine and devotion, *Institutes of the Christian Religion* was the classic statement of Protestantism, and his commentaries on Scripture—the first of their kind—are landmark works.

Calvin’s vision, learned from Luther and Augustine, that God sovereignly saves sinners, inspired great pastoral evangelists such as John Bunyan, George Whitefield, Jonathan Edwards, and Charles Haddon Spurgeon, along with pioneer missionaries such as the Baptist, William Carey. His view of the Christian life as a pilgrimage leading safely home by a predestined path of service and suffering, became a world view that has produced many humble heroes of faith.

Anchored in Geneva, Calvin was an international figure, advising and encouraging reformers in England, Scotland, France, the Low Countries and elsewhere. Geneva was a haven and inspiration to thousands of students and refugees. Calvinism shaped early America, and the modern West can hardly be understood without some knowledge of it.

John Calvin.

Who were the Pilgrim Fathers?

Early in the seventeenth century Protestants from England began to colonize North America, starting with settlements on the Atlantic coast. These pioneer colonists sometimes combined commerce with missionary zeal and a desire for freedom of worship. In 1607 a community was set up at Jamestown, Virginia, with an Episcopalian chaplain. However, the Episcopal church was never the most popular form of Christianity in the New World.

In 1620, the Pilgrim Fathers disembarked at Plymouth, New England. They were Puritans who had already left England to seek religious asylum in the Netherlands. Subsequently, they left Europe on board the *Mayflower* to find somewhere they could practice their faith freely and set up an ideal Christian community.

Religious conflict worsened in England under Charles I, and many more Puritans decided to leave the country. The Great Migration of 1629–1640 saw some 80,000 people leave England, about 20,000 migrating to each of Ireland, New England, the West Indies, and the Netherlands. By 1641, a total of around 200 ships arrived in New England, carrying about 21,000 immigrants, among them 129 clergymen and theologians.

Both the Pilgrims and the Massachusetts Bay Colony believed in the ideal of a Christian commonwealth governed by Christian principles, seeking to achieve on earth a version of the heavenly city. The first governor of Massachusetts Bay Colony, John Winthrop claimed: "We shall be as a city upon a hill, the eyes of all people are upon us."

Some settlers, such as Anne Hutchinson and Roger Williams, objected to what they felt to be a lack of freedom in the new colonies, and moved to frontier settlements where they could explore religious liberty. In 1636, Williams founded Providence Plantation on Rhode Island, where religious diversity was celebrated. The Baptists who settled there committed to another characteristic of the future in America: the separation of church and state. William Penn (1644–1718), a member of the Society of Friends, or Quakers, set up Pennsylvania as a refuge for his own group fleeing persecution in England.

Replica of the *Mayflower*.

Awakenings

During the seventeenth century a series of awakenings started in Germany and spread to Scandinavia and Switzerland, producing what we know as Pietism. These revivals were partly a reaction against spiritual deadness in many of the Protestant churches. Leaders of these revivals included Philipp Jakob Spener (1635-1705), August Francke (1663–1727), and Count Ludwig von Zinzendorf (1700–1760).

Cutting across class and creed, these Pietists emphasized New Testament simplicity and the need of a personal experience of Christ. They were also deeply concerned about mission and evangelism as well as Christian social ministry. The Moravian Church, founded by Zinzendorf in Germany, grew to become an intensely missionary-minded movement.

A similar pattern of revivals occurred in eighteenth-century Britain and North America. Dissatisfied with the coldness he experienced in the Church of England, and uncertain of his own salvation, John Wesley met a Moravian missionary during a visit to Georgia in 1735. Challenged to look to Christ alone for his salvation, Wesley finally found peace with God in a "heart-warming experience" in London in 1738.

Wesley's "new birth" was the impetus for a fresh wave of gospel preaching. Turning first to England's largely unevangelized population, John Wesley, with his hymn-writing brother Charles (1707-1788), soon won hundreds of thousands of converts. Many of them re-kindled the zeal of the Church of England, while others joined various denominations, including the Baptists and Congregationalists. The majority formed societies which shortly became the Methodist Church.

John Wesley

John Wesley (1703-1791) was born in Epworth, Yorkshire, England, the son of a clergyman. At the age of six he was rescued from his burning home; he later described himself as a "brand plucked from the burning." In 1729, John's younger brother, Charles Wesley, formed the "Holy Club" with fellow Oxford students; they were dubbed "Methodists" because of their methodical spiritual habits. In London, while attending a meeting in Aldersgate Street on 24 May 1738, Wesley listened to a reading from Luther, he felt his "heart strangely warmed." His "new birth" was the stimulus for a new career of preaching the gospel.

Wesley never hesitated to preach anywhere, even using his father's tombstone as a pulpit. He continued his itinerant ministry for fifty years, in fields, halls, cottages, and chapels, when churches were closed to him. Wesley and the Methodists were persecuted by clergymen and magistrates, and attacked in sermons, in print and by the mob. But Wesley regarded himself as commissioned by God to bring revival to the church, and opposition and persecution did not shake his resolve.

Wesley traveled continually, generally on horseback, preaching two or three times a day. He rose at four in the morning, lived simply, and was never idle if he could avoid it. Late in 1739, Wesley formed his followers into a separate society: "Thus without any previous plan, began the Methodist Society in England," he wrote. He opened chapels, commissioned preachers, organized charities, prescribed medicine and set up schools and orphanages.

John Wesley

What was the Great Awakening?

The Great Awakening, America's first major revival, was a momentous event in colonial America. The first evidence of revival appeared in the 1720s. In the Delaware Valley, an Irish Presbyterian named William Tennent spread religious enthusiasm, while the Dutch Reformed minister, Theodore Frelinghuysen, led revivals in the Raritan Valley, New Jersey. The Congregationalist, Solomon Stoddard, was experiencing revivals among his congregation in Northampton, Massachusetts, while between 1734 and the early 1740s, his grandson, Jonathan Edwards, inspired fervent conversions there and in frontier towns throughout the Connecticut Valley.

An extraordinary tour by the British evangelist George Whitefield, transformed these local happenings into a colonial phenomenon. Arriving from England in 1739, Whitefield preached from Savannah, Georgia, to York, Maine, both in churches and in the open air—sometimes to crowds of more than 20,000, and often defying the opposition of local clergymen. Whitefield achieved his greatest success in New England; by the time he left in 1741 he had created religious enthusiasm and revival throughout the colonies.

The Awakening peaked in the late 1730s and early 1740s, as other evangelists followed him. In 1741 Gilbert Tennent retraced Whitefield's revivalist route through New England; the Long Island preacher James Davenport (1716–1757) aroused enthusiasm in Connecticut and Massachusetts; and the German Nikolaus Ludwig von Zinzendorf arrived in Pennsylvania and encouraged revival among German settlers.

Initially the Awakening was most powerful in the middle and northern colonies. It developed later and more slowly in the South, hindered by unsympathetic Episcopalian clergymen, but in the late 1740s and 1750s itinerant preachers ignited the Awakening there too.

These revivals appealed to men and women of all regions, classes, and all Protestant denominations and churches. Their egalitarian, anti-authoritarian nature was particularly popular in inland rural areas.

George Whitefield

George Whitefield (1714–1770) was an Englishman considered by many to have been the greatest evangelist since the apostle Paul. Although he was an ordained Church of England clergyman, most of his preaching was outdoors: his congregations numbered thousands. From the age of twenty-two until his death at fifty-five, Whitefield preached three and four times a day. His ministry took him to every region of England, often to Wales, fifteen times to Scotland, and twice to Ireland. He was also devoted to the American colonies, visiting seven times, and evangelizing repeatedly from New Hampshire in the north to Georgia in the south. Whitefield was the first leader of the Evangelical Revival that transformed Britain, and the chief figure in the Great Awakening in America. He preached so he could be understood by the poor and unlearned, but also ministered to audiences consisting of the English nobility, and was heard by many of the great in America. Whitefield's much-repeated message to humankind was, "You must be born again!" which attracted the wrath and contempt of many, an opposition he met only with kindness.

George Whitefield.

Jonathan Edwards

Jonathan Edwards (1703-1758) a man of great intelligence and a major Calvinist theologian and philosopher, was converted at the age of seventeen. From the time he became pastor at Northampton, Massachusetts, until his death, brought about by complications from a smallpox injection, he played a dominant role in the Great Awakening and in defending Calvinism. Following disagreements with the church, he became a missionary to the Indians at Stockbridge, Massachusetts, where he published *The Freedom of the Will.*

Jonathan Edwards is important not only for his pastoral insight, saintliness and intellect; he is also almost unique in the history of the church to have been granted a virtually complete integration of "heart" and "head." His writings—setting out and defending the evangelical faith—are of lasting value to the church.

A Second Awakening

Between the 1790s and the 1830s a further series of nationwide religious revivals—the Second Great Awakening—made revivalism an enduring feature of American Christianity. This later movement was linked closely to the westward expansion of the newly independent nation.

The Second Awakening started in rural Connecticut and New Hampshire in the late 1790s. In New England it gained strength when Yale College students attended revivals in 1801 and then spread revivalism throughout the churches of this region. Revivalism here led to the formation of many voluntary societies—missions, charities, and reform groups. Stimulated by the Awakening, Yale and Andover graduates became missionaries and educators in New York and Ohio.

Another Awakening occurred in the 1790s among the Americans crossing the Cumberland Gap into Kentucky and Tennessee. Revivals were held in 1799 and 1800 at Muddy River, Red River, and Caspar River, south-western Kentucky. A huge camp meeting at Cane Ridge in 1801, attended by some 10,000 people, lasted a whole week. Preachers present at this "Great Revival" went on to hold camp meetings across Kentucky, Tennessee, and southern Ohio.

These gatherings spread Protestantism throughout the region. Charles Grandison Finney and other leaders conducted countless revivals in New York State during the 1820s and early 1830s, creating an intense atmosphere of evangelism, reform, and experiment which resulted in its being called the "burned-over district."

Although the revivals eventually subsided, their impact did not. The Awakenings helped shape the religious and cultural life of the United States profoundly and enduringly. Spiritual renewal continued in other places and in other forms. In the late nineteenth century, Dwight L. Moody (1837–1899) and Billy Sunday (1862–1935), the former businessman and former Major League baseball player, drew large crowds to their evangelistic meetings.

The English Methodists William (1829–1912) and Catherine Booth (1829–1890), who believed their denomination had become too "respectable," founded the Salvation Army in 1878 in London's poverty-stricken East End in order to reach the down-and-out for Jesus. In the process, they established not only a dynamic evangelistic society but also the world's most efficient and compassionate welfare agency. Other revivals took place, for instance in Scotland in the late 1830s, in France in the 1840s, and in Wales in 1859–1860 and 1904–1906.

How did Pentecostalism arise?

Pentecostal practices first appeared in America in churches and camp meetings from the mid-1860s onwards. As the twentieth century approached, increasing numbers of people were speaking in tongues and showing other physical signs of the Holy Spirit's gifts.

The first Pentecostal churches started before 1901, including the mainly African American Church of God in Christ, the Pentecostal Holiness Church, and the Church of God. According to their own tradition, on 1 January 1901, the first "Pentecostals" are said to have appeared at Charles Parham's Bethel Bible College, Topeka, Kansas, when Agnes Ozman received the baptism of the Holy Spirit and spoke in tongues. Parham then

D. L. Moody

By the second half of the nineteenth century, steamships had brought the continents nearer. Railways had spread across America and Britain. Cities were growing vast through increased mobility, high birth-rate and multiplying industries. All of which made mass evangelism possible. A man was needed who could proclaim the name of Christ to many thousands together, so the churches would be revived.

The man who emerged was Dwight Lyman Moody (1837–1899), from a small farming community in New England. He was semi-educated, but of such stature that he could land in Britain in 1873 utterly obscure but leave in 1875 with Scotland, England and Ireland at his feet. His story and personality commanded attention: rugged, delightful and compassionate, a man of integrity, he possessed a supreme gift for bringing New Testament Christianity before contemporary hearers and putting them to work for God.

D. L. Moody preaching.

Billy Graham

Probably the world's most famous preacher and evangelist, Billy Graham (1918–2018) joined Youth for Christ after graduating from Wheaton College, Illinois, and travelled throughout the United States and Europe as an evangelist. In 1949 he held a series of missions in Los Angeles, scheduled to last only three weeks, but extended to eight. In 1950 he founded the Billy Graham Evangelistic Association.

In 1957 Graham had successful missions in London and New York, in 1959 in Australia, and countless others elsewhere. Billy Graham would typically preach, then invite people to come forward in response. During the Cold War he spoke behind the Iron Curtain, during the apartheid era in South Africa, he refused to speak to segregated crowds. In all, Graham preached to live audiences of more than 210 million people in over 185 countries, and reached many more through television, video, film, and webcasts.

Billy Graham preaching.

began to teach that tongues was evidence of baptism in the Holy Spirit and a supernatural gift of human languages to aid in world evangelization.

Pentecostalism achieved worldwide attention in 1906 through the Azusa Street revival in Los Angeles, led by the African American preacher William Joseph Seymour. His mission conducted virtually continuous services, where thousands of people claimed to have received the gift of tongues and baptism in the Holy Spirit.

Apostolic Faith Mission, Azusa Street, Los Angeles.

Several holiness denominations soon joined the new movement. The African American Charles Harrison Mason carried the tongues experience back to his Church of God in Christ at Memphis, Tennessee, and as a result the denomination mushroomed. Having received tongues at Azusa Street in 1907, William H. Durham returned to Chicago, where he led thousands into the Pentecostal movement, which grew into the largely white Assemblies of God denomination in 1914.

How did modern missions begin?

The great revivals of the eighteenth century, especially the Wesleyan renewal in Britain, made possible one of the most significant developments in Christian history—the modern missionary movement.

The birth of modern missions is often traced to the English Baptist shoemaker, William Carey, who became convicted by the demand of Great Commission of Mark 16:15. Carey taught himself Latin, Greek, Hebrew, Dutch, and French, and sailed to India as a pioneering missionary, resulting in the formation of the Baptist Missionary Society. In 1795, Christians from several different denominations organized the London Missionary Society; and in 1797, Dutch Christians started the Netherlands Missionary Society. The Church Missionary Society was founded in 1799 by Christians in the Church of England.

In the US the beginning of modern missions dates from the founding of the American Board of Commissioners for Foreign Missions in 1810, a result of the Great Awakening. A group of students at Williams College, Massachusetts, committed to foreign missions. Among their recruits was the pioneer missionary to Burma, Adoniram Judson, who sailed to Asia in 1812.

Throughout the nineteenth century, missions sprang up from churches with a strong belief in their members participating in worldwide evangelization. Some churches were founded to promote mission: for instance, the Swedish Mission Covenant Church, in 1877, and Christian and Missionary Alliance (CMA), in 1897. A. B. Simpson, who started the CMA, was also founder of Nyack Missionary College, the earliest Bible institute (1882). Similar Bible institutes and colleges soon became vital centers for the training of ministers and missionaries.

Among new missions, some of which had a broader basis and utilized diverse talents, the China Inland Mission was particularly influential. It was a "faith mission"—depending on the voluntary support of people responding according to their belief, inclination, and ability, and eventually became the largest single Protestant mission in China.

This was a century of heroic missionary work. To list just a few other examples: Henry Martyn in India; Father Damien in Hawaii; David Livingstone in East Africa; Mary Slessor in West Africa; Father Charles Eugene de Foucauld in North Africa; C. T. Studd in China, India and Central Africa; and J. Hudson Taylor in China.

During the nineteenth century the United States became the major source of new Protestant missions and missionary personnel. By 1920 more than 20,000 young people had volunteered as missionaries, after having been challenged by members of the Student Volunteer Movement. There was also a mushrooming of the numbers of women missionaries. It was an age of great missionary organizers, innovative missionary organizations, and important missionary conferences. In 1854 a series of conventions led to the seminal World Missionary Conference in Edinburgh, Scotland, in 1910.

David Livingstone.

James Hudson Taylor.

William Carey

The English Baptist, William Carey (1761-1834), a village cobbler in Northamptonshire, became one of the pioneers of the modern Protestant missionary movement. He had read about the explorer Captain James Cook's voyages to Polynesia, and subsequently wrote his famous *An Enquiry into the Obligation of Christians to use Means for the Conversion of Heathen*, using available data to map and count all those who had never heard the gospel. After years of discouragement, in 1792, Carey persuaded his fellow Baptists to organize the Baptist Missionary Society, only the first of a number of such organizations in a growing missionary enterprise. Then, with Joshua Marshman and William Ward, Carey sailed to India as a missionary himself. Carey set about learning the local languages, translating the Bible, and making converts. Carey and his colleagues eventually printed parts or all the Bible in several different languages. A tireless worker, Carey never returned to Britain.

William Carey.

Major Missionaries of the modern age

Name	Nationality	Mission area	Mission society
Bartolomé de las Casas (1474-1566)	Spanish	Latin America	Dominican Order
Francis Xavier (1506-1552)	Spanish	India, Sri Lanka, East Indies, Japan	Jesuit Order
Matteo Ricci (1552-1610)	Italian	China	Jesuit Order
Robert de Nobili (1577-1656)	Italian	India	Jesuit Order
John Eliot (1604-1690)	English	Native Americans	Society for the Propagation of the Gospel in New England
Thomas Bray (1656-1730)	English	North America	Founded Society for Promoting Christian Knowledge, Society for the Propagation of the Gospel in Foreign Parts
Batholomaus Ziegenbalg (1684-1719)	German	India	Danish-Halle Mission
David Brainerd (1718-1747)	American	Native Americans	Scotch Society for Propagating Christian knowledge
Christian Friedrich Schwartz (1726-1798)	German	India	Danish-Halle Mission
William Carey (1761- 1834)	English	India	Founded Baptist Missionary Society
Henry Martyn (1781-1812)	English	India, Persia	British East India Company
Robert Morrison (1782-1834)	English	China	London Missionary Society
Adoniram Judson (1788-1850)	American	Burma (Myanmar)	American Board of Commissioners for Foreign Missions
Robert Moffat (1795-1883)	Scottish	South Africa	London Missionary Society
Elijah Bridgman (1801-1861)	American	China	American Board of Commissioners for Foreign Missions
Alexander Duff (1806-1878)	Scottish	India	Church of Scotland

Major Missionaries of the modern age

Name	Nationality	Mission area	Mission society
Samuel Crowther (1806-1891)	Nigerian	Nigeria	Church Missionary Society
Guglielmo Massaja (1809-1889)	Italian	Ethiopia	Capuchin Order
Johann Krapf (1810-1881)	German	East Africa	Church Missionary Society
David Livingstone (1813-1873)	Scottish	Africa	London Missionary Society
Johannes Rebmann (1819-1876)	German	East Africa	Church Missionary Society
John Paton (1824-1907)	Scottish	New Hebrides	Reformed Presbyterian Church of Scotland
Charles Lavigerie (1825-1892)	French	North Africa	Founded White Fathers Order
John Nevius (1829-1893)	American	China	Presbyterian Board of Foreign Missions
James Hudson Taylor (1832-1905)	English	China	Founded China Inland Mission
H. Grattan Guinness (1836-1910)	Irish	Congo	Founded Livingstone Inland Mission, North Africa Mission, Regions Beyond Missionary Union
Joseph Damien (1840-1889)	Belgian	Hawaii	Picpus Fathers
Mary Slessor (1848-1915)	Scottish	West Africa	United Presbyterian Church of Scotland
Charles de Foucauld (1858-1916)	French	North Africa	Trappist Order
C. T. Studd (1862-1931)	English	China, India, Congo	China Inland Mission, founded Heart of Africa Mission
Albert Schweitzer (1875-1965)	German	French Equatorial Africa	Paris Society of Evangelical Missions
Cameron Townsend (1896-1982)	American	Latin America	Founded Wycliffe Bible Translators
Jim Elliot (1927-1956)	American	Ecuador	

Bible Dictionary

Here is a concise lexicon of unusual names and words in the Bible. These are terms of particular cultural and theological significance, with meanings specific to Scripture, and clarifications of expressions that might appear to be ambiguous.

acacia Flowering tree with hard and durable wood. The Ark of the Covenant, altars, and other wooden furniture in the Tabernacle were made from acacia.

altar Raised structure made of rocks, packed earth, metal, or pottery, where sacrifices and offerings were presented to God, or to pagan gods (GENESIS 8:20; 13:18; 33:20).

Amalekites Nomadic nation living south and east of the Dead Sea, and who were enemies of Israel.

amen Hebrew word meaning "it is so" or "may it be so," used after a prayer or blessing, to affirm that what had been said was right and true.

Ammon Nation east of Israel.

Amorites Name for all non-Israelite nations who lived in Canaan. It sometimes refers to one nation scattered across Canaan.

angel Supernatural being who gives God's messages to people, or protects those who belong to God (GENESIS 16:7-12; NUMBERS 22:22-35; LUKE 1:11-28).

Angel of the LORD The angelic being who is closely identified in a number of Old Testament passages with the person of God himself (EXODUS 3:2; JUDGES 6:11ff). When he appears, he speaks with explicit divine power and authority (GENESIS 16:7ff; 22:11ff). In the New Testament he may be identified with the Holy Spirit (ACTS 8:26-29). Two primary functions of the Angel of the LORD are concerned with the enacting of divine judgement (2 SAMUEL 24:16) and deliverance (EXODUS 14:19).

anoint Pour or rub olive-oil on someone to honor them, or appoint them to special work in the service of God. The ritual also signified that the Spirit of God lay behind the anointing as the one who provided the spiritual power and authority to carry out the appointed task via the anointed one. Only three classes of people were anointed in the Old Testament: prophets, priests, and kings. Israelite kings were anointed when they took office, and the king was sometimes called "the anointed one." In the New Testament, all believers are anointed with the Holy Spirit.

Antichrist An expression that denotes someone who is implacably opposed to the person and work of Jesus Christ. The term only occurs in the letters of the Apostle John (e.g. 1 JOHN 2:18, 22; 4:3; 2 JOHN 7), but this sense of the term is widespread in Scripture.

apostle From the Greek word meaning "messenger." Person chosen and sent by Christ to take his message to others. The names of Christ's twelve apostles are in Matthew 10:2-4; Mark 3:16-19; Luke 6:14-16; Acts 1:12-13. Others became known as apostles later, for example Paul and James, the brother of Jesus.

Areopagus Hill in Athens where the city council once met. The council was known as "Areopagus" although it no longer met on the hill.

Ark of the Covenant Chest or box covered with gold, with two golden statues of winged creatures on the lid, containing two flat stones with the Ten Commandments written on them, kept in the Holy of Holies (EXODUS 25:10-22).

Asherah Goddess of fertility worshiped by the Canaanites.

Asia Roman province in what is modern Turkey.

assurance *See* **faith.**

Assyria Empire of Old Testament times whose capital city Nineveh was located in what is now modern, northern Iraq.

Atonement, Day of (Hebrew, "*Yom Kippur*") 10th day of the seventh month of the Hebrew calendar (around 1st October). On this one day of the year, the high priest was allowed to enter the Holy of Holies in the Temple and sprinkle blood from a sacrificed bull on the Ark of the Covenant, so the people's sins over the past year would be forgiven (LEVITICUS 16:1-34; NUMBERS 29:7-11).

Azazel A term that occurs only in the legislation applicable to the Day of Atonement, as recorded in Leviticus 25. This Hebrew term refers to the "scape-goat," on which the sins of the whole Israelite nation were symbolically placed. The animal was then released into the desert, signifying the permanent removal of the sins of the people of God. This ritual ceremony anticipates the atoning sacrifice of Jesus Christ on the cross for our sins.

Baal Word meaning "lord," originally used for local gods in Canaan. Later, it was used only for the chief god of Canaan, who was believed to give fertility to people, animals, and the earth. After the Hebrews invaded Canaan, many began to worship Baal.

Babylonia Large empire of Old Testament times, whose capital city, Babylon, was in what is today, Iraq.

Bashan Highlands and wooded hills of southern

Syria. Bashan was just north of Gilead and noted for its fat cattle and fine grain.

Beelzebub New Testament name for the devil, chief of the evil spirits.

blasphemy A term referring to the reviling or cursing of the holy name of God. Such an act of profound disrespect was punishable by death under the terms of the Law Covenant (LEVITICUS 24:10-13).

Booths, Festival of (Hebrew, *Sukkoth*), also called the Feast of Tabernacles. Festival celebrated by the Israelites in the fall, after harvest was over, to remind them of the years when their ancestors wandered in the wilderness.

breastplate Part of a soldier's armor, made of leather or metal. It covered the chest and sometimes the back, protecting against arrows and sword-blows.

bride/bridegroom Aside from the human institution of marriage between a man and a woman, these two terms are used in a powerful metaphorical sense to refer to Israel as the "bride" of the LORD in the prophetic literature of the Old Testament (JEREMIAH 2:2; 3:20; EZEKIEL 16:8; HOSEA 2:16). This metaphor paves the way for the New Covenant church to be described as the "bride of Christ" (EPHESIANS 5:25-27; REVELATION 19:7; 21:2; 22:17).

burnt offering Sacrifice in which every part of an animal was completely burnt on an altar, to obtain forgiveness for sin, and to please the Lord with the smell of the smoke (LEVITICUS 1).

Caesar Title of the Roman Emperor.

Canaan The area today covered by Israel, Gaza, the West Bank of Jordan, Lebanon, and southern Syria (NUMBERS 34:1-12). In the Bible it often refers only to the area south of Lebanon.

Canaanites The nations living in Canaan before the Israelites. Many continued to live there after the Israelites occupied the land.

chalcedony Semi precious stone, usually milky or gray in color.

chariot Two-wheeled cart, open at the back and pulled by horses. Often the sign of royalty or wealth (EXODUS 14:7; 2 KINGS 2:11).

cherubim Winged creatures symbolizing God's majesty and presence (EXODUS 25:18-20; EZEKIEL 1:5-13; REVELATION 4:6-9).

Christ Greek word meaning "Anointed One" or "Chosen One," used to translate the Hebrew word "Messiah." It often refers to the One many Jews believed God would send to rescue them from their enemies. Jesus was called "the Christ" because he was the one God chose, and sent as Savior and Lord of God's people, all believers—past, present, and future.

church The term denoting the universal people of God gathered for worship throughout the world. The Greek term for "church" (*ekklesia*) in the New Covenant age, is derived from the Hebrew term that refers to the "gathered assembly" of the people of Israel whenever they came to worship God under the Old Covenant.

circumcise To cut off the foreskin of the penis. Circumcision was performed on Israelite boys, eight days after birth, as a sign of God's covenant with his people (GENESIS 17:9-14).

cistern Hole or pit used for storing rainwater. Some cisterns were dug in the ground and lined with stones and plaster; others were cut into the rock.

clean/unclean Animals that were acceptable as food were called "clean"; those that were not acceptable were "unclean" (LEVITICUS 11:1-47; DEUTERONOMY 14:3-21). In Old Testament times, a person who was acceptable to worship God was "clean." A person who had certain diseases, who touched a dead body, or broke certain laws was "unclean," and not allowed to worship God, until restored to ritual cleanness.

cloud Alongside the natural meaning of this term, the phenomenon of the "cloud" was used to reveal the visible presence of the person of God to his people, Israel, in what was known as a "theophany"—the appearance of God in a visible form. God appeared in a cloud to guide his people through the wilderness, prior to their entering the land of Canaan, and the "cloud of his presence" was intimately associated with the Holy of Holies in the Tabernacle and Temple.

commandments Rules for God's people to live by. Best known are the Ten Commandments (EXODUS 20:1-17; DEUTERONOMY 5:6-21), which were given to Moses as the summary obligations of the entire Law Covenant-applicable to both Old and New Covenant ages.

concubine A woman servant who had sexual relations with her master.

covenant A solemn, binding relationship and agreement between people, or between God and an individual or group of people. There are six covenant stages of critical importance revealed throughout the Bible—all of them initiated, maintained, and fulfilled by God alone: Creation (Adam and Eve) (GENESIS 1-3); Noah (GENESIS 9:8-17); Abraham (GENESIS 12; 15; 17:1-8); Moses (EXODUS 19–40); David (2 SAMUEL 7); New Covenant-fulfilled in Jesus Christ. In the Old Testament it usually means the covenant in Moses' time between God and the people of Israel (EXODUS 24:4-8).

cross Wooden post on which the Romans nailed or tied condemned prisoners, to hang there till they died. It consisted of two lengths of timber crossed in the shape of a "T" "†" or "X". This common mode of Roman execution was referred to as crucifixion.

Cush Hebrew name for Ethiopia.

cymbals Pair of thin circular sheets of metal held in the hands and struck together to make a musical sound.

Dagon Main deity of the Philistines (JUDGES 16:23).

Dan One of the twelve tribes of Israel. When the Israelites left Egypt, the tribe of Dan occupied land west of Judah (JOSHUA 19:40-48). But after the Philistines took control of this area, part of the tribe moved to the northernmost region of Israel.

David's city In the Old Testament, this usually means the part of Jerusalem captured from the Jebusites by King David. In the New Testament, David's boyhood home of Bethlehem is known as David's town.

Day of the LORD A metaphorical expression with a profound prophetic and theological significance. The phrase occurs many times throughout the Old Testament, with a primary reference to both climactic expressions of God's punitive judgement against his people Israel, along with their enemies. In the New Testament it refers to the second coming of Christ.

Dedication, Festival of *See* **Hanukkah**.

defile Make someone unfit to worship God. *See* **clean/unclean**.

demon Evil spirit with the power to harm people, regarded as a messenger and servant of the devil. In the New Testament, demons are sometimes called "unclean spirits" because people controlled by them were regarded as unclean (MARK 5:1-13; 7:24-30).

devil Chief of the demons and evil spirits, also known as "Satan" (JOB 1:6-2:7; MATTHEW 4:1-11; LUKE 4:1-13; JOHN 8:44).

Diana Roman name for Artemis, the ancient goddess of fertility, worshiped especially in Asia Minor.

disciple Follower of John the Baptist, and especially of Jesus. The term often refers to his twelve apostles. *See* **apostle**.

divination Attempt to discover a message from God or the gods, for example, by examining marked stones or the liver of a sacrificed animal.

diviner Person who thought they could tell the future and what God wanted people to do by watching birds in flight, looking at the livers of animals, or rolling dice—all forbidden in Israel (2 KINGS 17:16-18; 21:4-6 ZECHARIAH 10:2).

dragon (also called "serpent") A picture of the Devil (REVELATION 12:3-13:4; 20:2-3).

Edomites Nation living in Edom, or Seir, an area south and southeast of the Dead Sea. The Edomites descended from Esau, Jacob's brother (GENESIS 36:1-43).

elders In the Old Testament, certain respected leaders of a tribe, nation, or city. In the New Testament, three groups are called elders: important Jewish religious leaders, some of them members of the Sanhedrin; Christian leaders responsible for the activity of the church (ACTS 11–21); 24 elders belong to God's heavenly court (REVELATION).

ephod Hebrew word usually referring to a piece of cloth worn over the shoulders by the high priest with Urim and Thummim attached to it. In some places, it refers to something people worshiped. In yet other passages, it seems to refer to something used to foretell the future.

Ephraim One of the largest tribes of Israel.

Epicureans Those who followed the teaching of Epicurus (died 270 BC), a Greek philosopher who taught that the highest good in life is happiness. Paul encountered some Epicureans in ACTS 17:18.

eternal life Life that is the gift of God and never ends (JOHN 3:16; 10:27-28; 11:25-26).

eunuch Man who cannot have normal sexual relations. In the courts of ancient kings, eunuchs often became important officials, who were put in charge of the royal harem.

evil spirits *See* **demon**.

Exile Period in Israel's history (597–539 BC) when the Babylonians took many people from Jerusalem and Judah as prisoners of war and forced them to live in Babylonia.

faith The fundamental prerequisite for salvation, and the full blessing of God upon one's life. Faith involves a whole-hearted commitment to belief, trust, obedience, and hope in the revealed word of God. In the New Covenant age, faith in the finished work of Christ's atonement on the cross is the key prerequisite for obtaining eternal life, and the forgiveness of one's sins.

fellowship offering Sacrifice offered to restore or maintain right relationship with God. Part of the sacrificial animal was burnt on the altar, the rest eaten by the worshipers or priests.

flax Small cultivated plant: fibers from its stem were spun into thread used to make linen cloth, utilized for many purposes, including priests' clothing.

forgiveness The action whereby God absolves those who confess their sins from the punishment for sin. Faith and trust in the person and work of Jesus Christ results in eternal forgiveness.

frankincense Valuable substance made from the sap of a tree, probably imported from Arabia. It gave a pleasant smell when burnt.

Gad One of the twelve tribes of Israel.

generation In the Bible, a generation is usually around 40 years.

gentile Person who is not a Jew.

Gethsemane Garden or olive grove on the Mount of Olives (MARK 14:32), where Jesus spent some time praying, with his disciples, immediately before his arrest, when Judas Iscariot betrayed him. *See also* **Mount of Olives**.

Gilead Region east of the Jordan River. Moab lay to the south of Gilead, and Bashan to the north.

Girgashites One of the nations that lived in Canaan before the Israelites.

glory Something seen, heard, or experienced that shows a person or thing is important, wondrous, or powerful. When God appeared, his glory was often seen as a brilliant light or as fire and smoke.

grace The expression of God's undeserved mercy and favor.

grain offering Sacrifice to give thanks to the Lord with a gift of grain (LEVITICUS 2).

guilt offering Sacrifice to put things right after a person had cheated someone, or the Lord (LEVITICUS 6:1-7).

Hades Greek word in the New Testament referring to the world of the dead.

Hanukkah Joyous Jewish festival when people remembered how Judas Maccabaeus rededicated the altar in the Temple in 165 BC. The festival began on the 25th day of the month Kislev (about December 10th) and lasted eight days. This festival (Feast of Dedication) is referred to in John 10:22, when Jesus was walking in the Temple area. It is also referred to in the title of Psalm 30.

harrow Metal frame used to break up and level the ground after it had been plowed.

Hebrew Old word for "Israelite" or "Jewish." Also, the language used by most Israelites until the Exile. After the people returned from Exile, more and more spoke Aramaic instead. Most of the Old Testament was written in Hebrew.

Herod's party Political party in New Testament times made up of Jews who wanted to be ruled by the family of Herod the Great rather than by a Roman governor.

High Priest Chief Jewish priest and president of the Sanhedrin council. Once a year, on the Day of Atonement, he entered the Holy of Holies in the Temple to offer a sacrifice for himself and for the sins of the people over the past year.

Hinnom Valley Valley west and south of Jerusalem, where in Old Testament times human sacrifice was sometimes made. *See* **Molech**.

Hittites Nation whose capital was located in what is now Turkey. Before 1200 BC, the Hittite empire at times controlled some kingdoms in Canaan. Many Hittites remained in Canaan after the Israelites arrived.

Hivites Nation that lived in Canaan before the Israelites, probably related to the Horites.

Holy of Holies The innermost room of the Tabernacle and the Temple. It was the holiest part of the Sanctuary that contained the "earthly dwelling place" of God, symbolized by the presence of the glory cloud. In the Tabernacle, the Holy of Holies housed only the Ark of the Covenant; in Solomon's Temple, it also held statues of winged creatures.

Holy One Name for God in the Old Testament (PSALMS 71:22; 89:18; ISAIAH 43:3). In the New Testament, for the promised Savior (MARK 1:24; LUKE 4:34; JOHN 6:69; ACTS 2:27; 13:35; 1 JOHN 2:20). *See also* **Savior**.

Holy Place The main room in the Tabernacle and the Temple, containing the shewbread, the golden altar of incense, and the golden lampstand. A priest entered the holy place once every morning and evening to burn incense on the altar.

Horites, also known as "Hurrians." Nation that lived in Canaan before the Israelites.

hyssop Bush with clusters of small branches. In religious ceremonies, hyssop was sometimes dipped in liquid and used to sprinkle people or objects (EXODUS 12:22).

incense Material that makes a sweet smell when burned, used in the worship of God (EXODUS 30:34-38).

Israel Nation made up of the twelve tribes descended from Jacob (*see* **twelve tribes of Israel**). Later, it referred to the northern kingdom, designating the ten tribes that broke away from the two tribes of Benjamin and Judah, following the death of Solomon (1 KINGS 12:1-20). *See also* **Judah**.

Issachar One of the twelve tribes of Israel.

Jebusites Group of Canaanite people who lived in Jebus, later known as Jerusalem (2 SAMUEL 5:6-9).

Jerusalem The capital city of the United Kingdom of Israel. After the separation of the United Kingdom into

Northern and Southern kingdoms (i.e. Israel and Judah respectively), following the reign of Solomon, Jerusalem remained the principal city of Judah in the South. In the Northern Kingdom, the principal city was Samaria.

Jew At first a geographical term, referring to people living in the territory of Judah. Later, a religious term, referring to anyone who followed the Jewish religion. *See also* **Hebrew**.

Jubilee, Year of The year that came every fifty years, when the Israelites were to return to the original owner any property they held. They were also to free their slaves and not cultivate their fields (LEVITICUS 25:8-54).

Judah One of the twelve tribes of Israel. When the ten northern tribes of Israel broke away following the death of Solomon, only the tribes of Judah and Benjamin were left, forming the southern kingdom, also called "Judah."

judges Leaders chosen by God for the Israelites after the time of Joshua, and before Saul became Israel's first king.

justification A judicial, or forensic term, which carries the sense of "acquit," "declare righteous." It is the very opposite of "condemn." And it is also God alone who determines the verdict of "justification" in respect of those who constitute his people—past, present, and future. In the New Testament (Covenant), faith and trust in Christ is the key criterion for justification in the sight of God (see ROMANS 3:23-26; 4:5-8; 5:18ff).

Law and the Prophets Term in the New Testament referring to the sacred writings of the Jews. They were two of the three sections of the Old Testament, but the expression sometimes refers to the entire Old Testament.

Leaven, or yeast. Substance added to dough to make it rise before being baked into bread. The term is also used metaphorically to refer to spiritual and moral corruption; e.g. in Jesus' rebuke of the Pharisees, in Matthew 16:5-12.

Levi One of the tribes of Israel, from whom the members of the priesthood were selected (i.e. the descendants of Aaron). Men of this tribe were special servants of the Lord (priests and Levites) in the Tabernacle, and later in the Temple; so this tribe was not given land. Instead, they were given towns scattered throughout the other twelve tribes. *See also* **Levite**.

Leviathan Legendary sea monster representing evil (PSALMS 74:13-14; 104:26; ISAIAH 27:1).

Levite Member of the tribe of Levi, and descendant of Aaron. Also, a man who helped the priests perform religious duties (NUMBERS 3:5-10).

locust Kind of grasshopper that comes in huge swarms and badly damages plants. In the prophecy of Joel, the locust plague is the vehicle of God's judgement against his sinful people—a sign of the coming of the dreadful Day of the LORD judgement (JOEL 1:2-2:11). *See also* **Day of the LORD**.

LORD In the Old Testament, the word "Lord" in capital letters stands for the Hebrew consonants YHWH, the personal name of God, often pronounced "Yahweh." It is not known for certain what vowel sounds were originally used with the consonants YHWH. The word "Lord" (in upper- and lower case letters) represents the Hebrew term *Adonai*, the usual word for "lord." By late Old Testament times, Jews felt God's personal name was too holy to be pronounced. So, they said *Adonai*, "Lord," whenever they read YHWH. When the Jewish scribes first translated the Hebrew Scriptures into ancient Greek, they translated the name of God as *Kurios*, "Lord."

lyre Type of harp.

magic *See* **sorcerer**.

Manasseh One of the twelve tribes of Israel.

manna Miraculous food, provided by God, and eaten by the Israelites during their wanderings in the wilderness. White and flaky, it looked like small coriander seeds, and tasted like wafers made with honey (EXODUS 16:14-34).

Medes Nation that lived in what is today northwest Iran. Their kingdom, Media, became one of the most important provinces in the Persian Empire. Persian laws were known as the "laws of the Medes and Persians" (ESTHER 1:19; DANIEL 6:8, 12, 15).

medium Person who believes he or she can communicate with the dead.

Mercury Deity of skillful speaking, and messenger of the Greek gods (ACTS 14:12).

Messiah ("the anointed one") Hebrew title given to the Savior whose coming was promised by the Hebrew prophets, as the Deliverer and Redeemer of the people of God; the Greek word "Christ" has the same meaning.

Midianites Nomadic nation that mainly lived in the desert, along the eastern shore of the Gulf of Aqaba.

Moab Nation that lived east of the Dead Sea. Its people were descended from Lot, the nephew of Abraham (19:30-38). In the Old Testament, Moab is sometimes seen as one of Israel's enemies (ISAIAH 15-16; JEREMIAH 48).

Molech One of the gods of the ancient people of Canaan.

Mount of Olives Hill just east of Jerusalem, across Kidron

Valley from the Temple. *See also* **Gethsemane**.

mustard Large plant that grows from a very small seed. This seed was used metaphorically by Jesus, when he described the huge, world-wide growth and extent of the Kingdom of Heaven in Matthew 13:31.

myrrh Sweet-smelling resin that was very valuable. It was used in perfume, as a medicine (MARK 15:23), and by the Jews when preparing bodies for burial (JOHN 19:39).

myrtle Kind of evergreen shrub or tree. It is referred to in the Old Testament as a plant symbolizing divine blessing and renewal (cf. ISAIAH 41:19; 55:13; ZECHARIAH 1:8-11).

Naphtali One of the twelve tribes of Israel.

Nazarene Someone from the town of Nazareth. The name was used as a title for Jesus, and sometimes for early Christians (ACTS 24:5).

Nazirite Man who made a special vow to serve God. Nazirites did not drink beer or wine, cut their hair, or touch a dead body (NUMBERS 6:1-21). The vow could be taken for a fixed period of time, but some were dedicated as Nazirites from birth, e.g. the judge, Samson (JUDGES 13-16).

Nebuchadnezzar Babylonian ruler who presided over the capture, destruction, and exile of the Judean kingdom from 605-587 BC.

Nineveh Ancient capital of the Assyrian Empire.

offerings *See* **sacrifices**

Olives, Mount of *See* **Mount of Olives.**

parable Story that teaches a spiritual truth, often told by Jesus.

paradise Name for heaven (LUKE 23:43; 2 CORINTHIANS 12:3).

Passover Hebrew, "*Pesach.*" Jewish festival held in early spring, when Israelites commemorated God rescuing them from slavery in Egypt (EXODUS 12:1-27; NUMBERS 28:16-25). The Angel of Death killed the first-born in the Egyptian homes but "passed over" Hebrew homes that were protected by the blood of sheep or goats, which God had commanded his people to smear over the doorframes of their houses. Failure to do so would have resulted in the death of their firstborn, just like that suffered by Egyptian families. This Passover ritual anticipated the atoning death of Jesus Christ on the cross, that obtained eternal salvation and absolute forgiveness of sin, via the shedding of his blood.

peace offering Sacrifice to request the Lord's blessing (LEVITICUS 3).

Peniel Place near the Jabbok River where Jacob wrestled with God, after which God changed Jacob's name to "Israel" (GENESIS 32:22-32).

Pentecost Greek name for the Israelite festival of wheat harvest. Pentecost means "fiftieth" —this feast was held fifty days after Passover.

Perizzites Nation that lived in the central hill country of Canaan before the Israelites.

Persia Huge empire of Old Testament times, whose capital was in what is now southern Iran.

Pharisees Jewish religious party that was particularly strict in obeying the Law of Moses and other rules, traditions, and teachings added through the centuries. They constituted the principal opponents of Jesus during his earthly ministry.

Pharaoh Traditional title for kings of Egypt during the entire duration of the Egyptian Empire, one that spanned over two millennia.

Philistines Name given to the people who controlled a strip of land along the Mediterranean coast called "Philistia." There were five main cities, each with its own ruler: Ashdod, Ashkelon, Ekron, Gath, and Gaza. The Philistines were frequently at war with Israel.

Phoenicia Territory along the Mediterranean Sea controlled by the cities of Tyre, Sidon, Arvad, and Byblos. The coast of modern Lebanon covers roughly the same area.

plague A term derived from several Hebrew and Greek words that denote, disease, death, and destruction of gigantic proportions. Plague was often utilized as an instrument of God's judgement against both his people, and their enemies (cf. EXODUS 7-12; JOEL).

Preparation, Day of The sixth day of the week (Friday), when the Jews prepared to keep the Sabbath (Saturday).

priest(s) These were men who led worship and offered sacrifices in the Tabernacle or Temple. They were chosen from the tribe of Levi– in particular, from the descendants of Aaron. More important priests were called "chief priests;" and the most important, the "high priest."

prophet Person who was anointed and appointed by God, to proclaim a message from God which could include telling what would happen in the future. Sometimes when the Spirit of God took control of a prophet, he lost control of his speech and actions, or became unaware of what was happening around him. Prophets were mainly particular men in the Old Testament, though the New Testament mentions prophets in the early church. John the Baptist is also called a prophet.

proverb Wise saying, pithy and easy to remember.

psalm Hebrew poem. Psalms were often written so they could be prayed or sung by an individual or a group. They formed part of the core public worship of God in

Old Testament times. Some psalms thank and praise God, others ask God to forgive sins, punish enemies, or to provide protection, comfort, and mercy.

Purim Jewish festival near the end of winter when the Jews celebrated deliverance from Haman, the evil prime minister of Persia, who planned to massacre them. The story is told in the book of Esther.

rabbi Hebrew word meaning "my teacher."

Red Sea Hebrew *yam suph*, "Sea of Reeds." One of the marshes or freshwater lakes near the eastern part of the Nile Delta (EXODUS 13:17–14:9). Sometimes in the Bible "Red Sea" is used for part of the sea now known as the Gulf of Suez (EXODUS 10:19) or the Gulf of Aqaba (EXODUS 23:31).

repentance When understood as a human response, repentance denotes the action of expressing sorrow for sin, along with a desire for forgiveness from God. Repentance also includes the mandatory response of "turning away" from one's sinful stance; it is not merely the verbal expression of sorrow, or regret.

Rephaim Perhaps a group of very large people who lived in Palestine before the Israelites (DEUTERONOMY 2:11, 20).

Reuben One of the twelve tribes of Israel.

righteousness One of the inherent qualities of the personhood of God, denoting moral perfection that incorporates perfect justice. It is also one of the key demands of godly living, characterized by just and fair interactions between individuals.

Roman Empire Political and military power that controlled the area around the Mediterranean Sea and Western Europe in New Testament times. Its capital was Rome.

Sabbath Seventh day of the week—from sunset on Friday to sunset on Saturday—a holy day under the Old Covenant, when no work was allowed (EXODUS 20:8-11; 23:10-12).

sackcloth Coarse cloth, made of goat- or camel hair, worn as a sign of mourning or distress.

sacrifices Gifts to God as acts of worship, that included prescribed animals, grain, fruit, and sweet-smelling spices. Israelites offered sacrifices to give thanks to God, to ask his forgiveness and blessing, and to pay for wrongdoing. Some were completely burned on the altar; others were partly burned on the altar, and the remainder eaten by priests or the worshipers who had offered them.

Sadducees Small, but powerful group of Jews in New Testament times who were closely connected with the high priests. They accepted only the first five books of the Old Testament as their Bible and did not believe in life after death.

salvation God's act of rescuing his people from the oppression of their enemies, the consequences of his people's sinfulness, and placing them under his care.

Samaria From the rule of King Omri (885–874 BC), the capital of the northern kingdom of Israel. In New Testament times, a district between Judea and Galilee, named for the city of Samaria. The people of this area, called "Samaritans," worshiped God differently from the Jews, resulting in bad feeling between them.

Samaritan *See* **Samaria.**

sanctification An Old Testament term denoting the state of being "set apart," or "dedicated" to the service of God. In the New Testament, sanctification refers to the process of gradual inward, spiritual transformation, under the operation of the Holy Spirit in the life of believers. In addition, the term "holiness" in the New Testament is used, rather than "sanctification" as such.

sanctuary *See* **temple.**

Sanhedrin The highest religious court of the Jews, made up of 70 leaders of the Jewish people. The leader was the high priest.

Satan *See* **Devil.**

save *See* **salvation.**

Savior God himself, or Jesus Christ, the one God sent to save people from sin.

scepter Decorated rod, often made of gold, held by a king as a sign of royal power.

scribe Person who wrote documents for others, or copied writings. In Old Testament times some scribes were employed by kings to prepare official documents and became important figures. In New Testament times, scribes taught and explained the teachings of the Old Testament, especially the first five books.

Scriptures In the New Testament, this means the Hebrew sacred writings known to Christians as the Old Testament (1 TIMOTHY 4:13; 2 TIMOTHY 3:15-17). Various names are used: "the Law" (or Law of Moses) **and the prophets**" (MATTHEW 5:17; 7:12; LUKE 2:22; 24:44); "the Holy Scriptures" (ROMANS 1:2; 2 TIMOTHY 3:15); and "the old covenant" (2 CORINTHIANS 3:14). The singular word "scripture" means a particular passage of the Old Testament.

scroll Roll of paper or thin leather used to write on. Scrolls were the universal vehicle for writing in the ancient world. It was not until the 2nd century AD that "books," as we know them, were invented. And, at first, they were known as "codexes."

serpent Name given to the dragon that appears in the New Testament as a picture of the Devil (REVELATION 12:3-17; 20:2-3). It is also derived from the Genesis account of the incarnation of Satan as the "serpent" who deceived Adam and Eve, and led them into rebellion against God (GENESIS 3).

Sheol In the Old Testament, a place of darkness to which all of the dead go, cut off from life and God.

Sidon *See* **Phoenicia.**

Simeon One of the twelve tribes of Israel.

sin Disobeying God by refusing to do what God requires.

Son of Man Title Jesus often used to refer to himself (MARK 8:31; 9:31; 10:45). This title is anticipated in the prophetic vision of Daniel 7:13ff, where one like a "Son of man" is described as "coming with the clouds of heaven" into the presence of God on his heavenly throne.

sorcerer Person who works magic for evil reasons. Sorcerers are consistently viewed in the Bible as those under the power and influence of the demonic world—implacably opposed to the person and work of the one, true, and living God.

Stoic Follower of a man named Zeno (died 262 BC), who taught that people should practice self-control and be guided by conscience. Paul encountered some Stoics in Acts 17:18, when he was in Athens.

synagogue Greek word meaning "gathering." Synagogues were places where Jews met every Sabbath for public worship and reading of Scripture (LUKE 4:16-30).

Tabernacle, or "Tent of Meeting." The large tent where the people of Israel worshiped God before the Temple was constructed (EXODUS 26). *See also* **sanctuary, temple.**

tassel Group of threads or cords fastened together at one end, but loose at the other. Israelites were required to wear them on their clothes (NUMBERS 15:37-41).

taxes Fees collected by rulers, usually a proportion of the value of a person's crops, property, or income. Taxes were collected at markets, city gates, ports, and border crossings. In New Testament times, Jews were hired by the Roman government to collect taxes from other Jews. Such tax-collectors were hated by their own people.

temple King Solomon built Israel's first temple in Jerusalem. Another temple was begun on its ruins following the return from exile in Babylonia (538 BC). In 20 BC Herod the Great began a new temple on the same site, but it was not entirely finished before Jerusalem was destroyed by the Romans in AD 70. Solomon's Temple was preceded by the Tabernacle, first constructed during the time of Moses, after the divine revelation of the terms of the Old Covenant on Mt Sinai, some 500 years or so earlier. The Tabernacle was a portable sanctuary, also described as the "Tent of Meeting," that accompanied the Israelites on their journey through the Wilderness, and on into the period of the occupation of Canaan. It only became a permanent worship center during the reign of King Solomon.

tenant In Bible times, a man who grew crops on land owned by someone else, and gave part of the harvest to the owner in payment for using the land.

Tent of Meeting *See* **Tabernacle.**

threshing Process of separating grain from its husks. Grain was spread out over a threshing place—a flat area of stone or packed earth. To remove the husks, people or animals walked on the grain, or dragged heavy boards across it. The grain and husks were then tossed into the air with a threshing fork. The wind would blow away the lighter husks, but the heavy grain would fall back on to the threshing place.

tithe One-tenth of a person's crops or income, given to God. In practice, the tithe was handed over to the Levites to manage, both for their own personal use and worship.

Trumpets, Feast of *See* **Feast of Trumpets.**

twelve tribes of Israel The Bible speaks of all those in a tribe as descended from one of the twelve sons of Jacob. The tribes of Ephraim and Manasseh were descended from the two sons of Joseph, one of Jacob's sons.

unclean *See* **clean.**

Urim and Thummim Two small objects used by Israelite priests to discover God's will.

vow Strong statement or promise, often made by calling on God to punish the speaker if the statement was untrue or the promise broken.

winnowing shovel Tool like a shovel or large fork, used to separate grain from the husks.

yoke Heavy bar of wood fitted over the necks of two oxen to enable them to pull a plow or cart.

Zeus The supreme Greek god.

Zion Originally a name for the "City of David," the Jebusite stronghold captured by King David. Later used to refer to the hill where the Jerusalem temple stood.

Acknowledgments

9. The Temple Institute, Jerusalem. 11. Wikikati. 12. Jim Padgett: Distant Shores Media/Sweet Publishing. 13. James Tissot. 14. Jim Padgett: Distant Shores Media/Sweet Publishing. 15a. James Tissot. 15b. Tim Dowley Associates Ltd. 16. Jim Padgett: Distant Shores Media/Sweet Publishing. 17. Cigoli. 18. Jim Padgett: Distant Shores Media/Sweet Publishing. 19a. James Tissot. 19b. Jocelyn Erskine-Kellie: Creative Commons Attribution 2.0 Generic. 20. Jim Padgett: Distant Shores Media/Sweet Publishing. 21a. Julius Schnorr von Carolsfeld. 21b. James Tissot. 22. Tim Dowley Associates Ltd. 25. Jim Padgett: Distant Shores Media/Sweet Publishing. 26. Basilica San Marco, Venice. 27. Ooman: Creative Commons Attribution-Share Alike 3.0. 28a. Jim Padgett: Distant Shores Media/Sweet Publishing. 28b. James Tissot. 30. St. Mungo Museum of Religious Life and Art, Glasgow: Creative Commons Attribution-Share Alike 3.0. 32. Tim Dowley Associates Ltd. 33a, 33b Tim Dowley Associates Ltd. 34. Tim Dowley Associates Ltd. 36. James Tissot. 39. James Tissot. 40. Tim Dowley Associates Ltd. 41. Domenico Fetti. 42. Tim Dowley Associates Ltd. 43. Dreamstime. 44. Jim Padgett: Distant Shores Media/Sweet Publishing. 46. Jim Padgett: Distant Shores Media/Sweet Publishing. 56. Dreamstime. 57. Gerhard van Honthorst. 58. James Tissot. 60. James Tissot. 61. Zev Radovan. 63. Tim Dowley Associates Ltd. 64. Jim Padgett: Distant Shores Media/Sweet Publishing. 65. James Tissot. 66. James Tissot. 67. Jörg Bittner Unna: Creative Commons Attribution 3.0 Unported. 68. Pieter Lastman. 69. Luis Rizo. 70. James Tissot. 71. Carole Raddato: Creative Commons Attribution 2.0 Generic. 72. Tim Dowley Associates Ltd. 73. Tim Dowley Associates Ltd. 74. Dreamstime. 75. Edward Burne-Jones: Creative Commons Attribution-Share Alike 4.0 International. 77. Tim Dowley Associates Ltd. 79. Tim Dowley Associates Ltd. 80. Tim Dowley Associates Ltd. 81a. Richard Scott: Tim Dowley Associates Ltd.. 81b. Unknown artist, c. 1420, Museu Nacional d'Art de Catalunya, Barcelona. 83. Fallaner: unknown artist, c. 1420, Museu Nacional d'Art de Catalunya, Barcelona. 85. Jim Padgett: Distant Shores Media/Sweet Publishing. 87. Jim Padgett: Distant Shores Media/Sweet Publishing. 88. Dreamstime. 89a. Nero: cjh1452000, Creative Commons Attribution 3.0 Unported. 89b. Titus: Bibi Saint-Pol. 89c. Siege of Jerusalem: David Roberts. 89d. Coliseum: FeaturedPics, Creative Commons Attribution-Share Alike 4.0 International. 89e. Boudicca: Colin Smith, Creative Commons Attribution 2.0 Generic. 91. Jim Padgett: Distant Shores Media/Sweet Publishing. 92. Jim Padgett: Distant Shores Media/Sweet Publishing. 93. Jim Padgett: Distant Shores Media/Sweet Publishing. 97. Leonardo da Vinci. 98. Dreamstime. 99. William Hole. 101. Jim Padgett: Distant Shores Media/Sweet Publishing. 103. Tim Dowley Associates Ltd. 104. Creative Commons Attribution 2.0 Generic, Dreamstime. 105. Tim Dowley Associates Ltd. 106. Jim Padgett: Distant Shores Media/Sweet Publishing. 107. Tim Dowley Associates Ltd. 109. Tim Dowley Associates Ltd. 111. Tim Dowley Associates Ltd. 112. Jim Padgett: Distant Shores Media/Sweet Publishing. 113. Tim Dowley Associates Ltd. 114. Jim Padgett: Distant Shores Media/Sweet Publishing. 116–117. Tim Dowley Associates Ltd. 118a. cjh1452000: Creative Commons Attribution 3.0 Unported. 118b. Dreamstime. 119. Jim Padgett: Distant Shores Media/Sweet Publishing. 125a. Dreamstime. 125b. James Tissot. 126. Tim Dowley Associates Ltd. 128. Dreamstime. 130. Jim Padgett: Distant Shores Media/Sweet Publishing. 132a. Jim Padgett: Distant Shores Media/Sweet Publishing. 132b. Rembrandt: kQHX7sr3-DICHA. 136. Dreamstime. 138. Tim Dowley Associates Ltd. 139. Dreamstime. 140. Sun Ladder: Creative Commons CC0 1.0 Universal Public Domain Dedication. 141. Caddetgray: Creative Commons Attribution 3.0 Unported. 142. Jacques Blanchard. 152. Jim Padgett: Distant Shores Media/Sweet Publishing. 153. George P. A. Healy. 155. Dreamstime. 156. Alan Parry, Tim Dowley Associates Ltd. 157. Tim Dowley Associates Ltd. 158. Alan Parry, Tim Dowley Associates Ltd. 159a. Alan Parry, Tim Dowley Associates Ltd. 159b. Tim Dowley Associates Ltd. 160a. Dreamstime. 160b. Tim Dowley Associates Ltd. 161. Alan Parry, Tim Dowley Associates Ltd. 162. Richard Scott, Tim Dowley Associates Ltd. 163. Dreamstime. 164. James Tissot. 165. Frank Baber, Tim Dowley Associates Ltd. 166a. Alan Parry, Tim Dowley Associates Ltd. 166b. Richard Scott, Tim Dowley Associates Ltd. 167. Alan Parry, Tim Dowley Associates Ltd. 168. Alan Parry, Tim Dowley Associates Ltd. 169. Jeremy Gower, Tim Dowley Associates Ltd. 170. Alan Parry, Tim Dowley Associates Ltd. 171a. Bill Corbett, Tim Dowley Associates Ltd. 171b. Richard Scott, Tim Dowley Associates Ltd. 172. Tim Dowley Associates Ltd. 173. Dreamstime. 174. Tim Dowley Associates Ltd. 175. Martin Bustamente, Tim Dowley Associates Ltd. 177. Dreamstime. 178a. Tim Dowley Associates Ltd. 178b. Richard Scott, Tim Dowley Associates Ltd. 179a. Dreamstime. 179b. Dreamstime. 180. Richard Scott, Tim Dowley Associates Ltd. 181. Tim Dowley Associates Ltd. 182. Dreamstime. 183. Richard Scott, Tim Dowley Associates Ltd. 184a. Dreamstime. 184b. Peter Dennis, Tim Dowley Associates Ltd. 185. Tim Dowley Associates Ltd. 186. Tim Dowley Associates Ltd. 187. Bernini. 189. Tim Dowley Associates Ltd. 190. Dreamstime. 191a. Wolfgang Menzel. 191b. Dreamstime. 192. David Roberts. 193 Tim Dowley Associates Ltd. 194a. Zev Radovan. 194b. Dreamstime. 196a. Dreamstime. 196b. Dreamstime. 197. Dreamstime. 198. Paul Wyart, Tim Dowley Associates Ltd. 199. Donald Harley, Tim Dowley Associates Ltd. 200. Tim Dowley Associates Ltd. 201. Tim Dowley Associates Ltd. 202a. Lucas Cranach: Creative Commons CC0 1.0 Universal Public Domain. 202b. Tim Dowley Associates Ltd. 203. Dreamstime. 204. Tim Dowley Associates Ltd. 205. National Library of Wales. 207a. Tim Dowley Associates Ltd. 207b. Billy Graham Evangelistic Association. 208. Nswinton. 209a. Tim Dowley Associates Ltd. 209b. Tim Dowley Associates Ltd. 209c. Tim Dowley Associates Ltd.

Index

Page numbers in *italics* refer to maps.

Index

Index

Index